A CENTURY
of
HOLINESS
THEOLOGY

A CENTURY

of

HOLINESS THEOLOGY

THE DOCTRINE OF ENTIRE SANCTIFICATION IN THE CHURCH OF THE NAZARENE 1905 TO 2004

MARK R. QUANSTROM

Beacon Hill Press of Kansas City
Kansas City, Missouri

Library of Congress Cataloging-in-Publication Data

Quanstrom, Mark R., 1955-
  A century of holiness theology : the doctrine of entire sanctification in the Church of the Nazarene : 1905 to 2004 / Mark R. Quanstrom.
     p. cm.
  Includes bibliographical references.
  ISBN 0-8341-2116-6 (pbk.)
  1. Church of the Nazarene—Doctrines—History—20th century. 2. Holiness—Church of the Nazarene—History of doctrines—20th century. 3. Sanctification—Church of the Nazarene—History of doctrines—20th century. I. Title.
  BX8699.N35Q36 2004
   234'.8'08828799—dc22

                                                                                          2003023484

10 9 8 7 6 5 4 3

To Dwight Adams (1952-1977),
a very good friend, who considered seriously things theological

CONTENTS

ACKNOWLEDGMENTS

As everyone knows who commits to writing, it is never a solitary endeavor. It is always collaborative. Thus, I wish to acknowledge many who directly and indirectly contributed to this work.

I would like to thank Drs. Kenneth Parker and Beldon Lane, professors at St. Louis University, who recommended that I write a historical theology on the particular doctrine of the Church of the Nazarene and who offered invaluable encouragement, advice, and critique.

I would like to thank Drs. William Greathouse, Paul Bassett, H. Ray Dunning, J. Kenneth Grider, Rob Staples, and Stan Ingersol for their time and insightful commentary concerning the doctrine of entire sanctification and for their clarification of issues and details.

I would like to thank Bonnie Perry for her constant encouragement.

I would like to thank the church I pastor, the First Church of the Nazarene in Belleville, Illinois, for being so graciously generous with their pastor while I was researching and writing this work.

I am indebted to my father and mother, Dr. Roy F. and Shirley Quanstrom, for initially pressing me to this work and for being the first editors and reviewers.

I am so very grateful to and proud of my three sons, Lukas, Ryan, and Daniel, who understood their father's desire and love for study, researching, and writing and who graciously shared their dad with libraries and many books.

And there are not words large enough to convey the gratitude I have for Debi, my partner, without whom I am half of myself and, therefore, without whom I never would have been able to do this.

INTRODUCTION

This book will chart the gradual change in the understanding of the doctrine of entire sanctification in the Church of the Nazarene in the 20th century. The Church of the Nazarene understood its reason for being was the proclamation of the possibility of life without sin as a consequence of a second work of grace. As the century began, the explication of the doctrine reflected the optimistic hopes of society at large and, therefore, described the change effected by entire sanctification in extravagantly promising terms. The early explication reflected 19th-century holiness orthodoxy and emphasized entire sanctification as an instantaneous second work of grace that eradicated the sinful nature, conditioned only by faith and consecration which resulted in almost glorified human persons.

As the century wore on, the very optimistic expectations of entire sanctification became less and less credible in light of the apparently intractable nature of sin. By midcentury, the extravagant promises of the grace of entire sanctification began to be tempered. Theologians in the denomination began to define the sin that could be eradicated more narrowly and the infirmities that were an inescapable consequence of fallen humanity more expansively. This led to an increasing dissatisfaction with traditional formulations of the doctrine.

As a result, the doctrine as formulated by John Wesley in the 18th century was reexamined. A study of his writings, which were divergent from the 19th-century formulations at important points, resulted in a radical reformulation of the doctrine. This reformulation has resulted in two contemporaneous and competing definitions of entire sanctification in the Church of the Nazarene. Needless to say, this poses a problem for a denomination that understands its primary reason for being as the preservation and proclamation of a doctrine of entire sanctification.

1
PERPETUATING THE AMERICAN IDEAL

"DETERMINED TO CONQUER THIS LAND"

The Pentecostal Church of the Nazarene, at the beginning of the 20th century, could not have been more confident of its future. This small denomination had come into being as a result of intentional and aggressive merging of the many independent Holiness denominations and associations that were in existence in the late 19th and early 20th centuries. The history of the Church of the Nazarene, therefore, is a history of unions. In 1905, the Van Alstyne, Texas, Independent Holiness Church united with the Milan, Tennessee, New Testament Church of Christ to form the Holiness Church of Christ. In Chicago, in 1907, Dr. Phineas F. Bresee's Los Angeles Church of the Nazarene, which he had begun in 1895, joined with the 11-year-old Association of Pentecostal Churches of America in New York to form the Pentecostal Church of the Nazarene. On October 13, 1908, the day that would come to be considered the official birthday of the church, these two churches, the Holiness Church of Christ of Texas and the Pentecostal Church of the Nazarene, united at Pilot Point, Texas. In 1915, the Pentecostal Mission of Tennessee and the Pentecostal Church of Scotland joined the denomination and 7 years later, the Laymen's Holiness Association of Jamestown, North Dakota, was added.

This new denomination, called the Pentecostal Church of the Nazarene, inherited the theological tradition of the 19th-century Holiness Movement. These Holiness people believed that persons could be freed from sin through a work of grace called entire sanctification. In short, their distinctive doctrine stated that subsequent to initial salvation there was a second work of grace that cleansed one from all inbred sin. God had called men to live without sin and He had made provision for it. Persons could be made holy. The image of God could be restored to fallen man. The Pentecostal Church of the Nazarene's doctrinal statement on entire sanctification was succinct and reflected 19th-century holiness orthodoxy.

> Entire sanctification is that act of God, subsequent to justification, by which regenerate believers are made free from inbred sin, and brought into the state of entire devotement to God, and the holy obedience of love made perfect. It is provided through the blood of Jesus, and is wrought immediately by the gracious agency of the Holy Spirit, upon the full and final consecration of the believer, and

a definite act of appropriating faith; and to this work and state of grace the Holy Spirit bears witness.[1]

Many proponents of holiness in the 19th and early 20th century, however, not only believed that individuals could be freed from all inbred sin but that society could be freed from sin too. Several anticipated nothing less than a society made holy as a consequence of sanctified individuals. Charles Finney, the early 19th-century revivalistic promoter of holiness, expected the Holy Spirit to sanctify and empower the American churches to proclaim the full gospel to such an extent that God's love, peace, and justice would finally triumph.

> The great business of the church is to reform the world—to put away every kind of sin. . . . The very profession of Christianity implies the profession and virtually an oath to do all that can be done for the universal reformation of the world. The Christian Church was designed to make aggressive movements in every direction . . . to reform individuals, communities, and governments, and never rest until the Kingdom and the greatness of the Kingdom under the whole heaven shall be given to the saints of the Most High God—until every form of iniquity shall be driven from the earth.[2]

Phoebe Palmer, organizer of "The Tuesday Meetings for the Promotion of Holiness" and perhaps the most influential Methodist Holiness leader in the antebellum period, believed that the Spirit of Christ was bringing about a great transformation of the Church and the world. She wrote, "Are not these meetings for holiness . . . the germs, the dawnings of millennial glory? Are they not strikingly imitative of the pentecostal? Is not this the baptism now called for . . . ere the world blossoms as a rose."[3] Melvin Dieter writes concerning the 19th-century Holiness Movement:

> [A] factor in the total milieu was the idealism which inspired the American national destiny—a divine destiny whose goal was to create a new society, free from the ills which had plagued the societies left behind when immigrants set out for America. . . . The inherent optimism in this American dream was readily assimilated with the optimism of perfectionism in the holiness movement. . . . For the holiness advocate it was all a part of a *grand, divine plan* to usher in the most glorious and last dispensation.[4]

The consolidation of the Holiness Movement into a national denomination called the Pentecostal Church of the Nazarene, while half a century later than Finney or Palmer, was, in large part, an attempt to fulfill this "grand divine plan." Timothy Smith, author of the official history of the first 25 years of the Church of the Nazarene, wrote concerning these consolidations:

> Many believed . . . that the gospel of Christian perfection was

the key to a century of spiritual progress. . . . When the followers of Phineas F. Bresee, H. F. Reynolds, and C. B. Jernigan met in the tiny Texas town called Pilot Point to unite the fragments of the holiness movement, that doctrine had become an embattled creed. Graying divines cherished still the dream of an interdenominational crusade for a national Pentecost.[5]

Thus, when the leaders of the disparate Holiness groups met to consider uniting with each other, these millennial hopes were evident, and unbridled optimism characterized every early union. In the 1907 merger between the Los Angeles Church of the Nazarene and the Association of Pentecostal Churches of America, which formed the Pentecostal Church of the Nazarene, Chicago, the committee on the "state of the church" proclaimed:

> The Pentecostal Church of the Nazarene has a brief but glorious history. It is no man-made organization, but had its origin in the mind of God and has been shaped, nurtured, cherished and guided by Him to the present moment. . . . From the very beginning the manifest blessing of God has been upon us, and He has enabled us to establish centers of holy fire from Nova Scotia to the Gulf of California, and from the Atlantic to the Pacific. . . . Our opportunity is a glorious one, which angels might envy. Upon us has fallen the task and privilege of uniting the Holiness people of America, so that they may accomplish the grand work of re-christianizing the continent. . . . The time is near at hand when He will shake this continent and manifest Himself to this people on a more stupendous scale and with more glorious power than the world has ever before witnessed. Indeed, He has commenced to do it already. The great reforms which have recently taken place in our political and commercial institutions, the wonderful and sweeping advance of prohibition, the outpouring of the Holy Spirit in Wales, India and Korea, the steady growth of the Holiness movement, and the rapid rise and progress of the Pentecostal Church of the Nazarene, all unite in attesting and proclaiming that this is true.[6]

It is not insignificant that the Church of the Nazarene considers its official birthday to be October 13, 1908, and its birthplace to be Pilot Point, Texas. It was at Pilot Point, Texas, in 1908, that Holiness churches from *all* points of the compass—north, south, east, and west—were united in a great assembly, and it was this particular union that best symbolized the optimistic hopes and dreams of this perfectionist denomination.

This is evident in the firsthand accounts of the union of 1908. The *Holiness Evangel,* the denominational periodical, reported the event for the entire church.

> Rev. W. H. Hoople spoke on union, followed with enthusiastic speeches by R. B. Mitchum, John N. Short, J. B. Creighton, C. B.

Jernigan, H. B. Hosley and several others. Much enthusiasm was manifested, the brethren from the North and South hugging each other. The motion (for union) was put by Dr. Bresee and carried unanimously, amid a storm of cheers. The enthusiasm grew wilder when the choir began to sing the "Battle Hymn of the Assembly," a new song composed by Bros. I. G. Martin and L. Milton Williams for the occasion and sung to the tune of "Dixie." The enthusiasm grew until the tabernacle could no longer hold the surging throng. They burst out and all joined in a march around the outside of the tabernacle, ending in a great promenade in front of the tabernacle. Those who were present will never forget the indescribable joy and enthusiasm of that hour. Brethren from the North and South, East and West sections of our great country hugged each other, laughed, cried and shouted for joy, that the prayer of Jesus was being answered and His people were enjoying the blessing that really and truly makes His people one. Dr. Bresee was called for and spoke on the affect *(sic)* that this union of the people of God would have on the work of God in the destinies of souls in the years to come. This was followed by cheer after cheer and waving of handkerchiefs.[7]

An old man from South Texas, evidently still able to recall the scars of the Civil War, stood up and said, "This morning is the first time I ever hugged a Yankee."[8] The first two verses and chorus of the song written for the occasion reveal the expectations of the church.

The Holiness Bands from over these lands,
are fast coming in and all joining hands,
Praise God, Praise God, Praise God for Jesus!
With the Blood and the Fire We'll rout the foe and his black-winged host.
March on, March on, march on with Jesus.

With the Nazarene hosts and the Pentecostal band,
and all our folks from the old Southland—
Look out! Look out! Look out for victory!
This Gideon band unitedly stand and are determined to conquer this land
Right away, Right away, Right away for Jesus.

With forces all united, We'll win! We'll win.
We'll preach a Gospel over the land that fully saves from sin.
Praise God, Praise God, Praise God for Full Salvation.
Praise God, Praise God, Praise God for Full Salvation.[9]

P. F. Bresee reflecting on the occasion wrote:
> People were here from Nova Scotia to the Gulf of California, and from Puget Sound to the Gulf of Mexico; and all agreed that it was twice worth crossing the continent to be present. . . . It now seems a foregone conclusion that the holiness forces of this country will be very soon largely united in one organic body. Many things have gone before to prepare the way, and now this movement, at each progressive step, seems so providentially led, that one incoming wave seems to prepare the way for another. The work moves on with great strides, not according to any human forecast, but by a divine impulse, to the great joy of the bloodwashed host.[10]

An Optimistic Age

It was an optimistic age, no less for the Pentecostal Church of the Nazarene than for the culture at large. According to Vincent Synan, this idea that one could be perfected paralleled the general optimism that prevailed throughout all of American society.[11] He has rightly characterized the Holiness Movement as a "kind of 'evangelical transcendentalism' that thrived in the idealism of a young and growing America."[12] Perhaps no time in American history has there been such an unshakable and generally shared confidence in the future than there was at the end of the 19th and beginning of the 20th centuries. Political progressives, social reformers, social "gospellers," evangelical idealists, and many Holiness people, while fundamentally disagreeing over the means to achieve the "golden age," all agreed that the millennium was approaching. While they certainly did not share the same vision concerning the nature of the coming "millennial kingdom," and while their philosophical and theological presuppositions were oftentimes in conflict, they all agreed that with the right technique, program, effort, reform, or grace, America as the land of promise would be realized.

The utopian socialist vision was reflected in the best-selling novel, *Looking Backward.* In 1888, Edward Bellamy, a novelist and short story writer, wrote of what American society would look like in the year 2000. Primarily through national control of all aspects of the economy and with the advances of the industrial revolution, American society would evolve into a perfect rational state where peace and goodwill would reign among men. Julian West, a man who had awakened in Boston in the year 2000, was told by his host, among other things, that "no man any more has any care for the morrow, either for himself or his children, for the nation guarantees the nurture, education, and comfortable maintenance of every citizen from the cradle to the grave."[13] When Julian was told there was no corruption in society, he suggested that human nature must have changed quite drastically. His kind and patient host Dr. Leete informed him that "the conditions of human life have changed, and with them the motives of human action."[14] Indeed, "the solidarity of the race and the brotherhood of man, which to you were but fine phrases, are, to our thinking and feeling, ties as real and as vital as physical fraternity."[15] When Julian was feeling a bit homesick for his mid-19th-century Boston, he was consoled by Dr. Leete's attractive daughter with the words, "I know, as well as I know that the world now is heaven compared with what it was in your day, that the only feeling you will have after a little while will be one of thankfulness to God that your life in that age was so strangely cut off, to be returned to you in this."[16]

A moralistic prescription that would usher in the millennial kingdom was presented by a Topeka, Kansas, Congregational minister, in his 1897 best-seller, *In His Steps: What Would Jesus Do?* The novel ends with the pastor, who had called his people to imitate Jesus in every aspect of their lives, being granted a vision of what would be.

> And when this part of the vision slowly faded, he saw the figure of the Son of God beckoning to him and to all the other actors in his life history. An Angel Choir somewhere was singing. There was a sound as of many voices and a shout as of a great victory. And the figure of Jesus grew more and more splendid. He stood at the end of a long flight of steps. "Yes! Yes! O my Master, has not the time come for this dawn of the millennium of Christian history? Oh, break upon the Christendom of this age with the light and the truth! Help us to follow thee all the way!" He rose at last with the awe of one who has looked at heavenly things. He felt the human forces and the human sins of the world as never before. And with a hope that walks hand in hand with faith and love, Henry Maxwell, disciple of Jesus, laid him down to sleep and dreamed of the regeneration of Christendom.[17]

A variation of this evangelical vision concerned the conversion of the world. Not only would the United States become a "promised land," it would become the launching pad for world transformation. John R. Mott, chairman of the Student Volunteers, a mission enterprise, assured Protestant Christians in 1900, in *The Evangelization of the World in This Generation* that "if they would combine their forces in a wholly committed effort, his suggested goal (of world evangelization) was not impossible of attainment."[18]

In 1912, Walter Rauschenbusch, the Christian socialist, would go so far as to write in *Christianizing the Social Order:*

> The larger part of the work of Christianizing the social order is already accomplished, and the success which has attended it ought to create a victorious self-assertion in all who stake their faith on its effectiveness . . . Christianity works. Moreover every part of the social order which has come even a little under the law of Christ has imme-

diately served as a vantage ground for further progress. There has been a speeding up of redemption. When a man is gagged, bound and tied to a stake, the hardest part is to get one hand free: every further gain is easier and makes ultimate freedom surer. What is next?[19]

It was an age of optimism, of idealism, or as Rauschenbusch would write, of belief in the divinity of progress. Martin Marty commenting on the spirit of the age writes:

> To the American of the turn-of-the-century years, progress was a demonstrable fact. The American empire was extending itself, to have domain over inferior people. The landscape was being transformed by railroads and machines which helped people subdue distance and reform the created world. . . . In short, a kind of metaphysic of Progress was coming to dominate.[20]

It was such an age of optimism that not even the horrors of World War I could temper it. Indeed, the confidence of the people of the United States in the early decades of this century was so pronounced that the World War, which would eventually be known as just the first of many in the century, was understood at the time as the *war to end all wars*. Instead of war calling into question the almost universal optimism of the age, it became simply another means by which divinely ordained and inevitable progress would continue. *The Christian Century* editor Charles Clayton Morrison exulted when, in 1918, the Pact of Paris was signed. "Today international war was banished from civilization."[21] Reverend Lyman Abbott, pastor of the Plymouth Church, Brooklyn, while acknowledging the misfortune of the war, nonetheless reflected the spirit of the age when he declared, "The human race falls down occasionally, bruises itself, and weeps some bitter tears; but picks itself up and goes on walking, and persistently in the right direction."[22] It was such an age of heady optimism that a world war could not even change it.

A POIGNANT SYMBOL

In Kansas City, just a few miles from the headquarters of the Church of the Nazarene, stands a monument that is a telling symbol of the optimism of the age. It is called *The Liberty Memorial,* and it was built to commemorate the war that was supposed to end all wars.

Before the war ended on November 11, 1918, "a mighty impulse took root in the consciousness of the people of Kansas City—a demand that an adequate memorial be erected in gratitude and in appreciation of . . . those who served in the World War."[23] An association was formed 18 days after the armistice was signed to build a monument to that Great War. The people of the city were so enamored with commemorating the historic event of what they believed would be the last war, that the following year the association was able to raise in just 10 days $2,368,826.41 for the project. A nationwide architectural competition was conducted and H. Van Buren Magonigle's architectural firm was awarded the contract. This Bostonian architect conceived of a monument consisting of a tower, 217 feet tall, two sphinxes symbolizing "memory" and "future," two museum buildings, a great stone frieze wall, and a memorial wall, surrounded by courtyards, stairways, and gardens. On November 1, 1921, over 200,000 people came to a hill just south of downtown to see and hear the five allied leaders of the First World War dedicate the ground for the monument, and it was the only time in history that General Jacques of Belgium, General Diaz of Italy, Marshal Foch of France, General Pershing of the United States, and Admiral Lord Beatty of Great Britain were all together in one place. The Liberty Memorial opened just three years later, on Armistice Day (November 11), 1926, with President Calvin Coolidge delivering the dedicatory address. Edward Stone, the master architect, said, "The Liberty Memorial is one of the country's great memorials, in a class with the Lincoln and Jefferson Memorials. It is like the Acropolis in Athens, with its great wall setting, or the monumental planning of Paris."[24] Four separate scripture verses were combined to make up the sculpted saying above the carved frieze. In King James English were the words:

> Behold a pale horse and his name that sat on him was death and hell followed him. Violence shall no more be heard in thy land —wasting nor destruction within thy borders. What doth the Lord require of thee but to do justly and to love mercy and to walk humbly with thy God. Then shall the earth yield her increase and God even our own God shall bless us.[25]

The inscription at the base of the Memorial Tower still states for what purpose the monument was intended: IN HONOR OF THOSE WHO SERVED IN THE WORLD WAR IN DEFENSE OF LIBERTY AND OUR COUNTRY. It was such an age of optimism that not even a world war could change it.

Needless to say, the hopes of those who celebrated the building of the *Liberty Memorial* were not realized. Those who participated in its creation and dedication could not know that the monument to the World War would be obsolete less than 15 years after its dedication, and that the American century would be a century of not one world war but two, with the second even more horrific than the first. Before the century was out, the United States would have not just one extended armed conflict to memorialize but four. In less than 3 years from the time of the monument's dedication, the United States economy would enter its worst depression and the Liberty Association would not even be able to raise the money needed to starkly maintain the monument. Subsequent generations to visit the Liberty Memorial would be astonished to learn that such optimism existed among Americans in the first part of this century and would even consider those who held such hopes to be quaintly naive.

The monument closed in 1994. It had fallen into such disrepair that a chain-link fence was erected surrounding the grounds preventing anyone from approaching the tower and reading the inscription. The doors to the museums were locked. The crumbling concrete, vacant courtyards and absent gardens all reflected decades of neglect. The Kansas City Board of Parks and Recreation had been forced to close the monument because of its deteriorating condition and thus, for many years, this monument built to commemorate the last world war stood as a poignant and perhaps more appropriate commentary on the unrealized hopes of those who inspired it.

Still Confident

In 1919, within weeks of the time that money was being raised for the *Liberty Memorial* and less than one mile east of where the memorial would stand, on the corner of Troost and 24th Street, the 11-year-old Protestant Holiness denomination, the Pentecostal Church of the Nazarene, was holding their fifth General Assembly in one of their churches. It was important for many reasons. To start, it was the first without P. F. Bresee, who had died in 1915, and the first after a series of serious conflicts that had threatened to undo the consolidations of the previous 11 years.[26] This assembly voted to drop the word *Pentecostal* from the church's name, thus clearly distinguishing itself from the "tongues" churches. This assembly also voted to add a previously missing statement of belief concerning the resurrection from the dead to their doctrinal statement. And the new leadership intensified their efforts to justify the new denomination and clarify its mission, particularly in light of the passing of several of their formative leaders. In the prefatory address in the 1919 *Manual,* so that there might be no mistaking the mission of the Church of the Nazarene, the three general superintendents, H. F. Reynolds, John W. Goodwin, and Roy T. Williams, declared:

> It seems evident that God has called our Church into existence for a definite purpose, namely, to propagate the Gospel of the Son of God throughout the world, seeking the conversion of sinners, the reclamation of backsliders, the sanctification of believers, especially emphasizing the great doctrine of full salvation. We do not wish to exist as a denomination merely for the purpose of existence, but rather for the purpose of the evangelization and the conserving of the results, which we believe can be accomplished only through a well organized church movement.[27]   *Amen.*

While this was the first General Assembly without many of the original leaders of the denomination, and while the young denomination struggled in the previous four years to preserve its consolidated gains, the delegates and leaders came to the assembly still confident that the particular mission to which God had called them would continue. The general superintendents, in their quadrennial address to the assembly, proclaimed that God had called them to spread scriptural holiness over the earth and that He had guided them across the greatest four years of their history.[28] Using a ready military analogy that reflected the anxiety of the church, the general superintendents ended their 1919 address to the (Pentecostal) Church of the Nazarene this way:

> We are a small people. Are we to give up because of this fact? In the late war, upon one occasion, the Germans had broken the French line and the word came to an American commander that the French were falling back and that the Germans were approaching the Americans from the rear, coming rapidly up the hill. "Hold them back!" came the command of the American officer to another American commander. "We will hold them, General, as long as one of us is left to fight!" They did. Three thousand Americans held thirty thousand Germans until reinforcements came, and at this moment the end began to appear in the great world war. Can we not be brave soldiers for God? We have the Truth, the Holy Ghost. We will hold the territory we have, but not stop with that. We are fighting an offensive warfare, for God, for holiness, for souls,—and we shall win.[29]

The Church of the Nazarene's early hopes have not yet been realized. The heady optimism, which characterized the participants of the mergers of these fledgling Holiness associations and denominations, was evaporating even as they were boldly asserting their faith in their divinely appointed mission. The millennial hopes were never shared by all of their Holiness people and, therefore, dissipated rather quickly. In that same address in which the general superintendents used the military analogy to encourage the church, they were forced to account for the less than expected growth of the denomination. The first third of that report consisted of reasons for that disappointment. The general superintendents cited the death of general officers, including three of the four general superintendents, an influenza epidemic that killed many pastors and closed several churches, the World War, and "the little disturbance in the church" that had threatened to fracture it. As reflected in the last lines of the prefatory remarks in the 1919 *Manual of the Church of the Nazarene*, as early as that fifth General Assembly, the church began to take a defensive posture, seeking to conserve the gains that had been made while striving to preserve their distinctive doctrine. In the beginning of the church's history, the mergers were understood as an aggressive attempt to fulfill millennial hopes, but they soon began to be appreciated as more necessary for the protection and preservation of the holiness doctrine of entire sanctification. As a result, it was not many years after the high expectations of the first and second general assemblies that the millennial hopes of some of these leaders were abandoned.

Even so, the church refused to forsake the distinctive doctrine of entire sanctification. If the church was not going to be used by God to help usher in the millennial kingdom, then the church was going to be used by God to preserve and defend the holiness doctrine. Persons could still be perfected even if society could not. Sin could be instantaneously eradicated from individuals even though it would remain a social reality. The doctrine would be militantly taught and defended, oftentimes in extravagant terms. But it, too, would undergo a reluctant and gradual change reflective of the loss of optimism that characterized most of the 20th century.

Timothy L. Smith concluded his history of the first 25 years of the Church of the Nazarene, titled *Called unto Holiness,* with a telling comment:

> The reader, therefore, must evaluate for himself the significance of the men and events which compose the history of the Nazarenes. We shall be content if in telling the story we have provided new and important information upon which thoughtful persons may ponder the meaning of American Christianity, the part played by the small denominational families . . . and the *relevance of Wesleyan perfectionism to a generation awed by its rediscovery of the deep sinfulness of man.*[30]

Thoughtful persons within the Church of the Nazarene have indeed pondered the impact of the "rediscovery of the deep sinfulness of man" on the distinctive doctrine that promised nothing less than the entire eradication of sin. The doctrine has been changed. In short, by the end of the century, entire sanctification would not be taught so much as an instantaneous change in the heart of the believer appropriated by consecration and faith, but rather more as an unremarkable event in a process of growth, if taught at all. The "eradication of the sinful nature" would be terminology that many Nazarenes would eschew, even though the words would remain in the Articles of Faith throughout the century. One of the latest Wesleyan theologies of the Church of the Nazarene would not emphasize the doctrine of entire sanctification as a distinct second work of grace, preferring to give "primary consideration to the substance rather than the structure of sanctification."[31] Pentecost, which was the biblical paradigm for the doctrine, would not be understood by very many as *the* occasion of a personal entire sanctification but either as a singular event in the context of salvation-history or as just one of many baptisms with the Holy Spirit. The high expectations concerning the positive consequences of entire sanctification would diminish drastically. While the Article of Faith would remain for the most part unchanged,[32] many in the Church of the Nazarene would understand the doctrine in a way that most early Holiness leaders of the movement would have lamented. These early Nazarenes' hopes for the propagation and preservation of the doctrine as they understood it have not been realized.

But those optimistic leaders of the Pentecostal Church of the Nazarene could not have known that the last significant union between holiness forces would be in 1922. They could not have known what effect a paralyzing depression, two world wars, a Korean war, a Vietnam war, the cold war, and the social upheavals of the '60s would have on the church's understanding of the nature of sin. Their cherished doctrine, which they thought was going to re-Christianize Christianity and convert the world, would instead remain a peculiar doctrine believed primarily by persons in relatively small Wesleyan denominations. Nazarenes in the last decades of the 20th century would be astonished to learn that such optimism had even existed among Holiness people in the first part of that century, and some would consider that those who held such high hopes were quaintly naive. As the Church of the Nazarene's early understanding of the doctrine of entire sanctification reflected the heady optimism of the late 19th century, so the Church of the Nazarene's most recent understanding of the doctrine has reflected the "theological realism" of the late 20th century, which among other things, takes into account the "deep sinfulness of man."

This book will chart this gradual change in the understanding of the doctrine. The second chapter will provide an explanation of the doctrine, as the "fathers" of the denomination understood it. This early explication reflected 19th-century holiness orthodoxy and emphasized entire sanctification as an instantaneous second work of grace that eradicated the sinful nature, conditioned only by faith and consecration. Entire sanctification was identified as the baptism with the Holy Spirit and that baptism with the Holy Spirit, according to these early descriptions, resulted in almost glorified human persons.

The third chapter is a summary of the theologies of the first two "systematic theologians" of the church, John Miley and A. M. Hills. Particular attention will be paid to their understanding of the freedom of the will and their almost complete rejection of total depravity. Changes in the denomination's Articles of Faith indicate that Miley and Hills were representative of the Church of the Nazarene's general understanding. This emphasis on a person's volition would be a recurring theme and, in these early years, reflected the incredible optimism of the culture at large.

The fourth chapter is a summary of H. Orton Wiley's explication of entire sanctification. He warrants a separate chapter because of his singular influence on the church's understanding of the doctrine of entire sanctification.

The fifth chapter notes a relative change in the explication of the doctrine. The extravagant promises of the grace of entire sanctification were beginning to be understood as unrealistic, in part as a result of the failure of persons to realize those promises. Consequently, the sin that could be eradicated was more narrowly defined and the infirmities that were an inescapable consequence of fallen humanity were more expansively defined. As a result, the promise of entire sanctification was tempered. At the same time, the denomination began more ardently to defend its historic articulation of the doctrine, insisting on the use of particular terminology to define the doctrine.

Chapter 6 shows that this tendency to define sin more narrowly and define infirmity more expansively continued in the sixth and seventh decades of the 20th century. Qualifications of the doctrine abound, resulting in increasing dissatisfaction with the traditional understanding of the doctrine in the church. This dissatisfaction with the traditional formulation compelled a study of Wesley's writings, which were understood as divergent from the 19th-century formulations at important points.

Chapter 7 reviews the radical reformulation of the doctrine in relational terms. This reformulation has resulted in two contemporaneous and competing definitions of entire sanctification in the Church of the Nazarene. Needless to say, this poses a problem for a denomination that understands its primary reason for being the preservation and proclamation of the doctrine of entire sanctification.

The final chapter provides no resolution. It does, however, outline in brief several positive steps persons in particular and the church in general are taking to better articulate a doctrine of entire sanctification for the 21st century that does indeed take into account "the deep sinfulness of man."

2

THE POSSIBILITIES OF GRACE

THE DISTINCTIVE DOCTRINE OF THE
CHURCH OF THE NAZARENE

In the *Manual of the Church of the Nazarene*, a ritual for receiving members into the church is provided. The ritual that is used today is fundamentally the same as that which was used in 1908. In this membership ritual, persons are asked three questions. They are asked, first, to assent to the shortest of creedal statements; second, if they know Jesus Christ as their personal Savior; third, if they will commit themselves to the church. The doctrinal statement written for this ritual is intentionally concise. In 1908, it read:

It is necessary that we be of one mind and heart. The doctrines *essential* to Christian experience upon which the Church rests are brief. We believe in God the Father, Son, and Holy Ghost; we especially emphasize the deity of Jesus Christ and the personality of the Holy Spirit. That man is born in sin; that he needs the work of the Holy Spirit in regeneration; that after the work of regeneration there is the further work of heart cleansing, or entire sanctification, which is effected by the Holy Ghost. And to each of these works of grace, the Holy Spirit gives witness. We believe in eternal destiny with its rewards and punishments. Do you heartily believe these truths?[1]

In the 1997 *Manual*, persons are asked, when joining the Church of the Nazarene, to agree to a doctrinal statement only slightly different from the 1908 statement.

The doctrines upon which the church rests as essential to Christian experience are brief. We believe in God the Father, Son, and Holy Spirit. We especially emphasize the deity of Jesus Christ and the personality of the Holy Spirit. We believe that human beings are born in sin; that they need the work of forgiveness through Christ and the new birth by the Holy Spirit; that subsequent to this there is the deeper work of heart cleansing or entire sanctification through the infilling of the Holy Spirit, and that to each of these works of grace the Holy Spirit gives witness. We believe that our Lord will return, the dead shall be raised, and that all shall come to final judgment with its rewards and punishments. Do you heartily believe these truths? If so, answer, "I do."[2]

27

There is much that persons desiring to unite with the Church of the Nazarene do not have to assent to. While it is presupposed that those joining the Church of the Nazarene are familiar with and agree to the doctrinal statements as found in the church constitution, which in the 1908 *Manual* included separate articles on God [the Father], Jesus Christ, The Holy Spirit, The Holy Scriptures, Inherited Depravity, Repentance, Justification, Regeneration, Sanctification, Destiny, Baptism, The Lord's Supper, and the Second Coming of Christ, the membership ritual indicated that the first and primary reason for union with the Church of the Nazarene was the church's understanding of entire sanctification. This was neither an oversight nor the result of inadequate consideration concerning what it should mean to belong to the Church of the Nazarene. The membership ritual's creedal statement was purposefully brief because the early Nazarenes held that unity with the denomination did not demand unity on a host of other doctrinal matters.

Holiness leaders at the turn of the century believed that they had found the secret for uniting all of Christendom. They believed that where other doctrinal issues caused division, holiness doctrine united. At the 1873 Landisville, Pennsylvania, National Holiness Camp Meeting, Dr. Edgar M. Levy, a Baptist, reflected the predominant belief of those in the Holiness Movement concerning differences in doctrinal matters. He preached:

> [A]t last we have discovered the basis for Christian unity. The sanctification of the believers of every name, create unity in the great Christian brotherhood, such as no creed has ever been able to accomplish. Here . . . we have . . . an exhibition of Christian unity as thrills one's soul to behold. A unity not in ordinances; a unity not in church government; a unity not in forms of worship; a unity not in mere letter of creed—but in . . . the baptism of the Holy Spirit. As it is the nature of sin to separate, disintegrate, and repel, it is the nature of holiness to unite and adjust and harmonize.[3]

J. A. Wood, a Methodist minister active in the Holiness Movement, exhorted in 1876: "Presbyterians, Baptists, Congregationalists, Lutherans, Episcopalians, and Methodists, LET US ALL BE HOLY; then shall the Protestant Church be mighty through God to the 'pulling down of strongholds,' and the setting up the Kingdom of Christ in the Earth."[4]

And so it was, that among the "founding fathers" of the Church of the Nazarene, there were Baptists, Presbyterians, Congregationalists, Friends, Methodists, and Advent Christians.[5] There were both premillennialists and postmillennialists. There were those who strongly advocated infant baptism and those that disdained the doctrine and practice. Some believed immersion was the only valid way to baptize while others believed the method indifferent.[6] There were slightly divergent beliefs concerning the Lord's Supper, with a corresponding difference of opinion concerning the frequency of its celebration. There were differences with regard to church polity. While many supported a congregational structure of church government, others believed an episcopal form would be best. Concerning the legislation of holy morals, the churches in the west pushed for silence on matters of personal behavior (attendance at theaters, for example) while those in the Midwest and South believed guidance in the form of special rules to be necessary.[7] The rallying cry of the early Nazarenes was "Unity in essentials; liberty in nonessentials." Essential Nazarene belief, that which was the ground for the mergers of these many independent Holiness groups and the hope for the union of all of Christendom, was a particular understanding of the doctrine of entire sanctification.

Entire sanctification in the Church of the Nazarene was taught as a second work of grace, subsequent to initial salvation, realized instantly by faith. It cleansed one from inbred sin, thus enabling believers to live free from sin "properly so called," that is, from willful transgression of known laws. God granted this sanctification when the two conditions of consecration and faith had been met. The Holy Spirit was then fully given to those who had been sanctified, just as He had been given to the disciples on the day of Pentecost, which was the biblical paradigm and evidence for the doctrine. Assurance that one had been sanctified wholly was to be found in believing the promise of God's Word and an internal witness of the Holy Spirit. Entire sanctification was the surest guarantee of further growth in grace and, therefore, was an experience to be sought early in the salvation process. "Saved and sanctified," as soon as possible, was the expectation for all believers in the Church of the Nazarene.

The two Articles of Faith that addressed this work of God were the articles on "Original Sin" and "Sanctification." In the 1908 *Manual of the Pentecostal Church of the Nazarene,* the respective statements were:

> Original Sin: Original Sin is that corruption of the nature of all who are engendered as the offspring of Adam, whereby everyone is very far gone from original righteousness, and is inclined to evil, and that continually. In the Scriptures it is designated as "The Carnal Mind," our "Old Man," "The flesh," "Sin that dwelleth in me," etc. It cannot be pardoned, and continues to exist with the new life of the regenerate until eradicated and destroyed by the baptism with the Holy Spirit.[8]

> Sanctification: Entire sanctification is that act of God, subsequent to justification, by which regenerate believers are made free from inbred sin, and brought into the state of entire devotement to God, and the holy obedience of love made perfect. It is provided

through the meritorious blood of Jesus, and wrought upon the full and final consecration of the believer, and a definite act of appropriating faith, by the gracious agency of the Holy Spirit; and to this work and state of grace the Holy Spirit bears witness. This experience is also known by various terms representing different phases of the experience, such as "Christian Perfection," "Perfect Love," "Heart Purity," "The Baptism with the Holy Spirit," "The fulness [sic] of the blessing," "Christian Holiness," etc.[9]

Following Dr. Bresee's lead, the founder of the Los Angeles Church of the Nazarene, the Pentecostal Church of the Nazarene had established a Ministerial Course of Study to educate its ministers and ensure agreement on the distinctive doctrine. The books recommended in this four-year course of independent study reflected the "authoritative" teaching of the church. Since 1908, this course of study has been reviewed approximately every four years and recommendations concerning which books should be added or omitted have been made by book committees appointed to the quadrennial general assemblies of the church. The books and authors included in the Ministerial Course of Study are used not only for independent study but also in the colleges and seminaries of the Church of the Nazarene and are indicative, therefore, of the "official" teaching of the church.[10]

The books recommended to Nazarenes in the early part of the 20th century were, for the most part, written by Methodists who were active in the Holiness Movement in the 19th century, and there was relative uniformity on the doctrine of entire sanctification among these authors. There was also incredible optimism concerning when a regenerated believer might expect to be sanctified wholly, how it was effected, and what entire sanctification accomplished.

ENTIRE SANCTIFICATION AS THE INSTANTANEOUS ERADICATION OF THE SINFUL NATURE

One of the first exclusively "holiness" books that appeared in the Ministerial Course of Study was written by John Allen Wood (1828—1905), published in 1876, and titled *Purity and Maturity*. Wood was a Methodist preacher who had become well known in the Holiness Movement for his first book *Perfect Love*. *Perfect Love* was written in 1861 and would sell more than 60,000 copies in Wood's lifetime. According to Wood, however, his second book, *Purity and Maturity* was a more complete explication of the doctrine of entire sanctification than was his first. On the first page of the introduction of *Purity and Maturity*, Wood wrote:

PERFECT LOVE was written sixteen years since, two years after the precious Saviour fully cleansed my heart: this is written after much more time for reflection, prayerful study, and the careful examination of every thing available on the subject. I am very willing to admit, CHRISTIAN PURITY is a SPECIALTY with me, and has been for nearly twenty years.[11]

J. A. Wood saw entire sanctification as the great need of the Church, and he was every bit as optimistic as other Holiness leaders concerning what effect a great "revival of personal holiness" would have on the world. He believed that it would do nothing less than usher in the millennial kingdom.

> Christian Purity is what the Church needs to qualify her to carry forward her great work of regenerating the world. . . . The Church numerically ought to duplicate herself every year; and *she would, if she were fully sanctified to God.* Did each member of the Church secure the salvation of *but one soul* a year . . . in less than seven years the WORLD WOULD BE CONVERTED, *and the millennial glory cover the whole earth.* Bishop Janes asserts—"A holy Church would soon make a holy world;" and Bishop Foster—"Let the Church attain to this, let Christians claim their privilege, and come up to the standard, and the world would be a speedy and easy conquest."[12]

Wood's primary thesis, contrary to what the title might have suggested, was that purity and maturity were not synonymous. Purity was not to be identified in any way with maturity. Wood was concerned with contesting the notion that holiness was a consequence of growth in grace. Holiness people believed that one of the greatest errors in the Church was the notion that holiness was a consequence of, or dependent on, a gradual growth in grace. Wood's book was written solely to distinguish between purity, which was the immediate gift of God's sanctifying grace, and maturity, which was growth in grace subsequent to entire sanctification.

> The opinion has become somewhat prevalent among Christian people, that deliverance from indwelling sin—a state of purity of heart—can be obtained by the ordinary process of *growth in grace.* This we regard as a serious mistake and productive of much evil. We view it as un-Scriptural and anti-Wesleyan.[13]

According to Wood, purity was not maturity. Purity was a quality of being in which there was freedom from all sin. So that there could be no mistake, he stated this definition countless times and in varying ways throughout his book. On the third page of his first chapter, he wrote,

> Purity or holiness significant of quality, implies entirety. It does not mean a mixture of purity and pollution, partly clean and partly defiled . . . he who is "cleansed" is entirely pure, is "clean," free from "all iniquity," "all unrighteousness," "all sin," "holy and without blame."[14]

His second chapter consisted of quotations from theological authorities in the Wesleyan tradition, such as John Wesley, John Fletcher, Adam Clarke, and Richard Watson, all of whom had defined purity as such. The third and fourth chapters consisted of scripture texts that he believed supported the Holiness Movement's definition of entire sanctification. His concluding commentary on the 38 passages he cited was that purity of heart was a consequence of entire sanctification and eradicated all sin from the life of the believer.

A "pure heart" is one that is cleansed from all indwelling sin, and is morally clean and right before God . . . and it cannot be clean until all inbred sin is removed by the cleansing blood of Christ. In the pure in heart all the Christian virtues exist to the exclusion of their opposite vices; as love without hatred, submission without rebellion, faith without unbelief, humility without pride, meekness without anger, patience without impatience, and peace with no strife.[15]

Contrary to what the above passage might suggest, Wood maintained that entire sanctification or purity of heart did not imply any fullness of grace. It was simply the absence of sin. "The idea of purifying is that of the removal of something, i.e. impurity from the soul; rather than the introduction of anything into the soul."[16] Furthermore, this cleansing from all sin was not to be understood as being in any way exceptional.

We understand simple purity, as not a high state of grace, when compared with the privileges and possibilities in the divine life. Purity is only the base, the substratum of a grand Christian life, and the present duty and privilege of all Christians. "With me (said the saintly Fletcher) it is a small thing to be cleansed from all sin; but O! To be filled with all the fulness of God."[17]

This purity of heart and life, which was a consequence of entire sanctification, was granted in an instant to the regenerated believer. Wood concluded the two chapters of scripture texts in which he defined purity as the absence of all sin by also proving the instantaneous nature of sanctification.

"Not a (scriptural) *figure* or *term* used, significant of purification, has any *limitation* to teach that the work may not be completed at once,—instantaneously wrought by the supernatural power of God. The (scripture) words "all," "wholly," "whole," and the like, express a *finished* work in those *"purified, made white, and tried."* Sanctification is a *plain, single, simple definite cleansing*, wrought by God himself, in the *soul itself*. And these passages are a standing rebuke to that gradualism, which pushes this whole subject into indefinite generalities, without a distinct work of cleansing.[18]

Since sanctification was wrought in an instant in the life of the regenerated believer by the "supernatural power of God," there was no need to wait for this gift. Because purity (holiness) was not the culmination of a long process of Christian maturity, it should be expected early in the Christian life. Echoing Phoebe Palmer, a 19th-century promoter of holiness in the Methodist Church, Wood wrote, "It is a short way from *pardon* to *purity* to him who WALKS IN THE LIGHT."[19] It was the "present duty and privilege" of all Christians. Indeed, the sooner one was made pure, the sooner one would become mature. Entire sanctification was the greatest guarantee of continued growth in grace. "The greater part of our growth in grace, and advancement in the divine life, should be subsequent to our entire sanctification."[20] Wood never denied a need for growth in grace or a need for maturation. He simply believed that it was best accomplished after the soul had been sanctified.

Growth in grace is essentially the same before and after sanctification. The only difference being in the former case, the reign of grace is somewhat limited, having a powerful inward foe to antagonize in addition to enemies from without. In the latter, grace has unlimited dominion in the soul, and its growth is unimpeded by anything within the hearts. . . . Every sanctified soul knows that after his purification, growth in grace is far more easy and rapid.[21]

To reiterate, J. A. Wood believed one could never mature into purity. Entire sanctification was that act of God, subsequent to justification, by which regenerate believers were made free from inbred sin, and it was most certainly an experience to be sought early in the salvation process. "Saved and sanctified" as soon as possible was J. A. Wood's understanding of the doctrine, and it was the expectation for all believers in the Pentecostal Church of the Nazarene.[22]

PENTECOST AS THE OCCASION FOR ENTIRE SANCTIFICATION

The biblical paradigm for the Holiness Movement's understanding of entire sanctification at the end of the 19th century was Pentecost. According to Donald Dayton, the "Pentecostal" formulation of entire sanctification, which was not used by John Wesley, took strong root in the years just before and after the Civil War.[23] Among Holiness people, Pentecost was not understood as a singular event in the context of salvation-history. Instead, Pentecost was a personal event that was to be a part of every believer's salvation experience. A "personal Pentecost" became normative for all believers according to holiness teaching, and this personal baptism of the Holy Spirit was considered the occasion of entire sanctification. By the end of the 19th century, the explanation of entire sanctification, with Pentecost as its model, was universal among those in the Holiness Movement.[24] According to the 1908 *Manual of the Pentecostal Church of the Nazarene*, the Article of Faith on "Original Sin" succinctly stated the doctrine. "[Original Sin] cannot be pardoned, and continues to exist with the new life of the regenerate until eradicated and destroyed by the baptism of the Holy Spirit."[25]

In 1908, the year of the birthday of the Pentecostal Church of the Nazarene, Daniel Steele's *The Gospel of the Comforter* became required reading for fourth year students in the Ministerial Course of Study and remained there until 1932. Daniel Steele (1824—1914) was a Methodist pastor and educator. He was the first president of Syracuse University and then professor of systematic theology at Boston University from 1887 to 1890. According to Richard Taylor, the editor of a volume of leading Wesleyan thinkers, "Few if any theologians have had a more extensive or enduring influence on the modern holiness movement than Daniel Steele."[26] *The Gospel of the Comforter*, which was published in 1897, was a book about the work and ministry of the Holy Spirit. In this work, Steele did not argue so much as assume that Pentecost, or the baptism of the Holy Ghost, was the occasion of entire sanctification.

Daniel Steele saw the baptism of the Holy Spirit (entire sanctification) as the great need of the Church. He believed that the reason for the Church's continuing lack of power and effectiveness in the world was the neglect of appropriating the baptism of the Holy Spirit. Early in his book, he wrote:

> The work of the Father . . . and the work of the Son . . . are completed past acts. But the work of the Spirit in each individual believer is incomplete. They very greatly mistake who suppose that He fully accomplished His mission to our world on the day of Pentecost. . . . The day of Pentecost was a pattern day; all the days of this dispensation should have been like it, or should have exceeded it. But alas! the Church has fallen down to the state in which it was before this blessing had been bestowed, and it is necessary for us to ask Christ to begin all over again. . . . We need a baptism of the Spirit as much as the apostles did at the time of Christ's resurrection.[27]

He was as optimistic as any in the Holiness Movement concerning what could be accomplished if the Church would only permit itself this fresh baptism. The Church could be at the threshold of millennial glory.

> Let the entire Church come to a full realization that the Comforter came to abide and that He is now descending in personal Pentecosts as certainly and as demonstrably in the consciousness of every perfect believer as He did in the upper room in Jerusalem, then will the glory of the dispensation of the Spirit begin to be generally seen. . . . There are indications of the dawn of that returning day of Pentecost when the Spirit shall be poured out in His fullness upon all who "know the exceeding greatness of Christ's power to usward who

believe." The eastern sky has streaks of light betokening the sunrise of a day of power. Christians of every name, lone watchers on the mountaintops, now see the edge of the ascending disk, and are shouting to the inhabitants of the dark valleys below to awake and arise and behold the splendors of the King of day.[28]

He was convinced that the baptism of the Holy Spirit was the greatest hope for uniting all of Christendom.

The various sects which divide the Christian world can keep the unity of the Spirit and swell in peace so long as they are filled with true charity. How can this fulness be insured . . . ? We may ask for the presence of the Comforter in our hearts, whose office it is "to shed abroad the love of God, . . ." Here is the real basis of Christian unity. It is spiritual and not ecclesiastical; not theological beyond the basal truths of orthodoxy; not sacramental and ceremonial. The manner and significance of water baptism, the Lord's Supper and the number and gradation of ordinations should be regarded as in the sphere of liberty. Is God revealed in His divine Son, Jesus Christ, the only Saviour, and does He communicate Himself to believers in the personal Holy Spirit, the only Sanctifier. This is a doctrinal basis sufficient for the unity of all Christians.[29]

Steele was very clear concerning what the baptism of the Holy Spirit accomplished. It did nothing less than destroy the carnal nature. "The entire eradication of the propensity to sin is by the direct and instantaneous act of the Holy Spirit responsive to a special act of faith in Christ claiming the full heritage of the believer."[30] He was as adamant as J. A. Wood concerning the instantaneous nature of the baptism. Quoting an anonymous "eminent expositor," Steele wrote: "[I]n the New Testament, we never read expressly and unmistakably of sanctification as a gradual process. . . . It was accomplished by the Spirit in an instant, and not by the processes of growth."[31]

Interpreting Pentecost as the moment of entire sanctification was fundamental to the Holiness Movement's argument concerning the nature of the doctrine. With Pentecost interpreted as the occasion of entire sanctification, there was biblical evidence that sanctification was what they believed it to be, that is, a second work of grace wrought instantaneously in the heart of the regenerated believer, cleansing that believer from all sin by a supernatural act of God. With Pentecost, they had a pivotal biblical model for the doctrine. According to Steele, this is what happened to the disciples at the first Pentecost. They were entirely sanctified. The historical evidence for this was found in the disciples' relative ineffectiveness subsequent to the Resurrection and prior to Pentecost and their amazing change after Pentecost.

Pentecost as the pivotal biblical model of the doctrine of Entire Sanctification

We do not read that the company of disciples was at all increased by the story of the resurrection of Christ. . . . This bare historic fact made no converts. . . . For seven weeks the company of believers had all the facts of the gospel except the ascension complete, and for ten days they had the climax, the ascension of Christ, but here was no increase of their numbers. But on the fiftieth day three thousand believed on Jesus as the divine Saviour. Something must have happened.[32]

That something was the baptism of the Holy Spirit in His purifying power. Steele was quite clear that the primary purpose in the giving of the Holy Spirit was for purity and not merely for power, as some supposed. At the turn of the century, there were others espousing the need for "personal Pentecosts" who were emphasizing that what the Holy Spirit bestowed at Pentecost was power. While Steele recognized that this was indeed true, it was not the Holy Spirit's first office.

They who urge believers to seek the baptism of the Spirit for service . . . are doing a good service to the Church; but they who proclaim this baptism for entire sanctification first . . . act more wisely, because the natural and scriptural order is cleansing before filling.[33]

Entire sanctification and the baptism of the Holy Ghost, according to Holiness people at the turn of the century, were synonymous terms. Pentecost was understood as the paradigm for the experience. And the Article of Faith on sanctification in the 1908 Pentecostal Church of the Nazarene stated such: "Entire sanctification is that act of God . . . by which believers are made free from inbred sin . . . by the gracious agency of the Holy Spirit. This experience is also known by various terms . . . such as 'The Baptism with the Holy Spirit.'"[34]

FAITH AND CONSECRATION AS THE PRIMARY CONDITIONS FOR ENTIRE SANCTIFICATION

In 1911, the General Assembly of the Church of the Nazarene added *Holiness and Power* by A. M. Hills (1848—1935) to its Ministerial Course of Study where it remained until 1964. A. M. Hills, who had studied at Oberlin under Charles Finney and Asa Mahan, was a Congregational pastor whose involvement in the Holiness Movement was primarily as an educator. In 1899, after teaching at Asbury College in Kentucky, he became the first president of Peniel College, the college of the Holiness Association of Texas. He was president of Central Holiness University in Oskaloosa, Iowa, and one of the founders of the Illinois Holiness University at Olivet, Illinois, which would become a Nazarene college in 1912. He was finally professor at the Nazarene College in Pasadena, California, which had been founded by P. F. Bresee. The book for which he is most known, *Holiness and Power*, was published in 1897 by Martin Wells Knapp and was written while Hills was engaged in evangelistic work. According to Richard Taylor, this book on holiness "is perhaps the most comprehensive collection of arguments, exposition, and documentation produced during that time."[35] The significance of the work for Nazarenes is evidenced by its inclusion in the course of study for a near-record 53 years.

He believed, as other Holiness leaders did, that the great need of the Church was the baptism of the Holy Ghost and he was no less optimistic than others concerning the consequences if persons were to receive this baptism.

Is it too much to say or believe that if the Protestant churches and ministry had a similar anointing of Holy Ghost power to-day, we could take the world for Christ in ten years? We now have thrones and governments and protection and favorable public sentiment, and hundreds of billions of money in the hands of Christians. We have established institutions and organizations and all needed facilities, the Bible printed in some four hundred languages, and a Christian literature in abundance, like the leaves of the forest. We have everything desirable for doing Christian work but the general enduement of Holy Spirit power. But without that, alas, how feeble, comparatively, when measured by that first century, are our Christian triumphs.[36]

Hills, as did Steele, Wood, and others in the Holiness Movement, believed that the baptism with the Holy Ghost or entire sanctification would be a unifying force for Christianity. In 1901, there was held in Chicago a General Holiness Assembly at which a call was issued for all of the disparate holiness organizations throughout the United States to unite. A. M. Hills was one of the coauthors of "The Official Call," as it was known. It stated:

Such a (holiness) Assembly, representing all of the evangelical Churches, will give a blessed opportunity of manifesting to the Church and to the world, the love they have for each other and for the various movements and denominations they represent. . . . The most devoted and prominent Christian workers have not been able to see things alike in all things, but, by the grace of God, they may be able to feel alike and work in perfect harmony regardless of their many differences. . . . We are on the eve of a great revival of Scriptural holiness . . . we believe it will be greatly used of God in bringing about the greatest revival of holiness witnessed since the days of the apostles; that the fire of God's love will sweep away all barriers that have kept the holiness people apart, and that the saints will be so occupied with God that they will lose sight of human creeds and forms and self importance and whatever else has hindered the out-pouring of God's Spirit.[37]

Hills was equally insistent concerning the instantaneous aspect of the doctrine. One could never grow into holiness. Basing his argument on God's promise of holiness for those who seek it, Hills wrote, "The reader will notice that every item of this promise stands before us as the exclusive work of God. . . . We are not sanctified gradually by our own poor, fitful and lifelong strivings, but by God's INSTANTANEOUS ACT of cleansing."[38] Quoting 1 Thessalonians 5:23, which was the favorite proof text of sanctification for Holiness writers,[39] Hills wrote: "Here is INSTANTANEOUS sanctification, not after death, nor at death, not by a process lifelong, nor by the growth method, if language can teach any such thing."[40]

Hills devoted an entire chapter of *Holiness and Power* to the teaching that entire sanctification eradicated the sinful nature. In the chapter titled "SANCTIFICATION THE CURE OF DEPRAVITY," Hills repeated over and over again this claim in rather extravagant terms.

> When the Holy Ghost came upon [the disciples] that "old man" of sin was crucified, and they were sanctified. He took the cowardice out of Peter, and the unbelief out of Thomas, and the overgrown ambitions out of James and John. The "Son of Thunder" became the "Apostle of Love." And right here we touch the meaning of SANCTIFICATION. It is the work of the Holy Spirit—the act of God's grace, by which "our old man is crucified" and the moral nature is "cleansed" of all "unrighteousness,"—unrightness, "proneness to sin," "sinful propensity."[41]

In a section comparing justification, regeneration, and sanctification, Hills made even more explicit his understanding of entire sanctification.

> [S]anctification is the work of God *purging* the whole being. . . . [S]anctification removes the *inclination* to sin in the future. . . . [S]anctification removes *inbred* sin, and, by correcting the nature of the whole being, confirms the will in obedience. . . . [S]anctification so "cleanses from filthiness and idols," and puts within the soul such a "new heart and a new spirit," that the whole man reinforces the will, and perfect obedience and a holy heart are secured. . . . [B]y sanctification, "we are transformed into the same image from glory to glory," and we are "made partakers of the divine nature." The longings for holiness and the image of God become realized.[42]

According to Hills and in complete agreement with Daniel Steele, the baptism with the Holy Ghost was the occasion of entire sanctification. Hills unquestionably believed that the gift of the Holy Spirit to the disciples on the Day of Pentecost was for their entire sanctification. While the disciples were clearly regenerate prior to Pentecost, they were still in need of a further work of grace.

But Jesus prayed that they might be "sanctified," and charged them to wait for the "Baptism with the Holy Ghost," which would be to them a sanctifying experience. This is no conjecture of ours. . . . That is exactly what we are insisting upon in this whole volume, and what the Bible teaches—that sanctification is the "cleansing of the heart by faith"—the result of a "Baptism with the Holy Ghost." And the after lives of those disciples prove that they were sanctified.[43]

For Hills, the baptism with the Holy Ghost was the moment of entire sanctification.

The value of the book *Holiness and Power*, in addition to being fully consistent with other holiness teachings, was found in its clear explanation of the means for obtaining the blessing. A full quarter of Hills's book was devoted to explaining precisely how regenerated believers were to be entirely sanctified. In this he was also in harmony with others in the Holiness Movement concerning the conditions necessary for receiving the baptism of the Holy Spirit.

Phoebe Palmer had declared a half century before that there were primarily two conditions for receiving this baptism. According to her and others in the tradition, the two were consecration and faith. In *Holiness and Power*, Hills didn't name just these two; he listed eight. However, the first five are quite preliminary when compared to consecration and faith and the sixth and seventh, which were respectively obedience and consecration, are difficult to distinguish from each other. Fortunately, he didn't concentrate on the five preliminary conditions, writing at times only a few paragraphs about each of them, and it is not necessary for this study to try to differentiate between obedience and consecration.

The first condition for entire sanctification, according to Hills, was discovering the need. There must first arise in regenerated believers grave dissatisfaction concerning the state of their salvation. Hills included personal testimonials of notable persons who had written of such dissatisfaction. One person thus quoted was Mrs. Harriet Beecher Stowe.

For some three or four years past there has been in my mind a subdued undercurrent of perplexity and unhappiness in regard to myself in my religious experience. I have often thought when sifting myself, 'Why am I thus restless? Why not at peace? I love God and Jesus Christ with a real and deep devotion, and in general I mean to conform my life to him. I am as consistent as many Christians, more; then why not satisfied?[44]

This "restlessness" would lead one to the discovery of the need for entire sanctification, and this was Hills's first condition. With this discovery, the second condition of repenting for not receiving the sanctifying Savior should be met along with a third: recognition of entire sanctification's importance. Of course, one must believe that entire sanctification is a possibility, and this was Hills's fourth condition for receiving the blessing. He then listed "hungering and thirsting" for it as the fifth indispensable condition.

Hills distinguished between the sixth and seventh conditions (obedience and consecration) although it is difficult to discern the distinctions that he made. Writing of obedience as a condition for entire sanctification, Hills stated, "Obedience means . . . absolute surrender of the will to the Lord about *all* things, for Jesus to take you and do what he pleases with you and yours."[45] When he wrote of consecration as a condition of entire sanctification, he used almost exactly the same language. "Consecration is the actual present surrender to God of the whole man and all we possess."[46] Regardless of the distinction in Hills's mind between obedience and consecration, he was quite consistent with holiness orthodoxy concerning the primary condition for receiving the blessing. After one was made conscious of the need for entire sanctification, one entered into the state by first of all, "surrendering" or "consecrating" oneself to God.

The act of consecration is to recognize Christ's ownership and to accept it. Say to him with the whole heart, "Lord, I am thine by right and I wish to be thine by choice. . . ." The blessing . . . is conferred gladly when we comply with the conditions, one of which is the absolute surrender of our WILL about EVERYTHING.[47]

And the surrender had to be absolute. "While there is a spark of insubordination or rebellion or dictation you will never get it. Truly submissive and obedient souls and loyal souls enter his kingdom."[48]

There were many ways to describe this entire consecration and there were many biblical images used. A favorite was "crucified with Christ," which came from Galatians 2:20.[49] Quoting General Booth, the founder of the Salvation Army, Hills wrote that being crucified with Christ meant:

Dying to all those pleasures and gratifications which flow from the undue love of self, the admiration of the world, the ownership of goods, and the inordinate love of kindred and friends which go together to make up the life and joy of the natural man. This may be painful; but we must be crucified with Christ if we are to live with him.[50]

The image used most for entire consecration came from Phoebe Palmer. Palmer (1807-74) was, without question, the most influential religious woman of her generation. Her writings and her "Tuesday Meetings for the Promotion of Holiness" made her the greatest promoter of entire sanctification in the century. Her primary contribution to the 19th-century Holiness Movement was her clear explanation of the method for obtaining the blessing. Using the last third of Exodus 29:37 and the last half of

[handwritten: Consecrated 1. Life + Faith, +obedience in Jesus]

Matthew 23:19 as her proof texts,[51] she taught that when believers conse-crated themselves on the altar, they were made holy. She wrote: "Christ is the CHRISTIAN'S ALTAR. Lay body, soul and spirit upon his merits."[52] Counseling one who was needing guidance into the state of entire sancti-fication, she wrote: "What you need, in order to bring you into this state, is an offering up of yourself through this purifying medium . . . [Make] the required sacrifice, it will be done unto you according to your faith."[53]

Hills himself used this image when describing consecration, and he was quite conscious of his indebtedness to Phoebe Palmer for this theolo-gy. He, too, counseled persons that by placing themselves on the altar of Christ and making a complete consecration, they would be made holy.

"The altar sanctifieth the gift." In this last quotation is a state-ment of a great fact. The altar is greater than the gift; and whatsoever *[handwritten: Jesus is the altar of faith]* is laid upon the altar (in faith) becomes sanctified and holy. It is the altar that does the work. The question arises: Who and what is the al-tar? In Heb. xiii. 10-12 we are told: "We have an altar. . . . Wherefore Jesus also that he might sanctify the people through his own blood, suffered without the gate." . . . his divine nature was the altar upon which the sacrifice was made. The Saviour, then, is the Christian's al-tar. Upon him I lay myself (in faith). The altar sanctifies the gift.[54]

Thus, complete consecration was absolutely necessary for entire sanctifi-cation, and it was a message that was found in all holiness literature of the period. Daniel Steele was equally clear concerning its necessity. He wrote, "God can do His perfect work in a soul only when the will is in the attitude of complete, trustful submission. . . . This highest upreaching of faith is possible only to the deepest submission of the human will.[55] J. A. Wood believed the same. "In every case (of entire sanctification), there is first a *full surrender to God,* acceptance of his will."[56] The Church of the Nazarene's Article of Faith on sanctification reflected the orthodox holi-ness teaching of the day. "[Entire sanctification] is provided through the meritorious blood of Jesus, and wrought upon the full and final consecra-tion of the believer."[57]

Hills reserved an entire chapter for the last condition for obtaining entire sanctification. As it turns out, one could take all seven steps that Hills had mentioned and still not receive the baptism of the Holy Spirit. To complete the work, one needed faith.

There are those who have consecrated all, and hungered and thirsted and yet have missed the blessing for years, simply because the last step was not taken. It is like marching across the desert to-ward Canaan, and halting on the wrong side of the Jordan. The swollen river was crossed by *faith.* Faith is the last step that brings the seeking soul to the "fulness of the blessing" of this Canaan of sanctification.[58]

Hills once again included testimonials of persons who supported the contention that entire sanctification was contingent finally on the faith of the believer. He quoted the experience of Dr. Carradine, who was a Methodist minister prominent in the Holiness Movement.

> I wanted perfect love to God and man, and a perfect rest in my soul all the time. . . . [I]t was cleansing, sin-eradication I craved. My prayer was for sanctification. After the battle of consecration came the battle of faith. Both precede the perfect victory of sanctification. *Vain is consecration without faith* to secure the blessing. Hence men can be perfectly consecrated all their lives, and never know the blessing of sanctification. I must believe there is such a work in order to realize the grace.[59]

"Believe and receive" is what the Holiness teachers taught. "Believe and receive" was the exact phrase they used. The victory of faith was the assurance of entire sanctification. Hills concluded the chapter on the need of faith for entire sanctification by suggesting four simple steps that one might take to realize the promise. Borrowed from a sermon preached at Moody Bible Institute by Andrew Murray, he wrote:

1. Say TO-NIGHT,   I MUST BE FILLED WITH THE SPIRIT. . . .
2.   I MAY be filled with the Spirit. . . .
3.   I WOULD be filled with the Spirit. . . .
4.   I SHALL be filled with the Spirit . . .

Dear reader, such language means INSTANTANEOUS SANCTIFICATION by faith, for you NOW.[60]

Faith as the final condition for entire sanctification was a fundamental teaching of Phoebe Palmer. Palmer believed that entire sanctification had to be received in the same manner that justification was received, namely, through faith. This "believe and receive" formula for entire sanctification guarded the Holiness people from any hint of a "works-righteousness" salvation. Palmer was so insistent on faith being the foremost condition for entire sanctification that she preferred to use the term "naked faith." A. M. Hills, in *Holiness and Power*, quoted the lengthy testimony of Phoebe Palmer's sanctification experience where she used the term "naked faith" to describe what had been required of her.

> I now saw what faith was in all its simplicity, and I replied, "I will come up before my Judge and in the face of an assembled universe say, 'The foundation of my faith was thy immutable word.'" The moment I came to this point, the Holy Spirit whispered, "This is just the way in which Abraham walked. . . . My faith was at once put to the test. I had expected that some wonderful manifestation would fol-

low. But I was shut up to *faith*—naked *faith* in a naked promise. I then took the advanced ground of confession. Giving God the glory due to his name I exclaimed: "Through thy grace alone I have been enabled to give myself wholly and forever to thee. Thou hast given thy word, assuring me that thou *dost receive.* I BELIEVE THAT WORD! Alleluia! Glory be to the Holy Spirit forever!" Oh, into what a region of light, glory and purity was my soul at this moment ushered![61]

Faith as the final condition for the baptism of the Holy Ghost was the teaching of Daniel Steele. "When we venture to believe . . . we find by happy experience that according to our faith it is done to us. . . . We feel that we are then holy in a sense unknown to us before."[62] Wood was equally unequivocal: "Purification by faith, the reader will see, is stated in most of the quotations we have given. Purity being only by faith, the reception of that which is conditioned on faith, can only be obtained by believing for it."[63]

With entire consecration and faith as the two primary conditions for being made entirely holy, there was then further evidence that this work of God was accomplished instantaneously. When these two conditions were met, entire sanctification was granted. Sin was eradicated and the Holy Spirit was given, for this was the promise of God's word. Consecration and faith as the two conditions for receiving the baptism of the Holy Ghost also supported the contention that being made entirely holy did not have to wait for any growth in grace. A brand-new believer could consecrate and believe for entire sanctification as easily as one who was not. There was therefore no excuse to not seek the blessing early in the Christian life. The Church of the Nazarene's Article of Faith on sanctification reflected this orthodox holiness teaching of the day: "[Entire sanctification] is provided through the meritorious blood of Jesus, and wrought upon the full and final consecration of the believer, and a definite act of appropriating faith, by the gracious agency of the Holy Spirit."[64]

THE RESULTS OF ENTIRE SANCTIFICATION

The Pentecostal Church of the Nazarene did not define the results of entire sanctification in negative terms only. The eradication of the sinful nature did not exhaust the consequences of this second work of grace. Sin was destroyed but holiness was imparted. Holiness books at the turn of the century included marvelous definitions and wonderful descriptions of this imparted holiness. Nowhere was the optimism of the church more pronounced than in their early convictions concerning what entire sanctification accomplished. The Article of Faith on sanctification in the 1908 *Manual of the Pentecostal Church of the Nazarene* condensed this positive description in two short phrases, but this abbreviated statement in no way encompassed all that these early Nazarenes believed about the doctrine. According to their statement of faith, "Entire sanctification is that act of God . . . by which regenerate believers are . . . brought into the state of entire devotement to God, and the holy obedience of love made perfect."[65]

In 1911, the General Assembly of the Pentecostal Church of the Nazarene added to the Ministerial Course of Study the book *Possibilities of Grace,* written by Rev. Asbury Lowrey, a Methodist elder, evangelist, and editor of the holiness periodical *Christian Standard.* The book would remain in the course of study for 45 years, almost as long as A. M. Hills's *Holiness and Power.* The book, as the title suggests, wonderfully proclaims the positive effects of entire sanctification in the life of the believer.

Asbury Lowrey believed, even more so than Wood, Steele, or Hills, that holiness was the great need of the Church. As a matter of fact, he taught unequivocally what other Holiness leaders would only intimate: that persons should not expect to be saved without the experience of entire sanctification. According to Lowrey, it really wasn't enough that persons were regenerated. If they were not entirely sanctified, they were in grave danger of condemnation. Lowrey unapologetically taught that it was either holiness or hell. Repeatedly in his 472-page tome, Lowrey declared this "holiness or hell" doctrine. He hints on the very first page what he explains on subsequent ones. "[H]oliness becomes a fundamental principle indispensable to all excellence. . . . Christians could not be Christians, angels could not be angels, and God could not be God, without it."[66] Commenting on the state of believers at the church of first-century Corinth, Lowrey made clear his understanding of those who were saved but not sanctified.

> They were "babes in Christ," that is, they had dishonored Christ and imperiled their justification, by living below the provisions of the atonement and the requirements of the Gospel. What is the legitimate inference? It is this: Not to leave the principles of the doctrine of Christ and go on to perfection, is to generate and foster sin in ourselves. . . . From which it appears that it is not necessary to lapse into positive sin in order to forfeit the favor of God and taint the soul. It is effectually done by simply neglecting the great salvation. . . . The continuance of a justified state hinges upon a subsequent thorough work.[67]

In particularly strong language, Lowrey essentially declared that the church at large was in a state of apostasy because it had rejected the doctrine of entire sanctification.

> No doubt the churches are today largely under condemnation growing out of this very delinquency [of seeking entire sanctification], while many Christians, who have shut their eyes and flung off conscious obligation, have really vitiated their title to heaven. They are living in willful disobedience, and, therefore, under guilt. If such is the alarming condition of

those who disregard holiness, what shall we say of those who antagonize it? Can such persons have any living hope of heaven? What is the difference between the rejection of pardon and the rejection of sanctification? According to Lowrey, there was no difference between one who rejected pardon and one who rejected sanctification. Lest there be any confusion over the matter, he wrote, in the concluding chapter of his book, ". . . [T]he passport into heaven is personal holiness . . . we must put on this wedding-garment, or never be admitted into the marriage-supper of the Lamb."[68]

The Pentecostal Church of the Nazarene did not officially endorse this aspect of holiness teaching. There is nothing in the doctrinal statements that would support this zealous "holiness or hell" theology. Nevertheless, much early Nazarene teaching reflected it, even among the most careful of Holiness writers. It was evident in A. M. Hills's assessment of a church that was ineffective in evangelism. According to Hills, because the church had not received the baptism of the Holy Ghost, "[T]hat church is training gospel-hardened candidates for damnation."[69] Daniel Steele did not hesitate to warn of the dangers of remaining in what he considered a strictly justified state. "We cannot believe that God is pleased with an average piety. . . . Let no man deem it profitable to hide from himself the evil lurking in his heart. The peace thus secured will not long endure. It is an illusion. No one can afford to rest in a treacherous peace."[70] J. A. Wood, throughout *Purity and Maturity,* continually referred to those who had been justified but not entirely sanctified as the "merely justified," so it is not surprising that he came very close to Lowrey's convictions in the matter.

> Living in a *partially purified state* in the light of Gospel provision, must be displeasing to God. Alas! what sad work this course is producing upon multitudes in all our churches! what *coldness!* what *darkness!* what *weakness!* what *death* . . . ! Dr. John Demptster says . . . *Apostasy or purity is the only possible alternative after regeneration.*[71]

In light of this "holiness or hell" theology, it is easy to understand why Lowrey and others believed that holiness was the greatest need of the Church.

Lowrey was as optimistic as any in the Holiness Movement concerning what would happen if the Church received this blessing. He believed that holiness was the reason for every great reformation in the history of the Church. According to Lowrey, had ministers been entirely sanctified already, the Church "would have been ablaze to-day, and heroically engaged in sweeping into the embrace of Jesus the lost millions of our race, more as nations than as individuals."[72]

Lowrey wrote even more extravagantly than Wood, Steele, or Hills of holiness as the eradication of all sin in the life of the believer. "Entire sanctification signifies deliverance from all sin, internal and external; that is, from all indwelling sin, as well as from its outward manifestations; not from its uprisings and guilty motions merely, but from its contaminations and inherent existence."[73] He understood, as did others, that Pentecost was the occasion for this second blessing. The baptism of the Holy Ghost and entire sanctification were synonymous terms for Lowrey also. Indeed, it was the Holy Spirit's particular office. "(The Holy Spirit's) special work was . . . to purge out all dross and (s)in from the heart."[74]

Lowrey devoted over 100 pages on how to obtain entire sanctification, and his analysis of the process paralleled A. M. Hills's understanding. First, one must believe in the possibility of sanctification. Then one must consecrate oneself to God and once again, Phoebe Palmer's influence is evident. "Another step toward entire sanctification is the act of self-surrender, by which we transfer ourselves and all that belongs to us into the hands of Jesus. This act of self-surrender is commonly spoken of as "placing all upon the altar."[75] The final step was faith. "It is the touch of faith alone that brings the healing virtue out of Christ by which the believer is made every whit whole."[76]

Lowrey's particular contribution to the teaching of entire sanctification, however, was his positive descriptions of the entirely sanctified state. While many others spoke in glowing terms of the baptism of the Holy Ghost and what it accomplished, none approached Lowrey's comprehensive description. In short, the language he used to describe the entirely sanctified believer was language that those outside the Holiness tradition had reserved for glorification. As stated above, Lowrey had a rather expansive view of what was eradicated by the grace of entire sanctification. All Holiness writers wrote of the sinful nature as that which was destroyed, but Lowrey pressed the definition. He hinted that not only was original sin gone but also God removed the residual effects of original sin from the life of the entirely sanctified. When discussing purification in the context of the Levitical sacrificial system, he wrote, "Nor is the meaning (of spiritual purification) restricted to the washing away of guilt alone, but also the removal of those depravities which have come upon us both by inheritance and involuntary transgression."[77] He did not elaborate on what those particular "depravities" were, but he wrote of them as obviously secondary to and as a consequence of original sin. This was not the only place he wrote of sanctification this way. He began his chapter on "Positive Holiness" using the same language.

Christian holiness . . . is a pure state of heart and mind, joined with and causing a pure life and character . . . it is a sinless condition. . . . Not merely unsinning in overt action . . . but unsinful in his being. The depravities and saturation of hereditary and contracted sinfulness are expunged.[78]

Entire sanctification did more than just remove evil and its effects. The baptism of the Holy Spirit imparted positive grace. According to Lowrey, entire sanctification restored the image of God to fallen man.

> By the process of redemption it is proposed to restore the primary, but now lost, rectitude of human nature. The original prototype—the image of God—is to be used as the standard. . . [The new man, then, is the moral character of God—the spirituality of His nature—the similitude of His grandest perfections. With this, all true believers are to be rehabilitated. It is to be done by a re-impression of the primeval type upon our sin-despoiled nature. Every marred feature shall be repaired—every faded lineament revived—every lost jewel returned—and the whole picture of divine loveliness reproduced.[79]

This impartation of the image of God is what expelled remaining sin and nothing less than the word *glory* was sufficient to describe this restored condition. The New Testament writers used the word *glory* "to denote that spiritual irradiation of the whole man which takes place when God reigns in him, when the image of God is realized in him."[80]

According to Lowrey, in entire sanctification, believers became as holy as God was holy. They did not merely approach God's holiness. They did not only approximate it. The only distinction between God's holiness and man's holiness was that God's holiness was inherent and man's was acquired.

> [H]oliness in men is identical in essence with the holiness of God. "Be ye holy; for I am holy," means incorporate My holiness into your being—be a "partaker of the Divine nature." It is a great mystery, and yet a glorious fact, that God can, will and does communicate Himself to His creatures, and when He does so, they become the incarnation of his holiness.[81]

The reason the believer became the "incarnation" of God the Father's holiness was because the believer received God the Holy Spirit. God's Holy Spirit fully dwelt within them as a consequence of the second work of grace, and it was the third person of the Trinity that imparted all of the Christian graces. Lowrey was equally generous in his description of what the Holy Spirit accomplished in the life of the entirely sanctified believer. It did not appear that there was anything unaffected by the Holy Spirit's presence.

> Dwelling within us, (the Holy Spirit) becomes a new teacher, a new faculty of discernment, a rich fellowship, a witness, a sanctifier, a producer of holy fruits, and an abiding Comforter. He puts sweetness into our spirits, wisdom and discretion into our ways, pathos

and sympathy into our accents, power into our words, melody into
our songs, and often a soft beaming light into our faces.[82]
At times, he could get quite poetic when explaining the Holy Spirit's be-
nevolences. When the Holy Spirit sanctified and took complete possession of the "purified temple," the heart was then converted "into a seat of
unbroken comfort, and (used) as a garden in which to produce His own
fruit of "love, joy, peace, long-suffering, gentleness, goodness, faith, meekness, temperance."[83]

In light of the fact that entire sanctification eradicated all sin, restored
the image of God to fallen man, incarnated God's holiness, and provided
an unhindered channel for the Holy Spirit to work, it is not surprising that
Lowrey believed that the grace of entire sanctification imparted nothing
less than a fully mature Christian character. According to his analysis of the
Greek word *teleios* to be sanctified was "*to be fully developed in spiritual
character,* i.e., *perfected in love.*"[84] This was not the only occasion that
Lowrey wrote of entire sanctification in terms of maturity as well as purity.
Slightly contradicting J. A. Wood in the matter, Lowrey wrote:

> The perfection here inculcated is a thorough resuscitation, de-
> velopment, and healthy exercising of the inner man. Every power is
> not only free from sin and rightly directed, but is continually at its
> best in the performance of its duty. It is a rounded Christian charac-
> ter, including the integrity of all the fruits of the Spirit in a state of
> maturity and full consecration to the service of God.[85]

It must be remembered that Lowrey was not describing the believer
who had been entirely sanctified and then had grown much in grace.
"Rounded Christian character" was what one should receive as a consequence of the instantaneous baptism of the Holy Spirit that every believer
could expect when the two conditions of consecration and faith were met.

This led Lowrey to some interesting conclusions when it came to his
analysis of temptation or the continued threat of sin. He believed that with
inbred sin removed, there would be instead a "repugnance" to sin and,
therefore, almost an inability to sin. The believer would hate the thought
of any sin and, while there might be temptations from the world or Satan,
there could be no inclination for sin arising from within the believer.
Temptation would find no access. "A heart charged with (sanctifying
grace) becomes a natural repellent of temptation . . . [T]he baptism of
fire, and of the Holy Ghost, makes the heart proof against the incursions
and havoc of temptation."[86]

This would seem to lead to the conclusion that after sanctification,
sin would be an impossibility. Lowrey could not bring himself to state this
but he came very close. He acknowledged that for every believer sin
would always be a possibility, but for the sanctified believer it would not

be very probable. "It must be conceded that entire sanctification brings with it a degree of security that does not attach to any lower state of grace. It is certified assurance and safety, *approximating* a state in which it is impossible to sin and fall."[87]

Entire sanctification would not only fundamentally change one's relationship to eternity but also change the believer's relationship to the world. One who was filled with the Holy Ghost would not be subject to the vicissitudes of life, rather one would become almost inured against them. "He may pass a whole life of conflict, trial, and suffering, like Daniel, Paul, Luther, and thousands more whose sufferings never gained notoriety, and yet in the midst of all, and continuously, in spite of all, he sings a paean of victory."[88] It sounded at times as though entire sanctification would make a heaven out of earth.

> The holiness of the Gospel develops a healthy manhood, and never touches but to ennoble. By it the family state and relations become more hallowed and precious, business pursuits more effective and enjoyable, Christian activities and benevolence more luxurious and inspiring, while all social intercourse and fellowships are made by it a thousand times more refined, delightful, and exalting.[89]

This kind of extravagant language was not unique to Asbury Lowrey. While John Wesley was very cautious in his explanations of what a believer might expect from the grace of entire sanctification, John Fletcher, the "theologian" of the early Wesleyan movement, was not so cautious. Many Holiness writers were quick to quote Fletcher's most familiar description of the entirely sanctified. Lowrey himself did so early in his book and it is not surprising, given the authority Fletcher carried, that Holiness writers expanded on his description.

> By Christian perfection, we mean nothing but the cluster and maturity of the graces which compose the Christian character in the Church militant. In other words, Christian perfection is a spiritual constellation made up of these gracious stars: perfect repentance, perfect faith, perfect humility, perfect meekness, perfect self-denial, perfect resignation, perfect hope, perfect charity, and, above all, perfect love.[90]

While Lowrey was one of the most optimistic of the Holiness writers concerning the promise of entire sanctification, he did not misrepresent the common understanding of most in the Holiness Movement. *Possibilities of Grace*, remaining in the Ministerial Course of Study until 1956, is evidence of the Pentecostal Church of the Nazarene's acceptance of his perspective. It should be noted that the claims he made concerning the second work of grace were found in other holiness literature of the period and certainly in the books already cited.

Because J. A. Wood's book, *Purity and Maturity,* was primarily concerned with distinguishing between the grace of entire sanctification and
growth in grace, it might be expected that Wood's understanding of the results of entire sanctification would be a bit tempered. It might be reasonable to expect that what Lowrey claimed for purity, Wood would claim for
maturity. For the most part, this was true. Yet at times, Wood described the
instantaneous effects of entire sanctification as extravagantly as had
Lowrey.

> Purity will give weight and spiritual power to our words, invita-
> tions and pious efforts. It will make Christian work natural and easy.
> . . . Purity wrought in the heart rectifies the constitution and charac-
> ter of man, as a moral being . . . restoring man's nature to its pristine
> *purity* and *love.*[91]

There are even occasions when Wood defined purity in terms that
seemed more appropriate to a definition of maturity.

> The soul is brought into complete harmony *with itself,* and *with
> God.* The reason, the conscience, the will, the affections and emo-
> tions are no longer antagonized against each other, but with a har-
> monious concurrence move together in delightful obedience to
> Christ.[92]

As glorious as was Lowrey's consistent description of the state of entire sanctification, even he did not approach Daniel Steele's occasional
descriptions. In *The Gospel of the Comforter,* Steele described the consequences of being entirely sanctified with reference to the presence of the
Holy Spirit. According to Steele, the Holy Spirit brought such a state to the
believer that "bliss" was the only word able to define it.

> He who is on so intimate terms with our ever blessed God will
> enjoy *the highest possible degree of happiness.* Fill (the soul's) infi-
> nite capacity with . . . the *pleroma,* "the fulness of him who filleth all
> in all," and bliss will be supreme and eternal. The vicissitudes of life,
> from health to sickness, from riches to poverty, from applause to
> abuse, may ripple the surface of this profound happiness, but they
> cannot disturb its immeasurable depths.[93]

Indeed, it brought nothing less than heaven on earth. "Hence we need not
die to know what are the felicities of saints in heaven. They flow from the
same fountain from which we are drinking in this world—'the joy of the
Holy Ghost.' The bliss of the Old Testament and of the New, of earth and
heaven, is the same."[94]

A. M. Hills was almost as equally promising. He concluded his book
Holiness and Power with a very explicit description of the results of entire
sanctification. Hills used Paul's description of the fruit of the Spirit found
in Galatians 5:22 as an outline for the chapter.[95] According to Hills, the

sanctified believer would be fully confident of God's love and his life would therefore be "as full of joy as a June morning."[96] Every doubt would be removed and in its place would be an unqualified constant assurance of God's salvation. As was his method throughout the book, he used personal testimonials to buttress his claims, and in the paragraph on peace as a consequence of entire sanctification, Hills wrote:

> Dr. Carradine says: "Sanctification has saved him from irritability of temper and disposition. . . . The hot, impatient flush, the hasty impulse to angry speech, the gunpowdery expression of thought and word—all have been taken away in a moment of time by the blessed Son of God.[97]

Sanctification did not just take care of a short temper; it cured irritability.

> Every regenerated man knows the set of circumstances that conspire to produce irritability. The coming home wearied and hungry, the aching head, the noisy children, the absent servant, the delayed meal, the fireless grate, the general influence of a cold, cloudy, rainy day, or a day of sweltering power. Here is a battlefield indeed, and here many a regenerated man goes down in temporary defeat. And here is the easy victory of the sanctified.[98]

The baptism of the Holy Ghost gave such self-control that sickness, disease, or pain could not compromise it. It made one's conscience so acutely sensitive that good and evil could be detected in what were typically considered amoral activities.

> Our power of moral discrimination may become so acute as to discern a moral element in acts now considered morally indifferent, such as the question, shall I ride to town or walk; shall I wear boots or shoes, gloves or mittens; take an umbrella or run the risk of rain.[99]

It gave spiritual knowledge, passion for souls, courage, and guaranteed unhindered growth in grace.

> This purifying Holy Spirit, coming into the heart, will make growth in grace as natural as the physical growth of a child. Here let me repeat, that the great growth of the soul into Christian maturity comes after the sanctifying gift of the Holy Spirit, but does not precede it. People do not grow into holiness; but they grow wonderfully after they receive it.[100]

Such were the marvelous definitions and wonderful descriptions of this second work of grace. Nowhere was the optimism of the church more pronounced than in their early convictions concerning what entire sanctification accomplished. These descriptions, and many others like them, were what early Nazarenes understood their statement of faith to mean. "Entire devotement to God, and the holy obedience of love made perfect" meant that entire sanctification or the baptism of the Holy Ghost restored the image of God to fallen man, incarnated God's holiness, provided a

pure dwelling for the Holy Spirit, made further sin highly unlikely, imparted in essence all the Christian graces, and, for the truly sanctified soul,
made a heaven out of earth. The words of one of the most loved of all
Nazarene hymns, composed by Nazarene songwriter Haldor Lillenas, testify to the marvelous effects of this second work of grace. Since 1917,
Nazarenes have sung:

"Glorious Freedom"
Once I was bound by sin's galling fetters;
    Chained like a slave, I struggled in vain.
But I received a glorious freedom
    When Jesus broke my fetters in twain.

Freedom from all the carnal affections;
    Freedom from envy, hatred, and strife;
Freedom from vain and worldly ambitions;
    Freedom from all that saddened my life!

Freedom from pride and all sinful follies;
    Freedom from love and glitter of gold;
Freedom from evil temper and anger—
    Glorious freedom, rapture untold!

Freedom from fear with all of its torments;
    Freedom from care with all of its pain;
Freedom in Christ, my blessed Redeemer,
    He who has rent my fetters in twain!

Refrain:
Glorious freedom! Wonderful freedom!
    No more in chains of sin I repine!
Jesus, the glorious Emancipator!
    Now and forever He shall be mine.[101]

3
THE RESPONSIBILITY OF GRACE

THE NEED FOR AN "OFFICIAL" NAZARENE THEOLOGY

Martin Marty, in the second volume of his history of American religion in the 20th century, titled *The Noise of the Conflict,* characterized the interwar years (1919-41) as years of conflict. He wrote:

> Instead of harmony and simplicity, conflict ruled. . . . Not since the Civil War had America been more torn. In matters specifically religious, the nation had never seemed more divided than it was in these interwar years . . . original-stock Protestants vs. everyone else; "100 percent Americans" vs. Communists and Slavs in the Red Scare; old-stock Anglo Saxons vs. Catholic or Jewish or Asian immigrants; the Ku Klux Klan vs. the same, plus liberals and blacks; white Christians vs. black Christians . . . Protestant Fundamentalists vs. Modernists . . . Protestant liberals vs. Protestant realists . . . and more.[1]

According to Marty, this resulted in a tightening of denominational lines and a "growth in rigidity" in various camps through these years of conflict."[2]

The characterization of the interwar years as a contentious time between religious groups resulting in a hardening of denominational identities characterized the Church of the Nazarene in these years. By the end of the second decade of the 20th century, the heady dreams of the first generation of Nazarenes were passing away along with them. The hope that the Holiness Movement might serve to re-Christianize Christianity was almost gone. According to Nazarene historian Timothy L. Smith, instead of an optimistic hope, there was a growing fear that the movement would not even outlive the second generation of Nazarenes.[3] The defensive need to preserve the inherited faith replaced the previous desire to aggressively propagate it. Consequently, as other denominations in this time period were doing, "the Nazarenes sharpened in this (interwar) period the lines of their separation from both the secular and the religious world around them."[4]

Some of this "sharpening [of] the lines of separation" occurred when the 1919 General Assembly dropped the adjective "Pentecostal" from its official name. The name "Pentecostal" had come to be identified with those churches that emphasized speaking in tongues as evidence of the gift of the Holy Spirit. In the Pentecostal Church of the Nazarene, Pentecost was the occasion of entire sanctification and speaking in tongues was not the evidence of that entire sanctification. Speaking in tongues, according to the Nazarenes, might have been a gift of the Holy Spirit appropriate to the Church of the 1st century, but certainly not the 20th. This charismatic gift was never allowed in the Pentecostal Church of the Nazarene. In 1906, when W. J. Seymour, a Pentecostal preacher and leader of the Azusa Street revival in Los Angeles, preached that speaking in tongues was evidence of the gift of the Holy Spirit at P. F. Bresee's Church of the Nazarene, he was locked out of the church and told never to come back.[5] With the growth of the Pentecostal movement in the early decades of the 20th century, the Pentecostal Church of the Nazarene, without much ado, decided in 1919 that it would be best if "Pentecostal" was dropped from its name.

Further clarification of the Church of the Nazarene's position concerning tongues was given in the denomination's periodicals and books. In 1926, the denomination began publishing a magazine for its preachers, appropriately titled *The Preacher's Magazine.* It was edited by J. B. Chapman, and in the third issue of the very first volume, H. Orton Wiley wrote a series of articles on the "tongues" movement, placing it in historical context for the Nazarene preachers. In the second paragraph of the first article, he wrote:

> One of the earliest appearances of the tongues apart from the apostolic age, is what is known as the "Devils of Loudun" which occurred during the Middle Ages when the soil seemed so fertile for all nervous and strange phenomena. Wild and errotic [sic] manifestations of a hysterical nature broke out in a convent of Ursuline nuns at Loudun about 1626. . . . The peculiarity of this manifestation of tongues lies in the fact that it was thought to be evidence of demon possession and those under its influence as in league with Satan. The same phenomenon is now regarded as an evidence of superior piety.[6]

 The Nazarenes were making sure that they were to be distinguished from their Pentecostal neighbors.

This young denomination also found itself having to address other religious controversies of the period, not only in matters that were directly challenging to its primary theological teaching, but also in matters apparently tangentially connected to it. The same year that the adjective "Pentecostal" was dropped from the church's name, the World's Christian Fundamentals Association was formed. This conservative interdenominational movement was a militant reaction to "modernism." Fundamentalism is exceedingly difficult to define, but it was, according to the fundamentalists, a reassertion of the "fundamentals" of the faith against the threat of Darwinism, German higher criticism, and the denial of the supernatural. All three of these threats called into question the authority of the Bible and thus the inerrancy of the Scriptures became one of the defining issues of the movement. Lyman Stewart, a California oil millionaire, had financed the publication of a series of pamphlets, titled *The Fundamentals,* with A. C. Dixon, pastor of Moody Church of Chicago, as first editor. From 1910 to 1915, 12 booklets were published, purporting to reassert the basic beliefs of the Christian faith. According to Ernest Sandeen, Lyman Stewart's fundamentalism included the unquestioning affirmation of these beliefs:

1. The verbal inspiration of the Bible "as originally given"
2. The deity of Christ
3. The vicarious death of Jesus
4. The personality of the Holy Spirit
5. The necessity of a personal infilling of the Spirit for victorious Christian living
6. The personal return of Christ
7. The urgency of speedy evangelization of the world[7]

In 1910, the Presbyterian General Assembly, representing an Old School Calvinist version of fundamentalism formulated five points of Christian belief that they declared necessary for every minister of the denomination to believe. They were: "(1) the inerrancy of the Bible, (2) the virgin birth of Christ, (3) Christ's atonement for sin, (4) his resurrection from the dead, and (5) his miracles."[8] Harry Emerson Fosdick, the "modernist" popular Baptist preacher, characterized the movement in a sermon preached in 1922 on the eve of a Baptist convention. In "Shall the Fundamentalists Win?", he cited their doctrinal tests. They were:

> (1) special miracles such as the Virgin Birth, (2) the inerrancy of Scripture. . . . (3) the "special theory" of substitutionary atonement, and (4) the second coming of Christ to set up a millennial kingdom.[9]

The Church of the Nazarene was not isolated from this national battle. While the Fundamentalist Movement did not cause the divisions in the Church of the Nazarene that it did in the Presbyterian and Baptist denominations, there was, according to Nazarene church historian Paul M. Bassett, a "fundamentalist leavening of the Holiness Movement" in these interwar years.[10] Marsden agreed. He wrote, in *Understanding Evangelicalism and Fundamentalism:* "Holiness groups, such as the Nazarenes and the Wesleyan Methodists, found their distinctive emphases being reshaped by the fundamentalist-led movement."[11]

The general superintendents of the Church of the Nazarene adopted fundamentalist terminology for their quadrennial addresses to the general assemblies in the second and third decades of the century. In successive general assemblies, the general superintendents celebrated the fact that the Church of the Nazarene was united on its "fundamentals." In 1923,

Generals J. W. Goodwin, H. F. Reynolds, and R. T. Williams declared to the Sixth General Assembly:

> *First,* we have to rejoice in repeating a statement that we face no doctrinal problems, nor divisions over fundamentals; on the subject of doctrine we have nothing to dread. Perhaps most of the ecclesiastical bodies face the sorrow of division over the fundamentals for which the movement is supposed to stand; but in this body today on the great fundamental truths of God's Word and of the church we stand solid without a single exception.[12]

In the 1928 General Assembly, this was repeated, even more strongly than before. The same three general superintendents proclaimed:

> First, we note with pleasure that there are no differences or divisions among us. We are a perfectly united denomination. In this General Assembly there will be no discussions of modernism or fundamentalism. We are all fundamentalists, we believe the Bible, we all believe in Christ, that He is truly the Son of God. We stand for the same great fundamentals and we will not be torn asunder nor be hurled into strife by arguments or contentions arising from the differences of opinion regarding the great underlying principles of Christianity. We are a united people![13]

In this address, a few paragraphs later, these general superintendents appeared to align themselves with the fundamentalists' view of Scripture, calling it "infallible." Under the heading, "Let Us Notice Some Principles That Will Guarantee Our Future," they wrote:

> We must stand for the whole Bible. We do not as a movement believe merely that the Bible contains the Word of God. We believe that the Bible is the Word of God. We believe it from Genesis to Revelation. We stand for it in life and death. The Bible has received the bitterest attack of the enemy for centuries, but today the Old Book stands as impregnable as the Rock of Gibraltar. . . . The church must stand first, last and all the time for the whole Bible, the inspired, infallible, revealed Word of God.[14]

In 1932, the quadrennial report by the now four general superintendents of the Church of the Nazarene declared the same. H. F. Reynolds, R. T. Williams, J. W. Goodwin, and J. B. Chapman wrote under the heading, "Some Outstanding Characteristics of the Church":

> First, it stands for the whole Bible. Our people not only believe that the Bible contains the Word of God, but we believe the Bible is the Word of God and we can preach it sincerely from Genesis to Revelation, and our preachers everywhere are preaching this grand old Book as the revealed will of God and plan of God for us, for our salvation and our activity. There is not a skeptic, a higher critic or a

modernist among the hundred thousand Nazarenes. We all believe in and stand for the grand old Book.[15]

Again, in the 1936 General Assembly, they declared that the Bible did not contain the Word of God but was the Word of God. While the words fundamental and fundamentalist did not appear in either the 1932 or 1936 addresses, the elected general leadership of the Church of the Nazarene was not afraid to adopt language that was similar to language the fundamentalists used when referencing the Bible.

In 1923, the General Assembly submitted to the districts a revised Constitution for their consideration and approval, to be voted on in the 1928 General Assembly. Among the recommended changes was the article of belief on the Holy Scriptures. Until 1923, it had read,

> By the Holy Scriptures we understand the sixty-six books of the Old and New Testaments, given by Divine inspiration, revealing the will of God concerning us in all things necessary to our salvation; so that whatever is not contained therein is not to be enjoined as an article of faith.[16]

At the 1928 General Assembly, the recommended changes were adopted and it now read:

> We believe in the plenary inspiration of the Holy Scriptures by which we understand the sixty-six books of the Old and New Testaments, given by divine inspiration, inerrantly revealing the will of God concerning us in all things necessary to salvation; so that whatever is not contained therein is not to be enjoined as an article of faith [emphases mine].[17]

Not only were the addresses by the general leadership punctuated with fundamentalist terminology, the denomination's Article of Faith on Scripture now included the one word that was central to Fundamentalism: inerrancy. Paul Bassett would write, concerning this "fundamentalist leavening" of the Church of the Nazarene:

> [I]n this period "second-blessing holiness" was not as critical to the denomination as it had earlier been. A fundamentalist orthodoxy with respect to the inspiration and authority of Scripture had become a *de facto* mark of the "good Nazarene."[18]

This may be overstating the case, but it is certainly evident that the Church of the Nazarene found itself having to address itself to the Fundamentalist/Modernist wars of the second, third, and fourth decades of the 20th century.

So that the denomination would have a clear theological identity, in 1919, on the eve of these religious controversies, the Church of the Nazarene commissioned an "official" theology. J. B. Chapman, who was president of the General Board of Education for the Church of the

Nazarene, asked H. Orton Wiley, president of Northwest Nazarene College, to write a systematic theology for the church. When Wiley's *Christian Theology* was finally completed, Dr. Chapman, in the introduction of the first volume, stated the reasons for the commission:

> As far back as 1919 those of us who were serving on the General Department of Education in the Church of the Nazarene felt keenly the need of a work on systematic theology of sufficient scope and thoroughness that it might serve as a standard of doctrine in connection with the development of the literature of our church and movement.[19]

The texts that the Pentecostal Church of the Nazarene had been using in the training of its ministers in the Course of Study and in the colleges were primarily 19th-century works written by Methodist theologians. The exception was a compendium of theology, written by E. P. Ellyson, one of the founding general superintendents of the Pentecostal Church of the Nazarene, to commemorate the 1908 merger of the holiness denominations. Although listed as a text for the first year course of study, it was hardly more than an outline and certainly not adequate for college-level study. The first comprehensive systematic theology to be used by the Pentecostal Church of the Nazarene was Samuel Wakefield's 1869 *A Complete System of Christian Theology*, itself a revision of the very first English Methodist systematic theology, Richard Watson's 1823 *Theological Institutes*. In 1911, Wakefield's theology was replaced by John Miley's *Systematic Theology*, which was the primary textbook in the Course of Study for upper level theology students until 1932. It was this text that the church sought to replace with Wiley's *Christian Theology*.

Clearly, the systematic theologies of Ellyson, Wakefield, and Miley were inadequate for the concerns of the church as it entered into the third decade of the 20th century. In 1919, when J. B. Chapman asked H. Orton Wiley to write an authoritative systematic theology for the Church of the Nazarene, it was because none in use adequately addressed the contemporary issues of their day.

Relevance was not the only reason the leaders of the Pentecostal Church of the Nazarene believed the denomination needed its own systematic theology. Secondly, and perhaps what is more important, the older Methodist theologies did not sufficiently emphasize the doctrine of entire sanctification, nor did they represent the doctrine as stated in the Articles of Faith of the Pentecostal Church of the Nazarene. John Miley's two volume *Systematic Theology* contained only 30 pages out of 1,057 on the doctrine of entire sanctification. In comparison, Wiley would devote 174 pages, out of 1,397, to the doctrine of entire sanctification. The older Methodist theologies did not stress the instantaneous nature of sanctification. They did not state strongly enough that sanctification accomplished nothing less than the eradication of the sinful nature. They did not use Pentecost as the paradigm or occasion of entire sanctification, and they certainly did not describe the results of entire sanctification in the extravagant terms of many of those in the Holiness Movement at the close of the 19th century. Miley's *Systematic Theology* held to an understanding of entire sanctification that those in the Holiness Movement had reacted against in forming their own associations and denominations. The 30 pages that Miley did devote to the doctrine were largely a polemic against the Holiness Movement's specific emphases!

Miley did acknowledge that sanctification could be understood as an instantaneous gift occasioned by faith. "The fullness of sanctification shall be instantly attained on the condition of faith, just as justification is attained; and there shall be a new experience of a great and gracious change, and just as consciously such as the experience in regeneration."[20] But he conditioned this orthodox holiness teaching with a caveat. According to Miley, it was not necessary to insist on the instantaneous aspect exclusively. Citing Wesley, Miley immediately followed the above statement with this qualification: "[W]e think it would be wrong to [Wesley] to say that he allowed no instances of entire sanctification except in this definite mode."[21] A few paragraphs later, he wrote more clearly concerning his understanding of the Wesleyan interpretation. "[Wesley's] own illustration of his doctrine points to a possible attainment in a gradual mode. . . . The instant consummation here emphasized does not exclude the gradual approach to it."[22]

Miley also did not insist that entire sanctification be strictly interpreted as the eradication of the sinful nature. In the first paragraph of the four that he devoted to the topic, he outlined the "repression theory," in which sanctification was understood primarily as power, enabling believers to live above sin and therefore able to live without sinning. This "repression theory," a holiness teaching whose origin was a holiness convention in Keswick, England, ignored the question of the destruction of the sinful nature. In a second paragraph, Miley mentioned the "eradication theory," which was the teaching embraced by most of those in the American Holiness Movement. In a third paragraph, he stated some objections to the "eradication theory," among them, the criticism that if all sin was eradicated from the life of a believer, there could be "no possible lapse from that state."[23] Miley thus indicated his preference for a theory other than the "eradication theory." In the final paragraph, he called into question the relevance or significance of the entire debate. He wrote:

> The reality of sanctification concerns us far more deeply than any
> question respecting the mode of the work within the soul . . . We
> know nothing more of the mode of this inner work than we know of

the mode of the Spirit in the work of regeneration. It may be in a more thorough subjugation of the sensuous and secular tendencies, or in a higher purification . . . or in a fuller presence and power of the Holy Spirit, or in all; but whether in one or another, or in all, the sanctification is entire when the spiritual life attains complete dominance.[24]

Furthermore, not only did Miley not describe the effects of sanctification as extravagantly as those in the Holiness Movement, he warned against such descriptions. With some of the popular Holiness authors in mind,[25] Miley pointedly wrote:

> The imagination, especially when warmed by the mystical temper, may picture a state of indifference to outward things; a state in which the soul is so lost in God as to be free from all anxiety and care, and even without wish of ease from pain; a state in which sickness and death are indifferent to the calm repose, and even the peril of souls awakens no solicitude; but such a reverie is far more replete with hallucination than with the truth and reality of sanctification. . . . The doctrine of sanctification must not be so interpreted as to be made a doctrine of despair to all Christians who have not consciously attained to such an experience, *particularly in the definite manner of the second-blessing theory.*[26]

This was clearly not an interpretation of entire sanctification that those in the American Holiness Movement or the Pentecostal Church of the Nazarene approved. As has been shown, the holiness books that the Nazarene church was using in colleges and in the course of study were much more insistent on a specific explication of their doctrine. Miley even had a few words for them. To those whom he believed were divisively dogmatic, he wrote:

> [W]e object to any insistence that [the instantaneous mode] is the only possible mode. Right here is the occasion of unfortunate differences among us. However, much of the evil consequence might easily be avoided . . . through a spirit of mutual forbearance. Let those who hold rigidly to the second-blessing view preach sanctification in their own way, but let them be tolerant of such as preach it in a manner somewhat different; and let such as hesitate respecting that special view be tolerant of those for whom it possesses great interest. . . . The doctrine itself, and not any rigid form into which we may cast it, is the real interest.[27]

Clearly, Miley's understanding of the doctrine of entire sanctification was not representative of the Pentecostal Church of the Nazarene's Article of Faith, and it was uniformly inconsistent with other holiness literature the church was using in its Course of Study and colleges. This would lead H. Ray Dunning, author of one of the Church of the Nazarene's most recent denominational theologies, to write in his dissertation on Nazarene ethics: "It is somewhat of an anomaly that Miley's theology . . . should remain in the curriculum for so long. His treatment of sanctification is quite different from most of the Nazarene writings . . . being best described as meliorating."[28]

When J. B. Chapman asked H. Orton Wiley to write an "official" theology for the Church of the Nazarene, it was because the "inherited" Methodist systematic theologies in use did not address the concerns of a church in the early decades of the 20th century, nor did they adequately represent the church's Articles of Faith. It was because the Church of the Nazarene needed a defining theology—a theology that distinguished the Church of the Nazarene from other evangelical and mainline denominations.

NATIVE ABILITY

Chapman, no doubt, expected that Wiley's *Christian Theology* would take several years to complete. No one expected that the church would have to wait two decades before the first volume of the three-volume work was completed. When Wiley was asked to write the theology, he was president of the struggling Nazarene College in Nampa, Idaho. He stayed at the college for 10 difficult years and, in 1928, assumed editorship of the denomination's periodical, the *Herald of Holiness.* In 1933, he became president of Pasadena College, the college that P. F. Bresee had started in 1902, and for the next 16 years was consumed with the stabilization of that school. The schools were small, and in addition to being the administrator, he was also a professor. These responsibilities and his desire to write a comprehensive historical, philosophic, and systematic theology kept him at the task for 20 years. In the preface to his first volume, he commented on the delay.

> Nearly twenty years ago I was asked by the Department of Education of the Church of the Nazarene, of which Dr. J. B. Chapman was then chairman, to prepare a work on Systematic Theology for use in the Course of Study for Licensed Ministers. I immediately set myself to the task but my range of vision was too narrow. I was constantly discovering new truth and each new discovery demanded a place in the plan of the work. Now after nearly twenty years of constant study and teaching, I am presenting to the church the result of these efforts in a work entitled *Christian Theology.*[29]

J. B. Chapman, in the introduction to the volume, commented on the delay also. He wrote:

> Pressed by many duties as college president, and for a time as editor of the *Herald of Holiness,* Dr. Wiley was unable to give the thought and attention to this subject that was necessary for its speedy completion. Sometimes we felt that he did not make sufficient

progress with the task to furnish ground for hope that he would live to complete it.[30]

In spite of this delay, Wiley's *Christian Theology* became "the" systematic theology of the Church of the Nazarene and remained in the Course of Study for more than 40 years. His *Introduction to Christian Theology* and the second volume of *Christian Theology* are still part of the required reading in the Course of Study for ministers.

Until 1932, however, while the church was waiting for Wiley, it continued to use Miley. Although Miley's explication of sanctification was wanting as far as the Church of the Nazarene was concerned, and although his theology did not address itself sufficiently to the issues of the early decades of the 20th century, his *Systematic Theology* was still valuable to the church. The reason for its continued use might be found in its strong emphasis on the moral responsibility of man. Man's responsibility to the experience of entire sanctification was an integral part of the church's understanding of the doctrine and Miley was consistent with the Nazarenes' emphasis on the import of the will for the attainment of holiness. *Amen*

Robert Chiles, in *Theological Transition in American Methodism: 1790—1935*, charted the changing emphases of Methodist theology throughout the 19th century and into the 20th. He traced this transition from John Wesley (1703-91) through three Methodist theologians: Richard Watson (1781—1833), John Miley (1813-95), and Albert Knudson (1873—1953). According to Chiles, as Methodist theology developed in the United States, there occurred modifications to the classical Wesleyan definitions. He noted three in particular and gave convincing evidence that Methodist theology, from Wesley to Knudson, changed decisively. In the realm of religious knowledge, Chiles charted a movement from dependence on revelation to emphasis on reason. In Methodist anthropology, there was a movement from understanding man as primarily sinful to understanding man as mostly moral. In Methodist soteriology, there was a movement from a reliance on God's gracious activity to a confidence on man's native ability. In the conclusion of his book, Chiles succinctly stated this transition.

> Thus scriptural revelation was compromised by reason's concern for evidence and logical implication; man was identified in terms of his moral capacity rather than by his captivity to sin; and the sovereignty of God's grace in salvation was qualified by man's intrinsic freedom.[31]

These later three themes, "reason's concern for evidence, man identified in terms of moral capacity, and man's intrinsic freedom" were all patently evident in Miley's *Systematic Theology*. He was clearly representative of the "transitioned" theology. In particular, freedom of choice, for

Miley, was the decisive and most fundamental principle of theology. He devoted successive chapters to free agency and man's ability to choose, and in these two chapters, Miley posited an absolute definition of freedom that was without constraint of any kind. Commenting on Miley's emphasis on moral freedom, Chiles wrote, "With its imposing claims made for the freedom of rational man, his theology of salvation represents . . . a decided departure from original Wesleyanism."[32] It could also be reasonably argued that his theology of salvation represented a decided departure from most of classical Protestant theology.

Free agency was fundamental for Miley because that was the only way persons could be held morally accountable. "If God is a moral ruler over responsible subjects, they must be morally free."[33] This led him to reject the classical doctrine of "moral inability" and compelled him to modify greatly the effects of the fall on the human race. According to Miley, persons were not in need of "prevenient grace" to choose the good, as Wesley had believed, but could, by virtue of their native ability, choose the good.   *Grace*

> If we choose the evil it is because we are pleased to choose it. The only bar to the choice of the good is that we are not pleased to choose it. Thus our choices are our own; and it is enough for our responsible freedom that they are made according to our own pleasure. In so choosing, no matter what or why, we choose freely and responsibly.[34]

The power to freely choose the good over the evil resided not in any divine aid counterbalancing the sinful nature, but resided in the native attribute of reason. He wrote: *No Grace*

> We are not constantly in some special motive state, or under some strong impulse, urgent for the volition which will carry us to its end. In the hours of mental quietude and self-command, duty in all its relations and requirements may be calmly considered and rules of right conduct settled. . . . It will thus be easy for us, even when suddenly brought under strong impulse or temptation, to pause and reflect and so take to ourselves strength from the weightiest reason against the wrong action to which we may be solicited. For so doing we need only the power which is intrinsic to rational agency.[35]

Miley at one point indicated that this moral ability was such that there was no difference between those who had made a habit of evil and those who had made a habit of good. Every person at every moment was every bit as able as every other person to choose the good. The playing field was always level when it came to choosing good over evil.

> The worldly mind can deeply concern itself with heavenly things. The sensual can apprehend the higher and diviner law of temperance and purity. The covetous and selfish can ponder the duty of

charity and realize its imperative claim. The hard and cruel can yield to the pathos of kindness and sympathy. . . . The prevalent habits of evil are no necessary result of an impotence of the moral nature.[36]

Miley did acknowledge that persons could be aided by the Holy Spirit but this was interpreted for the most part as enlightenment to reason or conscience. "The divine Spirit is ever present for our aid, and often active as a light in the moral reason and a quickening force in the conscience."[37] Concerning the question of "prevenient grace," which was so essential to Wesley's theology, Miley had the temerity to write: "As for the question of moral freedom, it is indifferent whether this capacity be native or gracious. For the consistency of Scripture truth it must have a gracious original."[38] This remarkable statement clearly indicates Miley's disposition. He gave lip service to the notion of enabling grace and he would write, more often than not, as if no grace were needed at all. In brief, salvation, according to Miley, was primarily conditioned on man's freedom and not on God's grace.

THE TRUE THEORY OF MORAL FREEDOM

When J. B. Chapman asked H. Orton Wiley to write a systematic theology for the Church of the Nazarene, A. M. Hills was disappointed that he hadn't been asked. Hills had joined the Church of the Nazarene in 1912, having been invited by P. F. Bresee himself.[39] Hills had been active in the Holiness Movement as a writer and as an evangelist, establishing colleges and Bible schools. He continued in that work after joining with the denomination, teaching at what would become Olivet Nazarene College in Kankakee, Illinois. In 1916, at the invitation of President H. Orton Wiley, he became a professor of systematic theology at Pasadena College where he served until his retirement in 1932. *Holiness and Power,* his work on the doctrine of entire sanctification, had been in use in the Church of the Nazarene's Ministerial Course of Study since 1911, and J. B. Chapman would ask if he would consider writing a textbook on homiletics and pastoral theology, which was included in the Course of Study from 1928 to 1940. It was not, therefore, unreasonable for him to have wanted or expected the commission to write a systematic theology. He was a respected and lauded Holiness preacher, writer, and teacher. When it went to the younger Wiley, Hills was not deterred. He set about revising the systematic theology he had already written between 1909 and 1915, hoping it would be found acceptable by the denominational leaders.[40] Even though there was widespread interest in the denomination for his systematic theology, the newly established Nazarene Publishing House would not agree to publish his revised two-volume work. With the influence of J. B. Chapman, Hills found an independent publisher and *Fundamental*

Christian Theology was published in 1930 in Pasadena by C. J. Kinne, a former manager of the Nazarene Publishing House. Hence it appeared a full 10 years prior to Wiley's work.

There were several reasons why H. Orton Wiley, instead of A. M. Hills, was asked to write the official systematic theology of the Church of the Nazarene, but there may have been one reason that eclipsed all the others. A. M. Hills was an ardent postmillennialist at a time when most Nazarenes were ardently premillennial. In 1932, H. Orton Wiley, who was still writing his theology, wrote to all the presidents of the Nazarene colleges and a few pastors, asking for their opinions concerning which systematic theology should be used for the ministerial course of study. Orval J. Nease, the President of Pasadena College, wrote expressing political considerations:

> Where is your theology? I had hoped it might be used. I would like to see Dr. Hills's text used but do not believe we could be consistent and do so. If I understand the situation correctly, the manuscript was rejected by the Reading committee of the Nazarene Publishing House. Now for us to place it in the course of study would be inconsistent. . . . I am sorry for this as I wish the "Old Doctors" book could be used. I fear lest the finance involved in the publication will break Bro. Kinne unless it is used someplace.[41]

The pastor of Calgary First Church of the Nazarene wrote expressing theological concerns:

> Happening to be in the meetings of the Gen. Assembly on education, I rather call to mind that the preference of the committee seemed to be in favor of Dr. Wiley's Theology. I have not had the opportunity of reading Dr. Hills' work, but am sure it would be wonderfully suited to our constituency but for one particular, and that is the millennial question.[42]

The question of whether one was premillennial or postmillennial had been a matter of indifference in the very young denomination. Some of the early leaders of the Holiness Movement, P. F. Bresee and Daniel Steele, to name just two, were postmillennial. They believed that with the advent of an interdenominational Holiness Movement, millennial hopes were finally capable of being realized. Because all in the Holiness Movement, particularly those in the South and Southeast, did not share this optimism, however, the Church of the Nazarene's Articles of Faith made no claim to any particular theory concerning Christ's return, except to say that He would. It was declared "adiaphora." The Article of Faith on the second coming of Christ, from 1907 to 1915, made a disclaimer concerning the Second Coming in a short second paragraph: "We do not, however, regard the numerous theories that gather around this Bible Doctrine as essential to salvation, and so we concede full liberty of belief among the members of the Pentecostal Church of the Nazarene."[43]

By the third decade of the 20th century, any remaining hopes that the church would help usher in the Christian millennium had dissipated for most Nazarenes. The World War, the depression, and the apparent failure of prohibition had helped to persuade most of them that society's salvation was going to have to be otherworldly. This and the "fundamentalist leavening" of the Holiness Movement, which was felt strongly in reference to their views of the Second Coming, made premillennialism the de facto doctrine of the church. The heady optimism of the early days of the church was gone. Timothy Smith observed, "Evangelists who had once proclaimed the approaching conversion of all mankind now professed to see no prospects for the kingdom of God save through the second coming of Christ."[44] It is not insignificant that the disclaimer that was included in the early Article of Faith on the second coming, stating that the church took no particular stand on any theory, was changed to a footnote in the *1915 Manual of the Church of the Nazarene* and finally dropped altogether in 1928.[45]

A. M. Hills, however, remained adamantly postmillennial. His minority views on the second coming of Christ had caused problems while he was president of Illinois Holiness University, and contributed to his dismissal there in 1910. His views on the Second Coming had been the source of some tension at Pasadena. Some of the students objected to Hills's teachings on "last things," and voiced their complaints to their pastors. Dr. A. O. Hendricks, president of Pasadena College from 1918 to 1923, hoping to preserve the good relationship between the local churches and the college, wrote Hills, demanding that he immediately stop teaching his views of the Second Coming, and warned him that if he did not stop, he would be terminated.

When, on Hills's own initiative, his *Fundamental Christian Theology* was finally published, it contained a chapter on the Second Coming that he did not write. In order for it to be more acceptable to the Church of the Nazarene, Hills allowed J. B. Chapman, who was by 1930 one of the general superintendents of the Church of the Nazarene, to write an apologetic for a premillennial interpretation of the Second Coming. This was followed by Hills's own postmillennial theory! In this "fundamental" systematic theology then, the church had two conflicting interpretations of the future of history, both presented as appropriate for Nazarenes. In A. M. Hills, there was the older and optimistic expectation that was representative of many of the early Nazarenes but which had become suspect with the course of time. Hills wrote in defense of postmillennialism:

> [Christ] never spoke one syllable about the insufficiency of the Holy Spirit and the gospel, and the present means of grace to win the

world and establish His kingdom. He never intimated that His preachers and teachers and missionaries should go in the power of the Holy Spirit, with the gospel and the means of grace, and labour in vain, because all these Christian instrumentalities were never intended to succeed! God inaugurated these means and they will succeed![46]

J. B. Chapman then gave seven reasons why he believed premillennialism was the most reasonable understanding of Christ's second coming. Reflecting the perspective of the majority of Nazarenes of the third decade of the 20th century, Chapman wrote:

> IT IS THE ONLY HOPE. 1. Christianity has utterly failed in the very countries where churches were planted by the apostles and their successors. . . . 2. The Reformation was speedily followed by rationalism, and the country that gave birth to the former is now home of the latter. . . . 4. The professors in universities and theological seminaries . . . seem determined to destroy the foundation of faith in the authority and certainty of God's word. . . . 5. The pew is in still more deplorable condition. . . . What a pitiful minority of our church members support the prayer-meetings, have family worship, and exhibit in their lives the marks of a deep and fervent piety! 6. Society is leprous all over. . . . The sin of impurity is enough to challenge the Omnipotent wrath which buried Sodom. 7. Neither the United States nor any other nation in Christendom possesses the elements of stability. The vile immoralities of men in public life, the determined and desperate socialism pervading the working classes, the rapid increase of crime and licentiousness and vice in every form are surely rotting away the foundations on which alone empires and republics stand. The masses hate the Church with the bitterest hatred. There is an absolute necessity for the personal coming of the Lord Jesus Christ to save an apostate Church and a Godless, undone world. Never has any former age terminated in more complete disaster and ruin than that which confronts the professing Christian body in this dispensation of the Spirit. The Coming of Christ is the sole hope of the world.[47]

In part, because A. M. Hills allowed J. B. Chapman to include an apologetic for the premillennial return of Christ, his *Fundamental Christian Theology* was published with the encouragement and influence of J. B. Chapman himself. It was subsequently recommended by the book committee, of which H. Orton Wiley was the chair, as the alternative systematic theology text in the Ministerial Course of Study from 1932 to 1940. While the church was waiting for Wiley to complete his work, they had used Miley's *Systematic Theology* and then, in 1932, recommended either Ralston's *Elements of Divinity*, which was an older Methodist theology along the lines of Miley, or A. M. Hills's *Fundamental Christian Theology* as an alternative.

In spite of Hills's minority views on the second coming of Christ, he was considered by many to have been the first "unofficial official" theologian of the church. In 1932 and 1936, he had three of his books, *Holiness and Power, Homiletics and Pastoral Theology,* and *Fundamental Christian Theology* included in the Ministerial Course of Study. H. Orton Wiley, in an article in the *Herald of Holiness* wrote, "Dr. Hills must be ever considered one of the great men of the American ministry."[48] Steven S. White, later editor of the same periodical, wrote in 1958: "A. M. Hills was perhaps the outstanding preacher . . . in the holiness movement . . . one of the best educated . . . of his day and one of the staunchest defenders of . . . fundamental beliefs."[49] While Hills's views on the millennium were not satisfactory to all and while some might quibble with his theory of inspiration,[50] he was thoroughly orthodox when it came to the holiness doctrine of the Church of the Nazarene. He preached, taught, and wrote what the Nazarenes believed about entire sanctification in the first few decades of the 20th century.

In A. M. Hills's *Fundamental Christian Theology,* there was a description of the effects of entire sanctification that was every bit as optimistic as *Holiness and Power* and other holiness literature of the period. However, in *Fundamental Christian Theology,* this idealistic expectation of the effects of entire sanctification was coupled with a doctrine of native moral ability. This led to the inevitable and intimidating conclusion that the attainment of entire sanctification and its concomitant benefits was dependent entirely on a person's ability to obey. The full realization of these beautiful descriptions of entire sanctification was a matter of the will!

Hills devoted two chapters to the doctrine of moral freedom, titling them, respectively, "Man's Moral Agency" and "The True Theory of Moral Freedom." These chapters are basically restatements of John Miley's and Charles G. Finney's views on moral freedom. Hills had studied at Oberlin under Finney, and these chapters are evidence that Hills adopted wholesale at least this aspect of Finney's theology. He freely quoted from Miley's *Systematic Theology* and Finney's *Theology* throughout the two chapters. According to Hills, who was quoting Finney:

> Man possesses the natural ability to obey all the requirements of God. The law of God ever requires obedience, so that must be possible. . . . We admit the sad effects of the fall upon our entire nature; but we deny the inference of moral inability to will so as to please God. . . . Our moral reason was injured and our intuitions; but we still have a moral reason sufficient to respond to the appeals of God. . . . The truth is, the whole theory of moral inability is a theo-

logical fiction, contrary to consciousness, conscience, moral reason, the voice of Scripture, and all the appeals of a just and holy God.[51]

Lest there be any doubts about the origin of man's ability to obey, Hills attacked directly the term "gracious ability." He wrote:

> Let us now consider the term GRACIOUS ABILITY. We find it often used in Methodist writings but we doubt the wisdom of using it. . . . We magnify *ability,* and rejoice in *grace;* but "gracious ability" means too much.[52]

Hills then abbreviated 12 pages from Finney's *Theology* proving that "gracious ability" was inconsistent with a doctrine of moral accountability. If men needed God's grace to obey, they could not logically be held accountable if they did not. "Moral obligation implies moral agency, and that moral agency implies freedom of will or, in other words, it implies a natural ability to comply with obligation. This ability is necessarily regarded . . . as the *sine qua non* of moral obligation."[53] Hills, quoting Finney, in an interesting reversal, defined grace as a gift dependent on and subsequent to the decision to obey! "The grace is great, just in proportion to the sinner's ability to comply with God's requirements."[54] And in a paragraph consistent with Miley's extraordinary statement: "As for the question of moral freedom, it is indifferent whether this capacity be native or gracious," Hills, quoting Finney, wrote:

> I reject the dogma of a gracious ability because it involves a denial of the true grace of the Gospel. I maintain that the Gospel, with all its influences, including the gift of the Holy Spirit, to convict, convert and sanctify the soul, is a system of grace throughout. But to maintain this, I must also maintain that God might justly have required obedience of men, *without making these provisions for them.* And to maintain the justice of God in requiring obedience, I must admit and maintain that obedience was possible to man *[emphasis mine].*[55]

Hills's commentary on this lengthy quotation from Finney was: "We think Finney's reasoning on this point unanswerable."[56]

Hills concluded the chapter, "The True Theory of Moral Freedom," by quoting from another theological textbook that was used in the Ministerial Course of Study for the Church of the Nazarene for first year students from 1911 to 1936. Amos Binney's *Theological Compendium* had been published in 1875 and revised and republished by Daniel Steele in 1902. It was a 195-page summary of Christian doctrine. According to Binney, Steele, and Hills:

> Though man is fallen and sadly depraved, so that there is in his nature a strong tendency toward sin, yet does he retain a Godlike attribute of freedom? In every volition of a moral nature, he is free to will the opposite. No decree of God, no chain of causation behind his will,

no combination of elements in his constitution, compel his moral acts. The gracious aid of the Holy Spirit is only suasive not necessitating.[57]

In *Fundamental Christian Theology*, there was a reinforcement of the doctrine of free agency that was current in late 19th-century Methodist theologies. In every compendium or systematic theology, from Binney to Miley to Ralston to Hills, the emphasis was placed on the power of a person's volition. To paraphrase what Hills had written: While there might have been rejoicing in grace, there was magnification of ability.

FROM DEPRAVITY TO FREE AGENCY

The Articles of Faith agreed upon in the 1908 merger of the several Holiness bodies in Pilot Point, Texas, contained two separate articles on the condition of fallen man. The first article was titled "Original Sin" and the second was titled "Inherited Depravity." The article on "Original Sin" was clearly intended to provide foundation for the denomination's doctrine of entire sanctification. It read:

Original Sin is that corruption of the nature of all who are engendered as the offspring of Adam, whereby everyone is very far gone from original righteousness, and is inclined to evil and that continually. In the Scriptures it is designated as "The Carnal Mind," our "Old Man," "The flesh," "Sin that dwelleth in me," etc. It cannot be pardoned, and continues to exist with the new life of the regenerate until eradicated and destroyed by the baptism with the Holy Spirit.[58]

The second Article of Faith addressing the condition of fallen man, titled "Inherited Depravity," was a strong statement indicating man's dependence on the grace of God for salvation. It read:

Since the sin and fall of Adam, all are without spiritual life, and by natural impulse and disposition are averse to God and holiness and inclined to sin. It is not possible that any should turn and prepare themselves by their own natural ability, to faith and calling upon God, or the doing of good works, acceptable and pleasing to Him, without the enabling Spirit and grace of God which are freely proffered to all men through our Lord Jesus Christ.[59]

This article was inherited from Bresee's Los Angeles Church of the Nazarene and was included, word for word, in the Articles of Faith of the 1908 merger. In 1911 however, the General Assembly voted to combine the two articles into one, titled "Original Sin—Depravity." The combined Article of Faith was reworded and slightly abbreviated but was without any substantial change. It now read:

Original sin, or depravity, is that corruption of the nature of all the offspring of Adam, by reason of which every one is very far gone from original righteousness, is averse to God, is without spiritual life, and is inclined to evil, and that continually. In the Scriptures it is designated as "the carnal mind," "our old man," "the flesh," "sin that dwelleth in me," etc. It continues to exist with the new life of the regenerate until eradicated and destroyed by the baptism of the Holy Spirit.

It is not possible that any should turn and prepare himself by his own natural ability to faith and calling upon God, or the doing of good works, acceptable and pleasing to Him, without the enabling Spirit and grace of God which are freely proffered to all men through our Lord Jesus Christ.[60]

These Articles of Faith were clearly in the Anglican/Methodist tradition. Phrases such as "very far gone from original righteousness," "inclined to evil and that continually," "no power to do good works, pleasing and acceptable to God," were phrases that were derivative of both the Thirty-nine Articles of the Church of England[61] and Wesley's Twenty-five Articles of Religion,[62] which were an abridgment of the Thirty-nine Articles.

In the 1923 General Assembly, this extended paragraph on "Original Sin—Depravity" was divided once again into two separate Articles of Faith. This time, however, the second paragraph of the combined Article of Faith, concerning a person's inability to turn to God by his own natural strength, was now found under the title "Free Will." The "new" Article of Faith was very similar in wording to the article that had once been titled "Inherited Depravity" in the 1908 *Manual.* It read:

> The condition of man after the fall of Adam is such that he cannot turn and prepare himself, by his own natural strength and works, to faith, and calling upon God; wherefore we have no power to do good works, pleasing and acceptable to God, without the grace of God by Christ assisting us."[63]

This change of title for this Article of Faith in and of itself is not significant, for in the Thirty-nine Articles of the Church of England and in Wesley's Articles of Religion, the articles (10 and 8 respectively) that concerned a person's inability to "turn and prepare himself, by his own natural strength and works," are also found under the heading, "Of Free Will." This was simply a return to a more historic expression of the Nazarene Articles of Faith.

This historic expression, however, lasted only five years, for among the recommended changes for the 1928 *Manual* was a reworking of this Article of Faith on "Free Will." The article, when it was found under "Inherited Depravity," did not cause Nazarenes alarm. If inability to turn to God was a condition of how very far fallen persons were, then so be it. If inability to turn to God was a condition of "Free Will," then that was a different matter. The Article of Faith as it was found in the 1923 *Manual* did not reflect the denomination's confidence in man's moral ability. According to Church of the Nazarene historian Timothy L. Smith, the delegates in 1928 recommended a statement that boldly declared that persons, in spite of the fall, retain a "godlike ability of freedom." "No decree of God, no chain of causation behind his will, no combination of elements in his constitution, compels his moral choice."[64] Evidently, the source for the recommended change to the Article of Faith on "Free Agency" in the 1928 General Assembly was a direct quote from Binney's *Compendium*. The delegates had read their theology, at least through the first year! After much debate, a tempered Article of Faith was adopted. The paragraph, which 20 years earlier had been titled "Inherited Depravity" was now titled, "Free Agency." It read:

> We believe that man's creation in godlikeness included ability to choose between right and wrong, and that thus he was made morally responsible; that through the fall of Adam he became depraved so that he can not now turn and prepare himself by his own natural strength and works to faith and calling upon God; but the grace of God through Jesus Christ is freely bestowed upon all men, enabling all who will to turn from sin to righteousness, believe on Jesus Christ for pardon and cleansing from sin, and follow good works pleasing and acceptable in His sight.[65]

Strictly speaking, this Article of Faith did acknowledge that persons needed the grace of God to "turn and prepare" themselves. However, by referencing "man's creation in godlikeness" at the very beginning of the article and by emphasizing that the grace of God through Christ "enables all who will to turn," the 1928 General Assembly, while acknowledging grace, placed the emphasis on free will. It certainly was a different article than when it had read, "the condition of man after the fall of Adam is such that he cannot turn and prepare himself . . . without the grace of God." In the original article, there was no mention of "godlike ability," "moral responsibility," or "enabling all who will to turn." As with Binney, Miley, and Hills, the important issue was man's moral responsibility, not God's gracious activity.

When this doctrine of moral ability was combined with the incredible promise of sanctification, there was a doctrine of holiness that was profoundly optimistic and perhaps quite intimidating, for all that the fullness of this promise was waiting for was an obedient will. Holiness was a magnificent gift of grace dependent on and subsequent to the simple decision to believe and obey. Thus, there was absolutely no excuse for members of the Church of the Nazarene not to realize the fullness of this promise. Indeed, if holiness in all its fullness was not realized, it was just evidence of an extremely pernicious will since all that was needed was a decision to believe and obey. The responsibility for this amazing grace was on the freely believing and obeying agent. The words of a beloved Nazarene hymn, sung at the close of a service as an invitation to receive this sanctifying grace, indicated the relationship between obedience and grace. Since 1905, Nazarenes have sung: "Is Your All on the Altar?"

You have longed for sweet peace, and for faith to increase,
   And have earnestly, fervently prayed;
But you cannot have rest or be perfectly blest
   Until all on the altar is laid.

Would you walk with the Lord, in the light of His Word,
   And have peace and contentment alway?
You must do His sweet will; to be free from all ill;
   On the altar your all you must lay.

Oh, we never can know what the Lord will bestow
   Of the blessings for which we have prayed
Till our body and soul He doth fully control,
   And our all on the altar is laid.

Refrain:
Is your all on the altar of sacrifice laid?
   Your heart does the Spirit control?
You can only be blest and have peace and sweet rest
   As you yield Him your body and soul.[66]

4
CHRISTIAN THEOLOGY FOR THE CHURCH OF THE NAZARENE

THE TASK OF H. ORTON WILEY

H. Orton Wiley finally published the first volume of his systematic theology in 1940, a full 20 years after J. B. Chapman had asked him to write it. In the preface to that first volume, Wiley acknowledged the length of time it had taken him to present it to the church by offering an explanation of sorts.

> Nearly twenty years ago I was asked . . . to prepare a work on Systematic Theology. . . . I immediately set myself to the task but my range of vision was too narrow. I was constantly discovering new truth and each new discovery demanded a place in the plan of the work. Now after nearly twenty years of constant study and teaching, I am presenting to the church the result of these efforts.[1]

In the preface, he also indicated the scope and purpose of the work.

> I have no thought of attempting any new contribution to modern theological science. My purpose and aim has been to review the field of theology in as simple a manner as possible for the use of those who, entering the ministry, desire to be informed concerning the great doctrines of the church.[2]

His "review of the field of theology in as simple a manner as possible" was almost 1,400 pages of comparative, historical, philosophical, biblical, and systematic theology. The index of his three-volume work reads like a historical theologian's list of Who's Who. In addition to recognizing the contributions of classical Methodist and Nazarene theologians such as John Wesley, John Fletcher, Adam Clarke, Samuel Wakefield, Richard Watson, Olin Curtis, William Pope, John Miley, P. F. Bresee, E. P. Ellyson, and A. M. Hills, Wiley freely acknowledged the contributions of theologians from other traditions. There are copious references to persons like Augustine, Cyprian, Gregory Nazianzen, Irenaeus, Origen, Tertullian, Erigena, Ambrose, Anselm, Luther, Aquinas, Melanchthon, Calvin, Zwingli, Arminius, Edwards, Hodge and Strong, to name just a few. He clearly sought to establish Nazarene holiness theology within the context of the entire Christian tradition, and he was unafraid to acknowledge the Holiness Movement's debt to the Church catholic. When he wrote in the preface, "I was constantly discovering new truth and each new discovery demanded a place in the plan of the work," it was no understatement. As a result of his 20 years of conscientious research, as recently as 1984, when 95 leading Wesleyan theologians were asked to identify the greatest influence on their own scholarly development, 25 cited Wiley as the person and 21 cited his *Christian Theology.*[3]

Neither was it an understatement when he wrote, "I have no thought of attempting any new contribution to modern theological science." H. Orton Wiley's *Christian Theology* was a conservative systematic theology that was faithful to the late 19th- and early 20th-century Holiness Movement. As John R. Tyson writes in *Handbook of Evangelical Theologians,* Wiley's chief partners in dialogue were theologians of the nineteenth century, writers of the old evangelicalism, and generally those who stood within the Wesleyan tradition."[4] Above all else, Wiley was faithful to the creedal statements of the Church of the Nazarene, quoting them verbatim at appropriate points in his work. As a result, his *Christian Theology* was the systematic theology in the Church of the Nazarene for over 40 years and his second volume (which includes his theology of entire sanctification) is still recommended reading in the Course of Study for ministers in the Church of the Nazarene.

This is not to say that his work was merely summary or simply descriptive of the prevailing currents of holiness theology, albeit with reference to its historical antecedents. His was not a "populist" theology. The historical and comparative methodology justified his tempering some of the more extravagant claims of some of the more sectarian elements of holiness theology, and his methodology permitted him to qualify and, in some instances, even jettison popularly held doctrines that were alien, in his mind, to an authentic Wesleyan-Holiness theology.

One such doctrine that Wiley felt was alien to an authentic Wesleyan-Holiness theology was the fundamentalist dogma concerning the inerrancy of the Scriptures. In the first volume of his *Christian Theology,* Wiley devoted two full chapters to a discussion of the inspiration and authority of the Scriptures. In the first of the two chapters, he carefully defined three theories of inspiration. The Mechanical or Dictation Theory, in which the authors were mere amanuenses and which lent itself most easily to an inerrant view of Scripture, Wiley rejected as supranatural and even docetic. According to Wiley, "this theory is . . . out of harmony with the known manner in which God works in the human soul."[5] The Intuition or Illumination theories, in which inspiration is understood as simply the elevation of man's natural insight, he rejected as too rationalistic and naturalistic. Wiley contended for a historic Methodist theory called the Dynamical. He wrote:

This is a mediating theory and is advanced in an effort to explain and preserve in proper harmony, both the divine and human factors in the inspiration of the Scriptures. It maintains that the sacred writers were given extraordinary aid without any interference with their personal characteristics or activities.[6]

This theory allowed Wiley to state that the Bible has a human element. "Not only did the Holy Spirit speak through David, David also spoke."[7] This did not compromise the Bible's authority for Wiley. It was fully inspired. Using the word that was added to the Church of the Nazarene's 1928 Article of Faith on the inspiration of the Holy Scriptures, Wiley wrote: "By *plenary* inspiration, we mean that the whole and every part is divinely inspired. This . . . presupposes . . . only that the results of that inspiration give us the Holy Scriptures as the final and authoritative rule of faith in the Church."[8]

This was not what the fundamentalists meant by inerrant. At the end of the second chapter devoted to the issue in his *Christian Theology,* Wiley cautiously clarified what he believed was the historic Wesleyan-Holiness position. "By the integrity of the Scriptures we mean that they have been kept intact and free from *essential* error, so that we may be assured of the truth originally given by the inspired authors."[9] According to Wiley, the Scriptures were not necessarily free from all error; they were free from *essential* error.

This was consistent with the Church of the Nazarene's revised Article of Faith on the Holy Scriptures. While the article adopted in 1928 did contain a form of the fundamentalist catchword ("inerrant," its placement in the Article of Faith decisively distinguished the denomination from fundamentalism, at least as far as the Articles of Faith were concerned. It read, "We believe in the plenary inspiration of the Holy Scriptures . . . given by divine inspiration, *inerrantly* revealing the will of God concerning us in all things necessary to salvation."[10]

The committee, which recommended the revision to the church and of which Wiley was a member, carefully worded it so that it meant just what it said; i.e., that the Bible was inerrant *in all matters necessary to salvation!* It did not say that the Bible was inerrant in all matters! This Article of Faith was an astutely worded and a politically sensitive statement, written in such a way so as to placate the fundamentalists in the denomination while at the same time preserving the historic position of the church.

Another critical doctrine that Wiley felt was alien to an authentic Wesleyan-Holiness theology concerned the doctrine of free moral agency, on which Miley and Hills had placed such emphasis. Wiley's *Christian Theology* was organized, as were many Protestant systematic theologies, on the pattern of Calvin's *Institutes of Christian Religion,* which meant that in Wiley's work, there were six divisions. Following the introduction were sections on the Doctrine of the Father, the Doctrine of the Son, the Doctrine of the Holy Spirit, the Doctrine of the Church, and the Doctrine of Last Things. Because Wiley understood the Holy Spirit as the administrator of redemption,[11] his soteriology was contained in the section on the doctrine of the Holy Spirit and he devoted an entire chapter, titled *The Preliminary States of Grace*,[12] to the matter of free will. Wiley never directly contradicted Miley or Hills by name, but he nevertheless clearly distinguished his theology from theirs. As a result, the "official" position of the Church of the Nazarene was that salvation was dependent on free grace and not on moral ability.

The chapter focused on the doctrine of "prevenient grace" and included a brief sketch of the 5th-century Pelagian/Augustinian debate over original sin and an extended historical account of the 17th-century debate between the Calvinists and the Remonstrants concerning the nature of grace. According to Wiley, James Arminius (1560—1609) held a mediating position between Pelagianism, which, by its denial of original sin, emphasized the doctrine of free moral agency, and Augustinian Calvinism, which, by its affirmation of total depravity, posited the doctrines of predestination and irresistible grace. Referencing the conclusions of the Synod of Dort that were faithfully represented in the Westminster Confession[13] and the "Five Points of Remonstrance,"[14] Wiley wrote, "The powerlessness and inability of man is everywhere assumed in the Scriptures. The question of total depravity, therefore, or the loss of the moral image of God, does not mark the dividing line between Arminianism and Calvinism."[15] Wiley, agreeing with Calvin, wrote that persons "in a state of nature" were incapable of any good apart from the grace of God. This however did not inevitably lead to the doctrines of predestination or irresistible grace. According to Wiley, there was no one who was in a state of nature alone, and this was what distinguished the Wesleyan-Arminian from the Calvinist. God's prevenient grace was universally bestowed. Furthermore, the Fall did not destroy man's power of volition. Thus, those who chose to respond to God's grace could respond, and conversely, those who chose to resist His grace could resist. Wiley believed that the Arminian doctrine of prevenient grace permitted both doctrines of total depravity and free moral agency.

> There is . . . a sinful bias, commonly known as a "bent to sinning" which determines the conduct by influencing the will. Thus grace is needed, not to restore to the will its power of volition . . . but to awaken the soul to the truth upon which religion rests, and to move upon the affections by enlisting the heart upon the side of truth. . . . The continuous co-operation of the human will with the

originating grace of the Spirit, merges prevenient grace directly into saving grace. . . . Arminianism maintains that through the prevenient grace of the Spirit, unconditionally bestowed upon all men, the power and responsibility of free agency exist from the first dawn of the moral life.[16]

Persons were free and, at the same time, entirely dependent on God's grace. This was of course a far cry from both Miley's "native ability" and Hills's "True Theory of Moral Freedom." Wiley had rejected the confidence that Miley and Hills had placed on a man's native moral freedom and replaced it with a confidence in God's freely bestowed grace. *Amen*

This care and precision in the explication of Wesleyan-Holiness doctrine characterized Wiley's entire work. *Christian Theology* provided precisely defined dogmas for a church whose existence was a consequence of successive mergers of disparate Holiness groups. At the same time, his theology was faithful to the Holiness tradition of the late 19th and early 20th centuries and in particular to the Articles of Faith of the 40-year-old denomination.

FAITHFUL TO THE DOCTRINE OF THE CHURCH

Wiley quoted the creedal statement of the church on entire sanctification in his 67-page chapter on the subject. After providing scriptural proof texts for the doctrine[17] and after a brief historical outline of the doctrine, Wiley wrote, under the heading "Definitions of Entire Sanctification:"

> We believe that entire sanctification is that act of God, subsequent to regeneration, by which believers are made free from original sin, or depravity, and brought into a state of entire devotement to God, and the holy obedience of love made perfect. It is wrought by the baptism with the Holy Spirit, and comprehends in one experience the cleansing of the heart from sin and the abiding, indwelling presence of the Holy Spirit, empowering the believer for life and service. Entire sanctification is provided by the blood of Jesus, is wrought instantaneously by faith, preceded by entire consecration; and to this work and state of grace the Holy Spirit bears witness. This experience is also known by various terms representing its different phases, such as "Christian Perfection," "Perfect Love," "Heart Purity," "The Baptism with the Holy Spirit," "The Fullness of the Blessing," and "Christian Holiness" (Creed, Art. X).[18]

He thus indicated his intention to remain fully consistent with the creedal statement of the Church of the Nazarene. There was to be nothing new. The authorities who Wiley quoted to substantiate the doctrine, in addition to the Methodist theologians, such as Wesley, Fletcher, Watson, and

Clarke and in addition to 19th-century Holiness theologians such as Lowrey, Wood, Peck, and Foster, were denominational leaders of the Church of the Nazarene. He referenced, among others, P. F. Bresee, E. P. Ellyson, E. F. Walker, R. T. Williams, J. B. Chapman, and H. V. Miller, who were all general superintendents of the Church of the Nazarene at different times during the years that Wiley was writing the systematic theology. *Christian Theology* was to be the theology of the Church of the Nazarene.

One of Wiley's intentions was to make certain that entire sanctification was understood in the church as an instantaneous act, a second work of grace. He began the chapter on entire sanctification by quoting scripture references that indicated to him this aspect of the teaching and, after quoting 2 Corinthians 7:1,[19] wrote, "Now this holiness already begun is to be perfected by the cleansing at a single stroke from inbred sin, and brings the soul to a constantly existing state of perfected obedience."[20] He continued the biblical exposition of the doctrine by using an argument first employed by Daniel Steele to prove the instantaneous nature of the grace. Whereas others in the Holiness Movement had used Pentecost as the biblical paradigm for the doctrine of entire sanctification, Wiley did not base the doctrine on this kind of interpretation of Acts 2. While Wiley believed that in entire sanctification the Holy Spirit was fully given, as happened on the Day of Pentecost,[21] he viewed entire sanctification as instantaneous because, when the verb *to sanctify* was used in the New Testament, it was most often used in the *aorist* tense. This is a tense that indicated a "momentary, completed act, without reference to time."[22] This he contrasted with the Greek present and imperfect tenses, which indicated continuous action and continuing past action, respectively. According to Steele and Wiley, the biblical writers' use of the aorist tense of the verb *to sanctify* was evidence that entire sanctification was to be understood as an instantaneous work of grace, a momentary, completed act, without reference to time. Wiley wrote (quoting 1 John 1:9):

> If we confess [present tense] *our sins, he is faithful and just to* forgive [aorist] *us our sins, and to cleanse* [aorist] *us from all unrighteousness* (I John 1:9). Here both the forgiveness and the cleansing are spoken of as completed acts, and there is no more reason grammatically for believing in a gradual sanctification than in a gradual justification.[23]

Entire sanctification was instantaneous because the New Testament writers used the aorist tense of the verb, to sanctify, when writing of the sanctifying work of God. It should be noted that Wiley, while rejecting fundamentalism at large, retained a "fundamentalist" hermeneutic when justifying the doctrine of entire sanctification. The Bible truly did inerrantly reveal the will of God concerning all things necessary to salvation. In the history of the doctrine in the Church of the Nazarene, this would not be the last time that biblical justification for the doctrine would substantially rest on the tense of the Greek verbs.

This did not mean that there was not a "progressive" or "gradual" element in the process of entire sanctification. There was, but this had to be carefully defined so that the distinctive doctrine of the instantaneous eradication of original sin would not be compromised. The Holiness Movement had identified the entire salvific process as sanctifying and had used terms like initial sanctification, partial sanctification, gradual sanctification, and continuous sanctification to describe the process. These terms however did not mean what they implied, i.e., that in the salvific process believers were gradually becoming more and more holy. So that there would be no mistaking the nature of the grace, Wiley devoted eight pages to a careful analysis of the nature of "progressive" sanctification and the meaning of these words.

He began by acknowledging that many Methodist theologians had come to emphasize sanctification as gradual instead of instantaneous. According to Wiley, this was because they had failed to recognize that sanctification was a work of grace alone. They failed to understand sufficiently that sanctification was an act of God and not an act of man. After quoting Alexander Pope on the matter, Wiley wrote:

> There is here a great truth which no student of theology can afford to overlook, and failure to emphasize this point, leads to confusion concerning the experience itself. But this point was not sufficiently guarded by Methodist theologians, and as a consequence, the emphasis came gradually to be placed upon the aspect of growth and development, rather than upon the crises which marked the different stages in personal experience.[24]

This was a crucial mistake and Wiley attempted to guarantee, that for Nazarenes, there would be no confusion concerning the instantaneous nature of this act of God.

This emphasis on the instantaneous act of God conditioned Wiley's explanation of the progressive nature of sanctification. In the third sentence of a section dedicated to an analysis of progressive sanctification, Wiley made clear that it was not to be identified in any way with "gradual" sanctification. Gradual sanctification implied that one could be made more and more holy. This Wiley rejected. According to Wiley, progressive sanctification simply meant:

> "the *temporal* aspect of the work of grace in the heart, as it takes place in successive stages. Each of these stages is marked by a *gradual approach* and an *instantaneous consummation* in experi-

ence, and the stages together mark the full scope of sanctifying grace" *(emphasis mine).*[25]

Progressive sanctification was to be strictly understood as the gradual approach in time toward the instantaneous sanctifying experience. Gradual sanctification, according to Wiley, was simply the growing awareness of the need for the instantaneous work of entire sanctification.

> While there is a gradual approach to sanctification . . . the sanctifying act by which we are made holy, must of necessity be instantaneous. In the words of Bishop Hamline, "It is gradually approached, but instantaneously bestowed." Dr. Adam Clarke states that "in no part of the Scriptures are we directed to seek holiness by gradation. We are to come to God for an instantaneous and complete purification from all sin."[26]

Furthermore, the temporal aspect of sanctification was not even integral to the process, for when the need for entire sanctification became apparent, the possibility for the grace could be realized.

> This gradual, preparatory work may be *cut short* in righteousness. When the sinner perfectly submits to the righteousness of Christ, and believes the promises of God, that moment he is justified and the Spirit imparts new life to his soul. When, also, the child of God through the Spirit, fully renounces inbred sin and trusts the blood of cleansing, that moment he may, by simple faith in Christ, be sanctified wholly *(emphasis mine).*[27]

Progressive sanctification, in spite of what the term might have suggested, was not to be understood as sanctifying! Progressive sanctification was simply a term used to describe the successive instantaneous acts of God in the life of the believer.

The first instantaneous act of God for Holiness people was called initial sanctification. This "first work of grace" was another word for conversion. Initial sanctification however, did not mean that one was made "partially holy" at conversion, even though that is what the term sanctification implied. "The term is not an indefinite one, referring to the cleansing away of more or less of the sinner's defilement. It is a definite term, and is limited strictly to that guilt and acquired depravity attaching to actual sins. . . . It does not refer to the cleansing from original sin."[28] Initial sanctification simply meant being forgiven. Past sins were "cleansed" in that moment.

Continuous sanctification, which Wiley identified as the sanctification that was subsequent to entire sanctification, or the "second work of grace," was not a continuing process whereby persons were made more and more holy. "Continuous" for Wiley meant "preserving." Continuous sanctification *kept* the work of that instantaneously completed act of grace.

> We mean by [continuous sanctification] that we are cleansed

from all sin, only as through faith, we are brought into a right relation to the atoning blood of Jesus Christ; and only as there is a continuous relation to atoning blood by faith, will there be a continuous cleansing, in the sense of a preservation in purity and holiness.[29] Progressive sanctification therefore, was not to be understood in any way as gradually sanctifying. Progressive sanctification was the term used to describe successive instantaneous acts of God. While much terminology, like initial, gradual, partial, or continuous seemed to indicate otherwise, there was only one way to be sanctified wholly, and that was to be sanctified instantaneously.

As others had before him, Wiley believed that this instantaneous act of God provided complete purification from all sin. Noting that in the Greek, "to sanctify" means "to make holy," Wiley wrote, in no uncertain terms, what entire sanctification accomplished.

The extent of cleansing according to the Scriptures, includes the complete removal of all sin. Sin is to be cleansed thoroughly, purged, extirpated, eradicated and crucified; not repressed, suppressed, counter-acted or made void, as these terms are commonly used. It is to be destroyed.[30]

After analyzing seven Greek words used to describe the sanctifying work of God in the life of the believer, Wiley concluded this short section on entire sanctification as purification from all sin by writing, "A careful study of these terms should convince every earnest believer that the Scriptures teach the complete cleansing of the heart from inbred sin—the utter destruction of the carnal mind."[31]

This complete cleansing of the heart from inbred sin, this destruction of the carnal mind, was accompanied by a divine empowering. Under the heading "Positive Devotement to God," which was derived from the phrase the Church of the Nazarene used in their article of faith to describe the grace of entire sanctification,[32] Wiley explained that in entire sanctification, the Holy Spirit of God possessed and filled the believer resulting in "positive devotement to God." This was nothing other than holy love. "While entire sanctification considered from the negative point of view is a cleansing from all sin, from the positive standpoint it is the infilling of divine love."[33] Purity and perfect love were what characterized the entirely sanctified believer.

Wiley, however, wanted to make clear that purity and perfect love—which were the results of cleansing and divine empowering respectively—when considered separately, were not sufficient in and of themselves to define the results of this grace. "Entire sanctification is something more than either purity or perfect love. Neither of these in the strictest sense of the term is holiness."[34] According to Wiley, the holiness, which was a consequence of this second work of grace and which was, in essence, the same as God's holiness,[35] was *the union* of these two aspects of the experience. A heart cleansed from all sin and a heart filled with divine love were two aspects of that same work of grace.

Purity and love are thus combined in a deeper, underlying nature, which does not so much appear to indicate any particular virtue, nor all of the virtues combined, as it does the recoil of a pure soul from sin, and a love of righteousness, indicative of a nature in perfect harmony with itself.[36]

As a result, the very nature of man was changed. When one was entirely sanctified, the holiness of God, which was characterized by purity and love, was imparted to persons without change in quality. Consequently, human nature was transformed and expressed nothing more and nothing less than this pure love. In a later section of the chapter, in a paragraph titled The Fundamental Concept of Christian Perfection, Wiley wrote:

Pure love reigns supreme without the antagonisms of sin. Love is the spring of every activity. The believer having entered into the fullness of the New Covenant, does by nature, the things contained in the law, and hence, the law is said to be written upon his heart.[37]

In an incredibly promising passage, Wiley combined the instantaneous aspect of the grace with this description of what the grace accomplished:

(The believer) finds, also, that God has promised a cleansing from all sin through the blood of Jesus. He lays hold of the promises of God, and in a moment, the Holy Spirit purifies his heart by faith. In that instant he lives the full life of love. In him love is made perfect . . . The law of God is written upon his heart.[38]

This pure love manifested itself in many ways. As other Holiness writers before him, Wiley quoted John Fletcher's description of the grace.

In other words, Christian perfection is a spiritual constellation, made up of these gracious stars: perfect repentance, perfect faith, perfect humility, perfect meekness, perfect self-denial, perfect resignation, perfect hope, perfect charity for our visible enemies, as well as our earthly relations; and, above all, perfect love for our invisible God, through the explicit knowledge of our Mediator, Jesus Christ.[39]

Wiley also made much of the fact that there would be a love for holiness and an animus toward evil in the entirely sanctified individual. "Holiness is such that it includes both [purity and perfect love] in a deeper nature—so completely renovated and adjusted by the work of the Spirit that its very expression is a love for righteousness and hatred of iniquity."[40]

This was all effected by consecration and faith. The means to this transforming grace was consecrating faith. "The scriptures are clear—it is always wrought by a simple faith in the atoning blood of Jesus Christ."[41] According to Wiley, this simple faith incorporated three elements:

(1) A consciousness of inbred sin, and a hungering and thirsting for full conformity to the image of Christ. (2) A firm conviction in the light of the scriptural provisions, that it is not only a privilege but a duty to be cleansed from all sin. (3) There must be perfect submission of the soul to God, commonly known as consecration, followed by an act of simple faith in Christ—a sure trust in Him for the promised blessing.[42]

Because simple consecrating faith was all that was necessary for entire sanctification, one could be entirely sanctified at any moment. A heart purified of all sin and filled with holy love was capable of being realized at any time, conditioned only by a simple act of consecrating faith.

What, then, is the appointed time. . . . It is the hour of submission to the baptism with the Holy Spirit, which purifies the heart from sin and fills it with divine love. There is no need here for an extended lapse of time. It is sufficient only that the believer come to feel his need and see his privileges in Christ Jesus.[43]

Entire sanctification, according to Wiley, was what the article of faith in the Church of the Nazarene said it was. It was an *act of God,* subsequent to regeneration, by which believers were made *free from original sin,* and brought into a state of *entire devotement to God,* and the holy obedience *of love made perfect.* It was wrought by the *baptism with the Holy Spirit,* and comprehended in one experience the *cleansing of the heart from sin* and the abiding, indwelling *presence of the Holy Spirit,* empowering the believer for life and service. Entire sanctification was provided by the blood of Jesus, was wrought *instantaneously by faith* and *preceded by entire consecration.*

SOME CLARIFYING DEFINITIONS

In addition to defining the doctrine of entire sanctification relative to the church at large and consistent with the denomination's Article of Faith, Wiley's careful explication included several pages of qualifications of the doctrine. In the Wesleyan-Holiness Movement, "Christian Perfection" was the term used to describe the state of one who had been entirely sanctified. This term, which Wesley had used, had resulted in much misunderstanding. Wiley, recognizing this, sought to temper some of the more extravagant descriptions of entire sanctification. Under the heading, "Misconceptions of Christian Perfection"[44] he wrote: "The term seems to connote a standard of excellence which those who are rightly informed never claimed for it."[45] He then wrote of what entire sanctification did not accomplish. He wrote of what Christian Perfection was not.

According to Wiley, there were primarily three important distinctions that needed to be made in order to preserve the doctrine from some of the more popular misconceptions. The first was the distinction between purity and maturity. Wiley believed that the failure to distinguish between purity and maturity was the reason for every objection to the doctrine. Echoing J. A. Wood, Wiley wrote:

> Purity is the result of a cleansing from the pollution of sin; maturity is due to growth in grace. Purity is accomplished by an instantaneous act; maturity is gradual and progressive, and is always indefinite and relative. When, therefore, we speak of perfect love, we have reference solely to its quality as being unmixed with sin, never to its degree or quantity. . . . A clear comprehension of the difference between purity and maturity will prevent confusion, both as to the doctrine and experience of Christian perfection.[46]

The second important distinction that needed to be made in order to preserve the doctrine from error was the difference between infirmities and sins. This was a crucial distinction for those in the Wesleyan-Holiness Movement. Sin, "properly so called," was strictly understood as *intentional* and *voluntary* transgressions. Intentional and voluntary sin brought guilt and condemnation and, as such, required repentance. Infirmities however, were understood as *involuntary* and *unintentional* transgressions of the divine law and were a result of ignorance and weakness as a consequence of the fall of man. Wiley quoted Wesley in a footnote concerning the matter.

> Not only sin, properly so called, that is, a voluntary transgression of a divine law; but sin, improperly so-called, that is, involuntary transgressions of a divine law, known or unknown, needs the atoning blood. I believe there is no such perfection in this life as excludes these involuntary transgressions, which I apprehend to be naturally consequent on the ignorance and mistakes inseparable from mortality. Therefore, sinless perfection is a phrase I never use, lest I should seem to contradict myself.[47]

A person who was entirely sanctified would never *intentionally* sin, and Christian perfection was the state of never sinning volitionally. Christian perfection did not mean however that one was exempt from sinning accidentally or involuntarily. That was considered sin "improperly so called." A person filled with the holy love of God himself would indeed transgress, however it would not be because of willful intention but because of weakness or ignorance.

The third important distinction that Wiley believed needed to be made concerned the possibility of temptation. Wiley held that all Christians, sanctified and not, were subject to temptation and that it was entirely consistent with Christian perfection since Christ himself was tempted. However, he believed, as others in the Holiness Movement before him had, that there was a qualitative difference between the temptation of those who were entirely sanctified and those who were not. "The difference lies in this, that in the latter, temptation stirs up the natural corruption of the heart with its bias toward sin; while in the former, the temptation is met with uniform resistance."[48] He acknowledged that it was hard to discern between those temptations that were prompted from the enemy without and those temptations that were prompted from the inbred sin within, but he believed that in the entirely sanctified individual the response to temptation would be immediate recoil and rejection. One could discern the source of temptation by how quickly it was dismissed.

Christian perfection therefore was not the absolute perfection of God himself, it was not the perfection of angels, and it was not even the perfection of Adam prior to the fall. The Christian perfection that the Holiness Movement proclaimed, according to Wiley, was a relative perfection, conditioned by the Fall, characterized by weakness and infirmities, capable of growth, and subject to temptation.

> It is true that this redeemed and perfected spirit, dwells in a body which is a member of a sinful race, but his spirit may be lifted from darkness to light, while his body remains the same "muddy vesture of decay" that it was before his spirit was redeemed. Consequently it is still beclouded with weakness, in that the soul is under the influence of material things, and will be until the creature itself shall have put on incorruption and immortality.[49]

This clarification of the doctrine of entire sanctification in terms of what it did not accomplish was not a major theme in much of the holiness literature the church had authorized for the course of study. Wesley, whom Wiley quoted, had written on the limits of entire sanctification in "A Plain Account of Christian Perfection." According to Wesley, the entirely sanctified were not free from ignorance or mistake. They were not infallible. They were not free from infirmities nor were they free from temptation.[50] And while this teaching of Wesley's had been faithfully reiterated in Wiley's *Christian Theology,* Wesley's clarifying treatment of the subject was not included in the ministerial course of study until 1952.

Wiley was not the first to carefully delimit the doctrine. Other Holiness writers had tried to faithfully represent some of these Wesleyan qualifications. With remarkable consistency however these other Holiness writers were more concerned with qualifying the qualifications of the doctrine than with qualifying the doctrine itself. C. W. Ruth, an early Nazarene evangelist and close friend of P. F. Bresee, had written a book on the doctrine, appropriately titled *Entire Sanctification.* In his 110-page book, which was required reading in the Ministerial Course of Study in 1908 (for the first and last time), he wrote how entire sanctification must be understood:

> Sanctification is not infallibility. A pure heart does not mean a perfect head. Sanctified people make mistakes. . . . A mistake is the thing you do because you do not know better; sin is the thing you do when you do know better. . . . Motive determines the morality of the act.[51]

But Ruth qualified the qualification. He stipulated that these mistakes would not occur very often for the entirely sanctified.

> While sanctified people are liable to mistakes because of mental infirmities and ignorance it is nevertheless true that the liabilities are not so great, and the mistakes perhaps not so numerous, owing to the fact that they are walking in the clear light of God, and hence have keener discernment, a clearer vision, and quicker moral perceptions.[52]

Daniel Steele, in *The Gospel of the Comforter*, briefly acknowledged that the gift of the Holy Spirit, which was concomitant with entire sanctification, did not prevent errors in judgment. But he too was quick to add that the Holy Spirit "indirectly helps us by delivering us from the dominance of appetites and passions inimical to clearness of intellect and calmness of judgment."[53] Thus he indicated that these errors of judgment would be much less likely in the entirely sanctified. A. M. Hills, in *Fundamental Christian Theology*, following Wesley, wrote of the *relative* perfection of entirely sanctified individuals. According to Hills,

> [Sanctification] does not bring angelic perfection. It does not bring us to the perfection of our own glorified state in the after-resurrection life. It does not bring us a *sinless perfection* in the sense that it makes it impossible for us to sin and fall. Entire sanctification does not imply or involve infallibility of knowledge, or judgment, or memory. It does not secure us from temptation. Sanctification does not end Christian growth.[54]

But in *Holiness and Power,* Hills followed his acknowledgment of a relative perfection with these words:

> Again and again, we must reiterate, it is God that giveth the ability, that does the sanctifying, that does the keeping. . . . Whatever man may not be able to do in his own strength, he can do when God commands it and girds with his own omnipotent strength. "If God should command me to fly," said John Wesley, "I would trust him for wings." Such an utterance is divinely wise.[55]

While others before Wiley had defined entire sanctification in terms of what it did not accomplish, this was a very minor theme in most of the holiness literature of the period prior to Wiley. These Holiness authors certainly did not give it the careful attention that Wiley gave it in his *Christian Theology*. As might be expected, the early Nazarene church was not too interested in defining their glorious doctrine in limiting terms. They were primarily interested in proclaiming the wonderful possibilities of this second work of grace. With Wiley, that had begun to change.

5
RIGHT CONCEPTIONS

KEEPING TO THE COURSE

One of the longest quadrennial addresses ever given by a general superintendent of the Church of the Nazarene was the one presented to the delegates at the 12th General Assembly in St. Louis in June of 1948. It was written by H. V. Miller, who had been elected to the general superintendency in 1940, and ran 23 pages. The tone of this 40th-anniversary address was slightly different from those that had been given in the first general assemblies of the Church of the Nazarene. Miller did not speak with the unbridled optimism that had characterized these earlier assembly addresses but instead spoke of the dangers that had threatened and were continuing to threaten the church. Using an analogy with which the delegates, who were just three years from the end of World War II, could easily identify, Miller said:

> Just four years ago our gospel ship sailed forth into turbulent seas. We had spent precious hours loading her cargo, replenishing supplies, checking her crew, making our ship as seaworthy as we could against the coming voyage. We lifted anchor, sailing forth into waters filled with treacherous current. Clouds of global strife hung low and threatening. The lightnings of war and the ominous signs of increasing storm on an already peril-filled sea threatened us as once again we set sail on our voyage of God-given destiny. Nonetheless our courage was strong for the voyage before us because we knew the Pilot we had on board.
>
> Another four years of tempest tossed seas have been voyaged and are now behind us. We have weathered the storm well, though our vessel has never sailed more boisterous seas or faced more adverse tides than those of the past quadrennium.[1]

Some of these "adverse tides" that the church had weathered were internal. Since the last general assembly, three of the most influential leaders of the denomination had died. Miller acknowledged the passing of one retired and two active general superintendents—J. W. Goodwin, R. T. Williams, and J. B. Chapman, respectively—by testifying to the sense of loss the church felt in their passing. "It is unlikely that any church has ever faced such losses in leadership in a given period of time as we have. One of the prevalent feelings of this gathering, spoken and unspoken, is the keen sense of this loss in leadership."[2] Another internal disappointment acknowledged in the address was the failure to realize attendance goals set at the previous general assembly. An internal "adverse tide" not mentioned in the report was the growing and oftentimes acrimonious debate over the place of special rules, such as the prohibition against the theater, in the denomination's constitution.[3]

Some of the adversities that threatened the church's culture and theology, however, were external. Three months before the 1948 General Assembly, a picture of Union Theological Seminary professor Reinhold Niebuhr was featured on the 25th-anniversary issue of *Time* magazine. The caption beneath the picture of an anxious-looking Niebuhr read, "Man's story is not a success story."[4] The article in the religious section of the magazine chronicled the change in American religious culture from a "hermetically smug optimism" in the "indefinite perfectibility" of man[5] to the tragedy of life and the inevitability of sin. Opining on the conditions of the day, the writer of the article wrote:

> The incomparable technological achievement is more and more dedicated to the task of destruction. Man's marvelous conquest of space has made total war a household experience and over vast reaches of the world, the commonest of childhood memories. The more abundance increases, the more resentment becomes the characteristic new look on 20th Century faces. The more production multiplies, the more scarcities become endemic. The faster science gains on disease, (which ultimately, seems always to elude it), the more the human race dies at the hands of living men. Men have never been so educated, but wisdom, even as an idea, has conspicuously vanished from the world.[6]

The article referred to Niebuhr's magnum opus, *The Nature and Destiny of Man,*[7] and outlined Niebuhr's theological anthropology, which assailed the very idea of the perfectibility of mankind. The first volume of the two-volume work, based on the Gifford Lectures he had given in Edinburgh in 1939, had been published in 1941, coincidently, the same year that H. Orton Wiley had published the first volume of his magnum opus, *Christian Theology.* In *The Nature and Destiny of Man,* however, in sharp contrast to Wiley's theology, there was no promise that man could escape his sinful condition while a captive of the fallen world. According to Niebuhr, while sin wasn't necessary, it was inevitable. As a matter of fact, the essence of sin was just this attempt to escape the limitations of human finitude.

> The real evil in the human situation . . . lies in man's unwillingness to recognize and acknowledge the weakness, finiteness and dependence of his position, in his inclination to grasp after a power and security which transcend the possibilities of human existence,

and in his effort to pretend a virtue and knowledge which are beyond the limits of mere creatures.[8]

Freedom from sin, both corporate and personal, will be possible only at the end of the age. Until then, man must live with the reality of an ever-present sinful hope, faith, and love.

Nothing that is worth doing can be achieved in our lifetime; therefore we must be saved by hope. Nothing which is true or beautiful or good makes complete sense in any immediate context of history; therefore we must be saved by faith. Nothing we do, however virtuous can be accomplished alone; therefore we are saved by love. No virtuous act is quite as virtuous from the standpoint of our friend or foe as it is from our standpoint. Therefore we must be saved by the final form of love which is forgiveness.[9]

The most influential theologian of the first half of the 20th century, whose face was on the cover of *Time* magazine the year the Church of the Nazarene celebrated its 40th birthday, was propagating a theology that was antithetical to the Church of the Nazarene's distinctive doctrine. Niebuhr's theology was certainly not a message to which the Church of the Nazarene would ever be sympathetic, but the "adverse tides" of historical circumstance, which had inspired Niebuhr's "theological realism," had the potential to adversely affect the holiness doctrine of entire sanctification and Christian perfection. The Church of the Nazarene was certainly not immune from the historical and cultural conditions that seemed to justify a doctrine of the inevitability of sin.

At the beginning of the century, as has already been shown, the leaders in the Church of the Nazarene had believed that the holiness message would "Christianize Christianity," unite denominations, transform American culture and eventually the world at large. The early explication of the doctrine of entire sanctification was a holiness manifestation of the heady optimism that Americans at large had been expressing at the beginning of the century and an evangelical counterpoint to the utopian hopes of liberal Protestantism. In the 40 years since the Pilot Point merger, however, national and world events had proven all optimism concerning the nature and destiny of man naive. The Bolshevik Revolution of 1917 had created an atheistic communistic state undermining hope in a relatively quick world evangelization. The stock market crash in 1929, which plunged the nation into a severe depression, called into question the ability of man to effectively orchestrate market forces and thus his economic well-being. The repeal of prohibition in 1933 effectively quenched any hope for massive moral social change. The Treaty at Versailles, which had promised world peace, had proven itself instrumental in involving the world in a Second World War, culminating in the dropping of atomic bombs on Hiroshima and Nagasaki. When Niebuhr's face appeared on the March 8, 1948, issue of *Time* magazine and when the general superintendents of the Church of the Nazarene were acknowledging the "storms of the peril-filled seas," in June of 1948, the United States was one of the principal adversaries in a nascent "cold war" that threatened the destruction of the entire world. These historical "adverse tides," as Miller had called them, had effectively killed any last vestige of hope that the holiness doctrine of the Church of the Nazarene might have become the agent for transforming American culture and then the world at large.

The greatest threat these adverse tides posed for the denomination at midcentury involved calling into question the distinctive doctrine of the Church of the Nazarene. The doctrine that persons could be freed from all sin could be compromised in light of the sobering social realities of the day. Consequently, throughout the decade of the 1940s, the leadership of the Church of the Nazarene continually called on the church to remain faithful to the doctrine. In 1948, in the address that recognized these threats, Miller wrote:

> One of the troubles of our present-day American life is that we too quickly lose sight of the price that it has cost in blood to maintain the liberty that makes our country unique. It is shockingly true that even now millions are all too soon forgetting the price that was so recently paid to hold our frontiers intact, so saving the freedom that we love. This tendency seems to run consistently through life. We, as a church, obviously face this same danger. A rich, though small, inheritance, has been passed to us. Will we squander this precious spiritual wealth, dissipating it through careless use and spiritual negligence? Or will we set a new precedent among men and pass on to another generation the inheritance given to us, not only intact but increased.[10]

Miller suggested that there was a parallel between the Methodists and the Nazarenes. This comparison was intended to alarm the delegates, for Nazarenes believed that the Methodists had abandoned the Wesleyan doctrine of entire sanctification and that one of the reasons for their own denomination's existence was due to the Methodists' failure to teach the doctrine as the Nazarenes had understood it. As far as the Church of the Nazarene was concerned, they were preserving the trust that the Methodists had forsaken. While Miller did not in any way imply that the Nazarenes were on the brink of becoming "Methodists," he did use this comparison to warn against any softening of the doctrine. He called on the preachers in particular to remain true to the distinctive doctrine of the Church of the Nazarene.

> Our preachers must major in scriptural holiness if we are to fill this unique place and complete this unique task to which God has

called us. Let our men read, pray, think, and sermonize in terms of scriptural freedom from sin and let them proclaim this truth with skill, versatility, persistency, and power.[11]

Four years earlier, J. B. Chapman had reminded the delegates that the only reason for the Nazarene denomination to exist at all was for the sake of the holiness doctrine. He declared:

[T]here is no complete escape from denominationalism, and the causes for the separateness of the Church of the Nazarene are the most fundamental possible, and we believe . . . that we came to the kingdom for "such a time as this." Ours has been the task to help keep alive the tenets of the "Faith of our Fathers," and to extend the testimony to vital salvation in terms of New Testament regeneration and Pentecostal sanctification.[12]

Four years before that, in 1940, at the 10th General Assembly, presiding General Superintendent R. T. Williams had also warned the delegates of several dangers facing the church in the years ahead. According to Williams, the first was the danger of forsaking the holiness message.

First, note the danger of losing sight of our central theme—holiness, the heart of the atonement. The doctrine of holiness is not only attractive and desirable, but absolutely essential to the life and usefulness of the church. A clear and intelligent understanding of this truth must extend to every corner of the denomination.[13]

In these addresses, the general superintendents were sure to declare that the doctrine of entire sanctification was alive and well. The church as of yet had not gone the way of the "Methodists" nor had the doctrine been compromised by the events that had prompted "theological realists" like Niebuhr. The possibility was always there however. Therefore, the leadership of the denomination called the church not only to faithfulness but also to continued indoctrination. In 1940, R. T. Williams, without apology, called on the church to make Nazarenes out of those who were joining the denomination. "Those who are received into membership, though saved and sanctified, must be transformed into workers with the Nazarene vision and spirit. . . . It is our duty tomorrow to get more members and to learn better how to develop them into real Nazarenes."[14] H. V. Miller, in 1948, reminded the church of the need for continuing instruction for new believers.

To make our heritage live in the tomorrows calls for true appreciation, sacrificial living, persistent indoctrination, and the wisest of planning. . . . No task confronts us requiring more painstaking effort than the passing on to another generation the same ideals and vision and full passion that moved our fathers. Along with line upon line of instruction and precept upon precept of doctrine must come revival tides of God's glory to illuminate and to confirm the truth of our teaching.[15]

This desire to make sure that the denomination's doctrine would be faithfully preserved manifested itself in the establishment of a graduate school seminary where Nazarene preachers might be trained for ministry in the Nazarene church. Discussion had been taking place among Nazarene leaders since the 1930s concerning the need for just such a graduate school seminary. H. Orton Wiley, as education secretary, in the 1940 General Board meeting encouraged the establishment of a seminary, and in the 1940 General Assembly quadrennial address, R. T. Williams made a careful recommendation to the delegates.

> Definite steps should be made toward the establishment of a seminary. The hour may not be here yet, but is not far distant, when such will be essential to the best interests of the church. Ministers, who have completed college and university courses, feel the need of work in this specialized field for highest efficiency. Many have sought seminary work in an atmosphere that has undermined their usefulness. The loss to the church from those who take seminary work in institutions unfavorable to the fundamental principles of our denomination is too heavy. We need to train our men in our own institutions for our own peculiar God-given task.[16]

The assembly voted to table the matter until the next general assembly. In early 1944, the general superintendents, acting on a recommendation made by the district superintendents at their annual conference, appointed a commission to make recommendations to the 1944 General Assembly concerning the seminary. The commission made clear the school's purpose in the second of 11 recommendations. "Finally, the primary purpose of the institution shall be to conserve, maintain, advocate and promulgate the great Bible doctrine of 'Entire Sanctification' as a second distinct work of divine grace wrought in the heart of the believer subsequent to regeneration."[17] The last recommendation left no doubt concerning the church's intention. "We recommend that the president and all professors of the Seminary must be in the experience of entire sanctification."[18] The delegates adopted the entire report without change amid enthusiastic applause. They then elected trustees for the school who went immediately to work, opening the seminary in the fall of 1945 with five full-time professors and 60 students.[19] Thus they provided for graduate level education consistent with their entrusted doctrine. They would not lose any preachers by virtue of their having to attend a seminary not sympathetic to the doctrine of entire sanctification as the Nazarenes understood it.

The Church of the Nazarene, in the mid-decades of the 20th century, was concerned that there not be any wavering concerning the doctrine of entire sanctification. In the quadrennial addresses, they applauded the lack of contention concerning the doctrine. They had recently received from the hands of H. Orton Wiley an authoritative systematic theology and had taken certain steps to provide orthodox graduate school education. They were intent on preserving as well as propagating her distinctive doctrine. H. V. Miller concluded the 1948 General Assembly quadrennial address the way he began it, with the forbidding allusion to that sailing ship. This time it was leaving the harbor, and once more, Miller called on the church to stay the course.

> And so in a very few short days we shall again put out to sea. . . . May we keep to the course and heed the compass we now set, regardless of gale or tide. There may be times, and probably will, when the skies will be black with not a star in sight. The seas will rage in their fury and hazards will surround us. Temptation may come to some to change course and seek some closer harbor of seeming safety. But may we not yield our course, but sail on to the shores that we are now choosing. May there never be a word on board that could be construed as the seed of mutiny nor a moment of slackening in diligence. May we all keep our appointed watches as though the sailing depended solely upon us. Remember, many other ships have long since broken upon treacherous rocks and hidden bars. Ships as seaworthy as our own have gone down before us. Careless watches, unwarranted changes in course, plausible excursions to attractive harbors looming into view, have brought about these tragedies. God help us to sail forth toward our desired haven of the will of God, carrying the precious cargo entrusted to us, rescuing as we go all to whom we can throw the line. Let us sail, Nazarenes. Our eternal Captain is on board.[20]

THE MEANING OF HOLINESS

The doctrine was affected by the historical circumstances. While the desire of the Church of the Nazarene was to "conserve, maintain, advocate and promulgate" the precious cargo to which they had been entrusted, subsequent explications of the doctrine reveal the subtle influence of a "theological realism." In addition to Wiley's *Christian Theology,* which was the primary theological textbook for all ministers in the church and was considered authoritative in its explication of entire sanctification, the church continued to publish and recommend works that focused exclusively on the holiness doctrine. The books that were added to the reading list in these decades, however, did not have the "triumphalist" titles or flavor that his earlier books had. In the early years, Nazarenes had read holiness books like A. M. Hills's *Holiness and Power,* Asbury Lowrey's *Possibilities of Grace,* R. S. Foster's *Christian Purity,* and J. A. Wood's *Perfect Love* that had made extravagant claims concerning what the grace could accomplish. While the denomination continued to include these works in the reading lists in the 1940s and 1950s, beginning in the fourth decade of the denomination's existence, Nazarene preachers were required to read books with carefully qualifying titles, like *Scriptural Freedom from Sin* by Henry E. Brockett, *A Right Conception of Sin* by Richard S. Taylor, *The Terminology of Holiness* by J. B. Chapman, *The Meaning of Holiness* by D. Shelby Corlett, and *Conflicting Concepts of Holiness* by W. T. Purkiser. These were works that were clinically precise in their definition concerning exactly what it was that was eradicated by the grace of entire sanctification, and they were not making the claims that earlier holiness works had. The doctrine in the middle decades of the 20th century, in the unavoidable light of the pervasive fallenness of the world, was being modified to account for that fallenness.

According to these later Holiness authors, the extravagantly unrealistic claims that earlier Holiness writers had made concerning what entire sanctification accomplished had caused great confusion and much misunderstanding. Henry E. Brockett, an English Holiness author, published *Scriptural Freedom from Sin* in 1940. It was quickly adopted in that same year as one of the books fourth year ministerial students were required to read, and it remained on the reading list until 1960. The foreword was written by a personal friend of Brockett, J. D. Drysdale, and in the first sentence of the foreword, Drysdale stated that "no truth has been so misrepresented and unscripturally assailed by its opponents as the glorious doctrine set forth in this heart-searching and inspiring volume."[21] In the brief two-and-a-half-page foreword, Drysdale acknowledged the mistake of other Holiness authors. He wrote: "I am forced to admit that amongst us there have often been sad and extravagant expressions [of the doctrine of entire sanctification], which doubtless have brought upon us much adverse criticism."[22] He believed Brockett's book would go a long way toward "vindicat[ing] the glorious doctrine of entire sanctification."[23] Brockett himself stated the same concerning the overly optimistic claims of some of the Holiness writers, just three pages into his work. He wrote: "We must beware of *exaggerating* the truth of deliverance from sin and thus falling into the error of thinking that it means either Adamic perfection or a fixed state of sinless perfection, that is, a state from which we can never fall or in which we can never be tempted."[24] He then proceeded to devote the whole of the sixth chapter, titled Holiness Truth Safeguards, to an explanation of what deliverance from sin did *not* mean. "It is necessary to be clear on these safeguards, so that we do not exaggerate the truth of God and thus fall into harmful error."[25] As other Wesleyan and Holiness writers had briefly done before him, Brockett stated that "scriptural freedom from sin" was neither the perfection of Adam nor was it the perfection of angels. In support of this definition, he quoted J. G. Morrison, who was an early Nazarene general superintendent, and whose book, *Our Lost Estate,* was in the course of study from 1932 to 1940.

> We do not profess to be angels, when we receive this great blessing, but just common men and women, woefully weak, still under the curse of the fall as to mental and physical powers, but pure and holy in the heart, and filled with perfect love. . . . Then again, entire sanctification is not, as we have intimated above, the sort of complete perfection that was the happy privilege of Adam and Eve. . . . Their bodies were perfect, while ours are full of the possibilities of pain, weakness, abnormal appetites and passions, decay and final death. Their minds were perfect and they needed not to learn. . . . The minds of human beings, even after they are wholly sanctified, are subject to weakness, frailty, imperfect judgment, poor memory, indecision and failure often to see the effect that will spring from a certain cause.[26]

Brockett however, "continued to qualify what was to be understood by *"scriptural* freedom from sin." At one point, Brockett had been asked to testify as to whether or not there was anything unholy in his life, and he had written a letter in response. He quoted a portion of this letter in his book as a way of clarifying what could be expected by entire sanctification.

> [E]ven with [Christ's] indwelling, I am not yet entirely freed from the effects of sin and the fall, being still in a fallen condition with a mortal, corruptible body that needs "keeping under," possessing very limited knowledge and with very imperfect powers of mind, judgment, etc., all through the fall. Even if I may not be conscious of sin, there may still be faults and failures in my life which the Lord may see but of which I may not be aware. From this point of view, I still fall short of the glory of God . . . I am only a sinner saved by grace. For these reasons, I would not make the unqualified statement, "There is nothing unholy in my life." It would be liable to be terribly misunderstood.[27]

Brockett therefore distinguished between being blameless and faultless. Using an example of a child's letter to his mother, which might be full of grammatical mistakes and yet still a perfect expression of pure love, Brockett wrote that while we may be blameless before God, we will never be faultless.

> By virtue of the fact that we are still in a fallen condition so far as our bodily and mental powers are concerned, we are subject to many infirmities, we lack the perfect knowledge of God's will in all things (this has to be learned by degrees). We are liable, therefore, to

errors of judgment, etc., and various other faults which may not be known to ourselves but are all seen by God. Hence the holiest Christian, from this point of view, may daily pray that humble prayer of confession, "Forgive us our debts, as we forgive our debtors."[28]

This distinction that entire sanctification enabled believers to be blameless before God but not necessarily faultless was a crucial one, and Brockett was by no means the only Holiness author to make it. There was a long tradition in the Holiness Movement of distinguishing between sin (blame) and infirmities (faults), between "willful transgressions of known laws," which would result in condemnation, and "mistakes," which were covered by the blood of Christ. Wesley himself was careful to distinguish between the two, and even the most optimistic Holiness authors, who wrote in the most extravagant terms concerning what sanctification accomplished, were sure to note it. But in the middle decades of the 20th century, explicating this distinction became much more prevalent. What had been a footnote in early holiness works became the subject of entire works by midcentury.

Another such representative book was Richard S. Taylor's *A Right Conception of Sin*. Richard S. Taylor was a pastor and evangelist in the Church of the Nazarene and would in 1953 earn a doctorate in theology from Boston University. In 1940, his book, which was primarily a polemic against Calvinism's definition of sin, was added to the course of study. The significance of his work to the Nazarenes' understanding of holiness is attested to by the book remaining in the course of study to the end of the century. In his 128-page treatise, Taylor carefully distinguished between the sinful nature and the human nature, between willful transgressions of known laws and infirmities, and in the language of Brockett, between that for which we will be blamed and that for which we will only be faulted.

Taylor began by claiming that the doctrine of sin was the central doctrine around which entire systems of theology were built. This led him to conclude:

> [I]f our conception of sin is faulty, our whole superstructure will be one error built on another, each one more absurd than the last, yet each one necessary if it is to fit in consistently with the whole erroneous scheme. If we are to end right we must begin right, and to begin right we must grapple with the question of sin in its doctrinal significance until we have grasped the scriptural facts relating to sin in all of its phases. We need to know exactly what sin is, of what kinds, how it acts, its effects, its relation to man, how it must be dealt with, and God's provision for it.[29]

He then briefly outlined the Calvinistic doctrines of unconditional election, irresistible grace, perseverance of saints, and imputed righteousness, showing how they are systematically dependent on one another. His first criticism of Calvinism was that it inevitably led to antinomianism. The individual, according to Taylor's interpretation of Calvinism, is not compelled to take any responsibility for his salvation at all. An individual can be assured of salvation without having to leave his life of sin. He concluded that Calvinism leaves persons in their sin. "In plain language, the Calvinistic system of predestination, grace, perseverance, and imputed righteousness, means that as a condition of getting to heaven complete deliverance from sin is unnecessary."[30]

This, of course, went right to the heart of the holiness matter, for Nazarenes believed that complete deliverance from sin was not only a possibility but an absolute necessity. Taylor then argued for the complete transformation of human nature, made possible through the infilling of the Holy Spirit in the second work of grace of entire sanctification.

> The mighty transformation in the disciples which took place on the day of Pentecost must not be forgotten as a further evidence of the complete renovation which is to follow regeneration. . . . The outstanding and most essential effect of the baptism with the Holy Ghost was this striking change in the believers themselves. As we meditate further we will recognize that the change was not mild or gradual, but radical and instantaneous. . . . After Pentecost [the disciples] were different. The cowardly became bold, the wayward became stable, the proud became humble. The motives were purified of self-seeking, dispositions were cleansed of malice, and devotion became an undivided and unquenchable flame.[31]

Taylor forcefully rejected again and again the Calvinistic error of a "sinning saint." Righteousness was not simply imputed to the Christian; it was instantaneously imparted in the grace of entire sanctification. Sin wasn't covered. Sin was erased. Christians could expect to live free from sin. Period.

> The most convincing evidence of the supernatural origin and power of Christianity is the miracle by which a weak profligate or ungodly worldling is instantly transformed into a sober, devoted saint, whose holy living now is as pronounced and natural as was his ungodliness before. It is this change of nature, effected by the Spirit in the crises of regeneration and entire sanctification, for which we are contending, lest it be buried beneath the debris of theological errors and lost to the Church.[32]

This promise of entire sanctification, however, demanded a right conception of sin, and the last half of the book was an explication of this correct understanding. After disposing of Calvinism, he wrote of the right conception, explaining "exactly what sin is, of what kinds, how it acts, its effects, its relation to man, how it must be dealt with, and God's provision for it."[33]

He addressed the matter forthrightly. In the very first sentence of the seventh chapter, titled "What Is an Act of Sin?" Taylor asked, "By the term 'sin' do we include every mistake in judgment, unknown offense, or other manifestation of human frailty and limitation?"[34] The answer was clear. "Obviously not."[35] As had others in the Holiness Movement, so Taylor distinguished between humanity's infirmities, which were an inescapable consequence of the Fall, and sin "properly so called." "God's quarrel is not with our humanity, but with our disposition to set our will against his."[36] According to Taylor, for sin to be sin there had to be two conditions: the knowledge of sin accompanied by an intention to sin. If either knowledge or consent were lacking, there was no sin.

> *"Primarily,* the law is broken when the thing is decided upon in the heart. It is when an unrighteous motive, intention, or passion enters the secret chambers of the soul—when one is actuated by a spirit inwardly contrary to love. . . . On the other hand, the law may have been unwittingly transgressed without, but if it has been honestly kept within, no sin is ascribed."[37]

According to Taylor, Christians would never intentionally transgress the known law of God but there were occasions when they did "wrong" out of ignorance or mistake. If one did "wrong" out of ignorance, then the condition of knowledge was lacking and the act was not considered sin. If one mistakenly did "wrong," then the condition of intentionality was missing and the act was not considered sin. Indeed, according to Taylor, "grace . . . takes into full consideration the circumstances and emotions and motives involved. If it was unintentional, unforeseen, and inescapable commission or omission, grace pronounces the man innocent."[38]

This was entirely in keeping with what others in the Holiness Movement at large understood about sin. Christians who had consecrated themselves to God in faith and whose sinful nature had been instantaneously eradicated by the Pentecostal Baptism of the Holy Spirit could live without sin, provided sin was clearly defined to include knowledge and volition. It wasn't sin if either was lacking.

This led Richard Taylor, in the second to the last chapter of his book, to distinguish between infirmity, which was a permanent human condition due to the Fall, and inbred sin, which was not a permanent condition of the Fall. The former compelled Christians to contend with their deficiencies their entire lives while the latter could be completely destroyed in entire sanctification, enabling Christians to live sinlessly deficient.

The difference between infirmity and inbred sin was sometimes difficult to discern, and Taylor was not remiss in acknowledging the difficulty.

"In practical everyday life it is not always easy to distinguish between car-nality and infirmity, as the line between them is sometimes very fine to outward appearances."[39] For the doctrine of entire sanctification to be cor-rectly understood, however, this distinction between infirmity and sin had to be made.

According to Taylor, infirmity was a consequence of the separation from the presence of God due to Adam's willful transgression of the known law. This loss of health and perfection, which Taylor identified as depravity, permanently impaired mankind's mind and body. As a conse-quence, "[persons have] become subject to countless mistakes of judg-ment, deficiency of knowledge, lapse of memory, faulty reasoning and perceptive faculties, physical deformities, abnormalities and peculiarities of temperament, disease, pain, and decay."[40]

Since these mistakes, deficiencies, lapses, abnormalities and peculi-arities were inevitable, there could be no culpability, and according to Taylor, actions resulting from such mistakes were not considered sinful. Nor should the condition that would lead to such a mistake be considered sinful. "But since none of these infirmities have a moral quality in them, they must not be considered a part of the Adamic depraved moral nature, or inbred sin."[41]

Consequently, Taylor had to carefully qualify what could be expected from entirely sanctified individuals.

We do not say, then, that a pure man will always speak in just that tone of voice, or show just the exact facial expression, or act with just that degree of prudence and discernment which the occa-sion may warrant; but delinquency will be due not to a lack of Christlikeness in spirit or motive but to a lack of Christlikeness in un-derstanding and emotional balance. When due to the first lack, it is sinful; when due to the second, it is human.[42]

As Taylor had written, this line between infirmity and sin was some-times very fine.

[A]n ugly, angry spirit, that causes sharp, hot words, or a spirit which causes the blood to rush to the face in quick fury even though suppressed, is certainly different from an intense, excitable manner when contending for a truth or defending a conviction, or a jangled, upset condition of the nervous system which gives rise to a certain ir-ritability or undue quickness of speech. True, the nerves lie very close to the moral nature, and must be watched or they will cause us to commit sin; still, there is a difference between nerves and carnality.[43]

It was also impossible to discern from merely observable behavior whether an action was a consequence of sinfulness or fallenness. The behavior that could be attributed to sin might simply be a consequence of infirmity.

> Because we have this treasure in earthen vessels, the perfect love in our heart may be imperfectly expressed, and for that reason critical, unsympathetic persons may find many flaws. They will fall on us as did the man who said knowingly, "The trouble with your holiness brethren is, they get angry too quickly." Upon inquiring the reason for such an astounding assertion, it was found that the "angry" man, a godly minister, well known to the writer, was simply remonstrating against some flagrant disorder in the service! All of us, Calvinists and Arminians alike, need to learn that the real quality of a man's spirit is often difficult for us mortals to measure. God is the only one who can judge.[44]

Taylor insisted that these mistakes, deficiencies, lapses, abnormalities, and peculiarities, which were not sinful in and of themselves, still needed to be disciplined so that they might not become sinful. Entirely sanctified Christians could not afford to be cavalier concerning these infirmities. While he believed that entire sanctification would restore some deficiencies when the carnal nature was eradicated, many were not. These needed controlling and correction. "Even after having been purified, therefore, one may still have temperamental impulses which are unfortunate and hence need to be disciplined, and physical impulses which are natural and need to be controlled, yet none of which are essentially sinful."[45]

Thus, for Nazarenes, a right understanding of entire sanctification demanded not only a right conception of sin but a right conception of infirmity. Entire sanctification eradicated the sinful nature resulting in believers being able to live free from sin. Entire sanctification did not, however, restore the fallen condition. Entirely sanctified believers still had to contend with their mistakes, deficiencies, lapses, faults, deformities, abnormalities, peculiarities, diseases, pains, and decay. Since such persons were not responsible for this aspect of their fallen condition, moral culpability could not be attributed, and therefore, "deficiencies" could not be properly considered sin. Entire sanctification addressed itself to the eradication of sin, "properly so called," which was strictly defined as a nature inclined to a willful transgression of the known law or the transgression itself.

This led some Nazarene writers in the middle decades of the century to emphasize, more than earlier Holiness writers, the continued work of God in the life of believers *subsequent* to entire sanctification. One such author was D. Shelby Corlett. Corlett was the fourth editor of the denominational periodical, *Herald of Holiness,* serving from 1936 to 1948. He had preached a series of sermons on holiness at Pasadena College and at Olivet Nazarene College in 1942 that were then published in 1944 as the book *The Meaning of Holiness*. This was included in the Ministerial Course of Study from 1944 to 1956 as a book to be read by second year students. In these messages on holiness D. Shelby Corlett defined the second work of grace not only in reference to what might be expected from the grace but also in reference to what ought not to be expected. According to Corlett, there was much entire sanctification did not accomplish.

Corlett was fully consistent with the Church of the Nazarene's Articles of Faith on the doctrine. In his fourth sermon on the subject, titled "Holiness in Personal Experience," Corlett wrote:

> This work of entire sanctification is a definite experience, a mighty work of grace, wrought by God in the life of the Christian in response to faith. It is an experience that marks a definite second crisis in the spiritual life, purifying the heart, filling the life with the Holy Spirit, bringing a spiritual wholeness to life and the heart into full devotedness to God. A wonderful, mighty, glorious experience, renewing the inmost character or nature into the likeness of God— "in righteousness and true holiness" (Eph. 4:24).[46]

This definition was certainly in keeping with Nazarene orthodoxy. While Corlett repeatedly reinforced the distinctive doctrine of the Church of the Nazarene in these seven sermons, he was not simply interested in reiterating what others had preached and written before him but was primarily concerned to impress on young Nazarene minds the expectations of the life of holiness that were subsequent to the experience of entire sanctification. His emphasis was not so much on the experience of entire sanctification itself as on the fulfillment of that experience. In his fifth sermon on the subject, he stated:

> This vital experience of entire sanctification or fullness of the Spirit is not the ultimate purpose of God for human life, it is not the final work of the Spirit of holiness for man in this world. It is a high point in human experience, it is the completion of the initial work of salvation; but the purpose of God for man in this world is saintliness of life and Christlikeness in character. . . . As wonderful as is this experience of heart holiness it does not of itself bring the sanctified person immediately to that goal of saintliness of life or perfect Christian character.[47]

As far as Corlett was concerned, too many entirely sanctified individuals were living far below the holiness standard. Although cleansed from inbred sin, they were not proceeding as they should toward that goal of saintliness.

> The tragic fact faced today is that too few of those professing holiness are giving themselves as they should to a life of active ser-

vice to Christ and for others, hence they are experiencing far too little of the manifestation of the power of the Holy Spirit in their lives.[48]

Entire sanctification was not "the final work of the Spirit of holiness for man" because entire sanctification dealt with inbred sin only. It did not restore, in Richard Taylor's language, the mistakes, deficiencies, lapses, abnormalities, and peculiarities of the fallen human condition. As had Brockett and Taylor, so Corlett also made that distinction between sin, which was defined as either the inclination to willfully transgress or the transgression itself, and infirmity, which was understood as an inevitable condition of our depravity.

> "The earthen vessel which holds the priceless treasure," says Dr. James Denny, "is human nature as it is; man's body in its weakness, and liability to death; his mind with its limitations and confusions; his moral nature with its distortions and misconceptions, and its insight not half restored."[49]

Because sanctified Christians were still subject to these "infirmities," one could not expect that God's work was mostly done after one was entirely sanctified. Entire sanctification was not the completed work. According to Corlett, there was needed further confession, discipline, and growth!

Corlett quoted Brockett to justify the idea that entirely sanctified believers needed to confess.

> By virtue of the fact that we are still in a fallen condition so far as our bodily and mental powers are concerned, we are subject to many infirmities, we lack perfect knowledge of God's will in all things (this has to be learned by degrees), we are liable, therefore, to errors of judgment, etc., and various other faults which may not be known to ourselves but are seen by God. Hence the holiest Christian, from this point of view, may daily pray that humble prayer of confession, "Forgive us our debts, as we forgive our debtors."[50]

The appropriateness of this petition of the Lord's Prayer for entirely sanctified believers had been problematic for those in the Holiness Movement for obvious reasons. If all sin had been eradicated in the second work of grace, there would be no need for further confession. This is indeed what many in the Holiness Movement believed. Asbury Lowrey had written in *Possibilities of Grace* that entirely sanctified Christians did not need to consider themselves as confessing actual sin when repeating the Lord's Prayer. "It will be easy to show that a man does not necessarily confess that he is an actual sinner or personally sinful by repeating the Lord's Prayer."[51] According to Lowrey, the Lord's Prayer was a corporate prayer and as there would clearly be unsanctified Christians in the church, it would be appropriate to pray the petition for forgiveness generally. It would also be appropriate to pray this petition as a way of remembering sin that had already been forgiven. "The remembrance of past sin is always grievous to the best of Christians; and though consciously forgiven, the mind never recurs to them, but with profound contrition."[52] Lowrey did acknowledge however, as did Corlett, that even entirely sanctified believers could appropriately confess infirmities, even if they weren't sin.

> Original sin has darkened the understanding, warped the judgment, weakened the reason, made the body the seat of disease, pain and death . . . And from them many faults and shortcomings may arise which fall below the ideal divine law of absolute right. But these faults are not properly sins, because they are not transgressions of the law of grace by which Christians are judged. . . . On this account it is both a duty and privilege to remember this merciful provision in our prayers and confessions.[53]

However, some were anxious about this suggestion that infirmities needed confessing. W. T. Purkiser, in his *Conflicting Concepts of Holiness*, which has been a part of the Ministerial Course of Study since 1956, wrote even more strongly that Christians need not mean this petition when they pray it.

> [T]he Lord's Prayer is a social prayer, and includes those who may have sinned. The fact, however, that our Lord immediately coupled with this phrase the condition that we forgive those who trespass against us leads one to think that our continued forgiveness for past sins is conditioned on our spirit of forgiveness toward those who sin against us.[54]

In any event, Corlett did not refrain from suggesting that infirmities needed forgiveness, even though they were not sin, "properly so called."

Neither did Corlett hesitate to write of the value of discipline for entirely sanctified Christians. Those entirely sanctified needed to control their dispositions even though these dispositions were not sinful but just infirm.

> In this discipline or conquest there is the overcoming of prejudices, attitudes and mannerisms which may hinder the full and symmetrical manifestation of holiness in the life . . . There is also the conquest of one's natural dispositions. The naturally impetuous person must develop patience; the timid, hesitant, backward person must overcome these hindrances by the help of God; the natural critic or cynic must overcome that tendency and cultivate a charitable attitude toward others.[55]

According to Corlett, entirely sanctified Christians should expect to need to grow.

> Since this state or condition is a relative holiness, not absolute

or ideal holiness, and since it is manifested through human nature of differing educational, religious and moral backgrounds, there may be a difference in the manifestation of holiness; but in each case there will be development toward that mature or perfect man. . . . There is no limit to the progress possible in this life of holiness.[56]

It must be pointed out that there was nothing that either Brockett, Taylor or Corlett had written that could not have been found in earlier holiness works. J. A. Wood, Daniel Steele, A. M. Hills, Asbury Lowrey, and H. Orton Wiley had all distinguished between sin and infirmity in their writings, as had John Wesley himself. They had all written of the possibility for continued growth even after the second work of grace. John Wesley had done so himself. The distinction between the holiness writings that were recommended to Nazarene ministers in the course of study in the early years of the denomination's life and those writings recommended in midcentury is not to be found in any deviation from holiness dogma but in point of emphasis. As is evidenced by the works that were recommended in the 1940s and 1950s, over against those the denomination had inherited, there were the beginnings of defining entire sanctification in terms of what it did not accomplish as well as in terms of what it did. These second and third generation Holiness writers were not making the extravagant claims that earlier Holiness writers had concerning what entire sanctification accomplished, and they were much more explicit concerning the infirmities that entirely sanctified Christians would still be plagued with. Consequently, the promise was tempered. The expectations concerning the grace were becoming a bit more modest.

CARDINAL ELEMENTS

At the same time that the church was carefully clarifying what entire sanctification did not accomplish by virtue of distinguishing between sin and infirmity, it was reinforcing the doctrine's essential points. "Conserving, maintaining, advocating and promulgating" the precious cargo that had been entrusted to it not only resulted in an intentional effort to explain more precisely the doctrine of entire sanctification but also led to an intentional effort to forcefully reiterate the orthodox elements of the doctrine. Nothing essential was going to be lost by the clarifications that were being made, and several books dedicated to the doctrine of entire sanctification were recommended to guarantee continued orthodoxy.

Two such books were written by the first theology professor of the newly organized Nazarene Seminary. Steven S. White had graduated from Peniel Holiness College in Texas (which would later become Bethany Nazarene College in Bethany, Oklahoma) and then went on to earn a Bachelor of Divinity degree from Drew Theological Seminary, a Master of

Arts degree from Brown University, and a Ph.D. from the University of Chicago. He had been ordained in the Church of the Nazarene in 1914 and had served the church as pastor and educator. In 1945 he became the first theology professor of Nazarene Theological Seminary, and in 1948 he succeeded Corlett as editor of the *Herald of Holiness* where he served for 12 years. During this time as professor and editor, he wrote a series of short books on the doctrine of entire sanctification. The first in the series called *Studies in Holiness* was titled *Cardinal Elements in Sanctification*. His book, which was recommended in the Ministerial Course of Study from 1952 to 1960, was a summary of five of the essential truths of entire sanctification.

The first was that entire sanctification was a *second* work of grace. Using a methodology that he would use throughout the book, he began first by arguing from the Bible, quoting the standard holiness proof texts (1 Thessalonians 5:23; Ephesians 5:25-26; John 14:16-18; John 17:17). He then argued from reason. He defended the secondness of the experience of entire sanctification by distinguishing between acts of sin and the state of sin, reasoning that the former needed the grace of forgiveness while the latter required the grace of entire sanctification. He closed the chapter by sharing his own personal experience of being entirely sanctified, stating that the argument from experience was the most important evidence of all to the truth of the doctrine.

The above argument from experience is so important that I must give a description of what happened in more detail. I was first saved when I was in my middle teens. After a time I backslid. It was in this backslidden state that I entered Peniel College at Peniel, Texas. There I was soon blessedly reclaimed. And then near the close of this same school year I was wonderfully sanctified wholly. This came after quite a period of struggle as to a full and complete consecration. . . . This absolute surrender was necessary in order for God to fully and freely cleanse me from the sinful nature with which I was born. This cleansing was wrought by the baptism with the Holy Spirit and was entire sanctification. Altogether it was a glorious experience, going beyond anything that had ever happened to me before. The most noticeable effect was a peace that I had never known before. It was not peace *with* God . . . It was the peace *of* God, a peace that passeth all understanding. It seemed that God had turned a veritable Amazon River of peace into my soul.[57]

The second cardinal element of sanctification was that it was instantaneous. Scriptural justification of this aspect of the doctrine was found in the account of the Day of Pentecost. Since holiness orthodoxy stated that the Day of Pentecost was when the disciples were sanctified, White used this to support the contention that it was instantaneous. The denomination had also understood entire sanctification to be contingent on faith and since faith could be exercised in a moment, so could the grace be granted. In addition to these arguments, White tentatively used the argument of the Greek tenses. Since so many of the verbs which have to do with sanctification are in the aorist tense, which is the tense that principally indicates completed action, then the grace must be understood as happening instantaneously. After providing other justification for it being instantaneous, White concluded this chapter by appealing to his own personal experience of the grace, as he had in the first chapter. "The writer received this blessing instantaneously. . . . Finally, after much prayer, I made a full consecration, trusted God completely, and He did the work at once."[58]

The third and perhaps most important cardinal element of entire sanctification for White was that entire sanctification freed the believer from inbred sin. White was far from indifferent to the terminology that was used to describe this aspect of entire sanctification. He insisted that the definition of entire sanctification include the term *eradication* to make clear just how decisive a change the grace effected. According to White, no other word was sufficient to define the dramatic destruction of sin that was a consequence of entire sanctification.

The eradication of the carnal mind, the old man, or inbred sin is meant when it is held that entire sanctification frees from sin. In taking this position we oppose the "holy in Christ" theory, the Keswickism, or what some have called Calvinistic holiness. Those who are in this group believe in suppression, suspension, or counteraction rather than eradication. Actual or complete freedom from sin for them comes only by proxy. Christ's holiness is taken for ours and we have only positional or imputed cleansing. Wesleyan holiness, on the other hand, insists that purity is imparted to the heart of the individual through the blood of Jesus Christ and the precious agency of the Holy Spirit when the Christian consecrates his all and believes now that the work is done.[59]

The necessity of this term, *eradication,* to describe this change, was the entire subject of the second book White wrote in this series, appropriately titled *Eradication: Defined, Explained, Authenticated.* This even more forceful defense of the teaching of the Church of the Nazarene was included in the Ministerial Course of Study from 1956 to 1968. Hugh Benner, the first president of the Nazarene Theological Seminary and general superintendent from 1952 to 1968, wrote the foreword in which he commented on the imperative of the church to remain true to the entrusted doctrine and in particular to the use of this particular word to define the doctrine.

In the midst of subtle temptations to evade some of the more strenuous terms associated with the preaching of scriptural holiness, and attempts to find a more palatable phraseology for this doctrine and experience, it is refreshing and heartening to read this straight-forward declaration of the right and responsibility of those who adhere to the Wesleyan interpretation of this truth to use, without apology, this strong, applicable, appropriate, scriptural word—eradication.[60]

In *Eradication,* White was concerned to defend the idea that the sinful nature was entirely destroyed in the second work of grace. After countering some objections to the use of the term, White appealed to John Wesley for justification concerning the matter. Conceding that Wesley himself never used the particular word, he nonetheless argued that Wesley believed in the idea.

Did Wesley believe in the eradication or complete destruction of this . . . state of sin in which man is born? We believe that the evidence compels one to answer this in the affirmative. Here are a number of phrases which he used in stating what is done when a person is sanctified wholly: purification from sin, a heart that is purified from all sin, deliverance from inward as well as outward sin . . . salvation from all sin, inbred sin or the total corruption of man's nature taken away.[61]

He then argued against "suppressionist" theories that stated that the sinful nature could only be controlled but not destroyed, and he argued against the "growth in holiness" theories that stated that there was a gradual destruction of the sinful nature through discipline. As far as White was concerned, the true Wesleyan position, and therefore the true position, was the one that insisted on the instantaneous and absolute annihilation of the sinful nature, and this is what the term eradication indicated. "It is the Wesleyan position, which declares that man is freed from sin by the instantaneous eradication of the carnal mind, here and now, by the baptism of the Holy Spirit. Thus, the 'old man' is expelled, and Christ takes over the rule in our hearts."[62] And according to White, this was what the Bible taught.

Our final thought will be to list a few of the terms which describe God's method of dealing with the sin nature in the human heart. . . . They are so definite and far-reaching in their meaning that they could hardly be interpreted as teaching anything less than eradication. They are the terms crucify and crucified, which signify to destroy utterly (Gal 2:20; 5:24; 6:14). Along with these are those which are or could be translated mortify, kill, render extinct (Rom. 7:4; 8:13), destroy, annul, abolish, put an end to, annihilate (I John 3:8; Rom. 6:6), and cleanse, purify, cleanse thoroughly, purge (Acts 15:9; I Cor. 7:1; Tit. 2:14). Freedom from sin, or Christian perfection, is clearly implied by these Biblical words. . . . The teaching of Jesus affirms the possibility of freedom from sin; and there are many terms—especially in Paul's writings—which substantiate our belief in eradication.[63]

White did, however, caution against errors that "eradicationists" sometimes made. In *Cardinal Elements in Sanctification,* he warned against two errors. The first was the error of placing too much emphasis on the crisis nature of the experience of entire sanctification. According to White, those who place too much emphasis on the instantaneous eradication of the sinful nature can "feel that they do not have to do anything in order to keep sanctified."[64] White called for entirely sanctified Christians to continue to consecrate and continue to believe. "Moment by moment we must live the sanctified life."[65]

The second caution mentioned in *Cardinal Elements* was failing to make the distinction between infirmities and sin. Infirmities could not be eradicated. Sin could be. And in *Eradication,* White devoted an entire chapter to distinguishing between that which was eradicated by entire sanctification and that which was not. He again insisted on the need for the particular term. "The grace of entire sanctification is a radical work and cannot be designated with anything less than radical words."[66] But clarity concerning what was and was not eradicated was absolutely necessary. There was much that was not. According to White, humanity's finiteness was not eradicated. Entire sanctification would not make anyone godlike or angelic. It would not erase the effects of the fall on the human body and mind. Sickness, weariness, physical deformities, and mental infirmities would all remain in the entirely sanctified person. The effect of entire sanctification would even be relative to the individual.

> Entire sanctification does not regiment us. It does not make us all to be equally congenial. There will still be more natural fear in some than in others; and women will, as a rule, be more subject to modesty than men. There is . . . the probability that one who has had years in sin before getting saved and sanctified will have more memories to battle with as he lives his Christian life than he who was saved and sanctified early in life.[67]

Entirely sanctified persons were still human, affected by the Fall, and therefore subject to infirmities. White then distinguished, as had Brockett, Taylor, and Corlett, between sin and infirmity.

> This whole field of infirmity as over against sin is important, and should be better understood by our preachers and laymen. Infirmities are involuntary, or unintentional, deviations from the perfect law of God due to a physical and mental condition which has result-

ed from the fall. . . . In other words, we can never hope to reach a place in this life where every decision and act will be all that it should be from God's standpoint. . . . If infirmities are understood as they should be, they do not break one's communion with God. That is, if one realizes as he should that their outcome is mistakes and not sins, they do not bring condemnation and thus destroy our communion with God.[68]

White acknowledged that distinguishing behavior in others as either a consequence of sin or infirmities was difficult and in *Cardinal Elements in Sanctification* recommended suspension of judgment. He counseled: "At this point of determining between infirmities and sin, a man should be hard on himself and very charitable toward the other fellow."[69]

In *Eradication,* White wrote that it was a little more difficult to state precisely what was eradicated in entire sanctification than to state what wasn't. But it wasn't impossible. He quoted the 1952 Church of the Nazarene *Manual* which stated that it was original sin that was eradicated by the baptism with the Holy Spirit.[70] He then listed most of the euphemisms used to describe this "original sin."

It has been called a concupiscence, an incentive to sin, the inclination to sin, the bias toward sin, the bent toward sin, an inborn perversity, the hidden enemy in the heart, a moral perversion, the root of bitterness, a wrongness in human nature, the carnal mind, the old man of sin, "the sin which doth so easily beset us," the racial sin, inbred sin, a lawless wild beast in the heart of man, endemic evil in the heart of man, the Freudian Id, the radical evil in man, a hereditary sinful inclination, the abnormality in the native drives which are found in man—sex, food, etc., the evil state which results from the destruction of the moral or incidental image in man through the fall, a sinful disposition, the ego-urge or unsurrendered self, the spirit of antichrist in the heart, enmity against God, an innate corruption of the innermost nature of man, an evil root which bears like branches and like fruit, a trio of sinful tendencies—self-will, pride, and idolatry, unbelief and heart-idolatry, a natural propensity to sin, the stony heart, the body of sin, the sin that dwelleth in me, an evil heart of unbelief, lawlessness, a hateful intruder, a sinful power, a sinful master, the law of sin and death, filthiness of the flesh and the spirit, the Adamic nature, a proneness to wander from the path of right.[71]

This was what was eradicated in the grace of entire sanctification. As he had in the previous chapters of *Cardinal Elements*, White concluded his apology for the use of the term eradication when describing what happens to the sinful nature in the second work of grace, by testifying of his own experience. "I believe that when I was wholly sanctified the carnal mind was eradicated. God on the basis of the blood of Jesus Christ and through the agency of the Holy Spirit did the work when I fully met the conditions."[72] This third cardinal element was the most important as far as White was concerned. Entire sanctification eradicated the sinful nature.

The fourth cardinal element of entire sanctification mentioned in *Cardinal Elements* concerned its attainability in this life. It obviously was. White wrote: "The writer of this paper is still alive and he secured this blessing more than twenty-five years ago. This experience of entire sancti-fication is attainable in this life. The Bible, reason, and experience all testi-fy to this truth."[73]

The fifth concerned its identification with the baptism with the Holy Spirit. Pentecost was the occasion of the disciples' entire sanctification and so the baptism with the Holy Spirit was the occasion of entire sanctifi-cation. While merely regenerated persons could testify to having the Holy Spirit with them, the Holy Spirit came in his fullness when and only when a believer was entirely sanctified. According to White, "We obtain the Holy Spirit in a measure when we are converted. He is the efficient Cause of regeneration as well as of entire sanctification, but in the latter case He comes in His fullness."[74] He quoted Acts 15:8-9, which was a standard proof text to support this identification between entire sanctification and the Baptism of the Holy Spirit.[75] White was willing to acknowledge that the Day of Pentecost had historical significance as the birthday of the Church as well. He did recognize that it was more than just a paradigm for an individual's salvific experience.

> There was a sense in which Pentecost was the time and place of the formal inauguration of the Christian Church, but it was also the time and place when an individual blessing of great significance was bestowed on the followers of Jesus. The central happening of Pente-cost, the baptism with the Holy Spirit, from the standpoint of the in-dividual, can be repeated; and it brings with its coming the cleansing of the heart from its sinful nature.[76]

According to White, however, it was primarily to be understood as the oc-casion of the disciples' entire sanctification.

Entire sanctification, or the baptism of the Holy Spirit was nothing less than the instantaneous *eradication* of the sinful nature subsequent to regeneration and clearly prior to death. In 1952, the Church of the Naza-rene's Article of Faith on original sin was slightly changed to emphasize the point. From 1928 to 1948, the fifth Article of Faith had read:

> We believe that original sin, or depravity, is that corruption of the nature of all the offspring of Adam by reason of which every one is very far gone from original righteousness or the pure state of our first parents at the time of their creation, is averse to God, is without

spiritual life, and inclined to evil, and that continually; and that it continues to exist with the new life of the regenerate, until eradicated by the baptism with the Holy Spirit.[77]

The sentence in the Article of Faith that addressed eradication was the last clause in the paragraph, but in 1952, that clause was made into a separate sentence, and the words, "We further believe that original sin," were inserted. Since 1952, this paragraph has read:

We believe that original sin, or depravity, is that corruption of the nature of all the offspring of Adam by reason of which every one is very far gone from original righteousness or the pure state of our first parents at the time of their creation, is averse to God, is without spiritual life, and inclined to evil, and that continually. *We further believe that original sin* continues to exist with the new life of the regenerate, until eradicated by the baptism with the Holy Spirit.[78]

Thus, there were two movements in the Church of the Nazarene in the fourth and fifth decades of the church's existence, both a consequence of the changing historical circumstances. The unavoidable reality of the apparently inherent sinfulness of humanity resulted in clinical qualifications of the doctrine of entire sanctification that defined more of man's "fallen-ness" as infirmity instead of sin. At the same time, the threat of this "theological realism" compelled the denomination to a greater attention to "conserving, maintaining, advocating and promulgating" the precious doctrine with which it had been entrusted. Entire sanctification eradicated sin in its entirety, but sin in its entirety was understood quite particularly.

6
A Plain Account

━━━━━━━━━━━━━━━━━━━━━ ◆ ━━━━━━━━━━━━━━━━━━━━━

Called unto Holiness

In 1955, on the eve of the 50th anniversary of the Church of the Nazarene, the Board of General Superintendents appointed a Commission on Church History to write a history of the denomination. The commission asked Timothy L. Smith, who had been the chairman of the history department at Eastern Nazarene College and was at the time of their asking an associate professor of history and education at the University of Minnesota, to write the book. Smith had written a groundbreaking Ph.D. dissertation from Harvard University, titled *Revivalism and Social Reform*,[1] that (when published) became a prizewinning history of American Protestantism on the eve of the Civil War. The Commission's decision to enlist Smith to write the official history of the formative years of the Church of the Nazarene was judicious, for he brought to this project the same careful scholarship that had characterized his previous work. Smith provided the Church of the Nazarene with a significant and comprehensive social history of the denomination's first 25 years (1908-33). It was published in 1962 by the Nazarene Publishing House under the title *Called unto Holiness*, and was added to the Ministerial Course of Study in 1964, where it remains as a textbook for fourth year ministerial students to this day.

Smith concluded his history of the first 25 years of the Church of the Nazarene with a chapter titled A Forward Glance. Since Smith had only written of the first 25 years of the church's existence, in the last chapter he chose to summarize the progress of the church since 1933, recording its institutional growth and noting the church's continued faithfulness to its distinctive culture and doctrine. In the last two paragraphs of the last chapter, however, he addressed a provocative question to the people of the Church of the Nazarene. After asserting his faith that "God was at work in the affairs of men"[2] (and thus in the affairs of the Church of the Nazarene), he called on the church to consider the future of the denomination's particular theology. The concluding paragraph of this history of the first 25 years reads:

> The reader, therefore, must evaluate for himself the significance of the men and events which compose the history of the Nazarenes. We shall be content if in telling the story we have provided new and important information upon which thoughtful persons may ponder

the meaning of American Christianity, the part played by the small denominational families into which so much of it has recently been divided, and *the relevance of Wesleyan perfectionism to a generation awed by its rediscovery of the deep sinfulness of man.*[3]

Smith was calling the church, in this last sentence of the official history of the denomination, to a reassessment of holiness theology, one that would provide a more theologically realistic account of the "deep sinfulness of man." While most Nazarenes were not willing to concede to Smith the possible implication that Wesleyan perfectionism was irrelevant, they were continuing to take into consideration the continuing fact of the sin of the world. As has been previously stated, at the end of the 19th and beginning of the 20th centuries, Holiness teachers and leaders, like Asbury Lowrey, A. M. Hills, Daniel Steele, and J. A. Wood, understood themselves as part of a process whereby the whole world either could or would be made wholly Christian. Their writings were filled with optimistic descriptions of what the eradication of the sinful nature would accomplish, both personally and in the world at large. As the century wore on, these expectations began to appear unrealistic and were strictly qualified by subsequent Holiness authors. The qualifications to the doctrine that were made in the '40s and '50s continued to be made so that by the sixth and seventh decades of the 20th century, the expectations of what entire sanctification could accomplish, both personally and corporately, were a mere shadow of what had appeared in earlier declarations.

This "rediscovery of the deep sinfulness of man," as Smith called it, was even more evident in the quadrennial addresses of the general superintendents of the Church of the Nazarene in the 1960s and 1970s than it had been in the previous two decades. The elected leaders of the largest Holiness denomination did not hesitate to acknowledge the continuing pervasiveness of sin and their addresses in these decades reflected the anxious malaise of the culture at large. The confidence that early Nazarene leaders had exhibited concerning what the holiness message could accomplish was clearly gone and was replaced by an urgent call for the potentially fearful to keep the faith, in spite of the threatening circumstances. In 1968, Dr. V. H. Lewis, commenting on the state of the world to the delegates of the 17th General Assembly, wrote:

> The Church today is in the midst of a disturbed world. War is brutalizing humanity. Governments are uncertain. Economies are strained and often unsound. The erroneous belief that the social structure can be improved without a change in the hearts of those who make up society has increased the tensions among mankind. Law and order are threatened by those who try to settle social issues in the streets. The constituted authority's failure to enforce existing

laws and punish crime has resulted in devious means to thwart justice and increased lawlessness. . . .

The growth and exploitation of sex and lust under the guise of art, literature, advertising, and entertainment have brought a terrible harvest in decaying morals and ethics.

Education stressing unbelief in God and the Bible has plunged this generation into a trackless jungle, where it wanders uncertainly with no worthy purpose or defined path to follow.

The disregard of God's commandments and violation of the Sabbath are almost unbelievable. National spiritual life is tragically weak and at times seems almost nonexistent. . . .

The increasing tide of evil; the deluge of degrading literature; the vagrancy of society in breaking the Ten Commandments; the wasteland of much television and other so-called entertainments; the constant hammering of the sordid at our homes and lives; God-and-morals-forgetting theories of relativism, the "new morality"—all result in the decay of men and nations. That is what we face today. To be true to our faith and to our assignment we must meet the tide with courage and spiritual power.[4]

The 1972 quadrennial address, given by General Superintendent Dr. George Coulter, began with a quote from Charles Dickens's *A Tale of Two Cities:*

"It was the best of times, it was the worst of times, it was the age of wisdom, it was the age of foolishness, it was the epoch of belief, it was the epoch of incredulity, it was the season of Light, it was the season of Darkness, it was the spring of hope, it was the winter of despair, we had everything before us, we had nothing before us."

While Charles Dickens wrote these words in the late 1800's they seem strangely appropriate to our own day and time.

It is no longer shocking to say that this is an age of revolution. During this quadrennium minority groups in many lands have demanded equality of opportunity and compensation; crime has spread and has become more violent; militants have openly defied existing institutions; students have rebelled, and thousands of people have committed themselves to eliminating contemporary problems even at the price of the destruction of the whole social system.

Thoughtful people are expressing new concern about the pollution of natural resources, about the decline in moral standards, and the breakdown of law and order. Internationally, treaties are being made and broken rather easily; confrontations between nations still persist, and the threat of a final world conflagration is ever before us. While science continues to venture into new frontiers of the universe, the same human problems of fear, sorrow, frustration, and sin grip men's souls. One economist has described our world as a "small, rather crowded, spaceship hurtling through space, destination unknown. . . ."

For most people God and the Bible are no longer their Authority. Rioting and rebellion reveal that the state has ceased to be authority to many. Unless our civilization can be rallied around some common core of values, we are doomed.[5]

In 1976, General Superintendent Dr. Eugene Stowe addressed the 19th General Assembly of the Church of the Nazarene and described the state of the world using the apocalyptic imagery of the Bible. Perhaps no quadrennial address reveals how much had changed in the Church of the Nazarene's expectations for the future of the world as the one delivered by Stowe. It bears quoting at length.

At no period in history have the dire predictions of Christ recorded in the twenty-fourth chapter of Matthew's Gospel had a more contemporary ring about them. These signs of the end times, might well have been clipped from today's *Dallas News* or *Times-Herald:* "And ye shall hear of wars and rumours of wars: . . . nation shall rise against nation, and kingdom against kingdom: and there shall be famines, and pestilences, and earthquakes, in divers places" (Matthew 24:6a, 7).

The fall of South Vietnam and Cambodia to their Communist enemies has rewritten the map of southeast Asia and drastically altered the balance of power in that area. Nationalistic movements in Africa, Europe, and Latin America have toppled governments and brought major political changes to emerging nations. Nowhere has crisis been more continual than in the Middle East. This tinderbox has periodically been ignited by frictions between Israel and the Arab nations, and the uneasy truce presently existing could be broken at any moment. The worldwide energy crisis has thrown this area into an even more critical position, since the largest supplies of petroleum are located here. A struggle for this prize could well trigger the final holocaust. Small wonder that Billy Graham recently declared that "many world leaders will admit in private that they believe the world stands on the very edge of Armageddon" (*Christianity Today,* July 4, 1975, 3).

Every bit as serious as this pattern of violent change is the moral and ethical decay which threatens the foundations of our world society. . . .

No single event in the quadrennium has shocked America more than the sordid tragedy of Watergate. Nothing has displayed more graphically the moral bankruptcy of our culture than these revelations of deceit and fraud on the part of the president of the United States and other high officials who proved to be traitors to their trust. But this incident represents only the tip of the frighteningly destructive iceberg which threatens our world. Millions worship the golden calf of materialism and thereby fuel the fires of economic tension which have resulted from the widening extremes of prosperity and poverty which polarize mankind. A flood of pornographic literature and entertainment protected by a false concept of personal freedom has risen to an unbelievable level. One of the by-products of the immoral brainwashing is the erosion of traditional standards of sexual conduct. Premarital and extramarital sex are increasingly condoned and even sanctioned. The basic institution of society, the home, stands in very real jeopardy. Homosexuality shamelessly flaunts itself and has even won the acceptance of some religious groups. Shades of Sodom and Gomorrah!

These samples of change are representative of the downward direction which our world is taking. The outlook is not bright, but God's Word never promised that it would be. J. B. Phillips observes, "You simply cannot read the New Testament fairly and come to the conclusion that the world is going to become better and better until at last God congratulates mankind on the splendid job they have made of it!" (The Ring of Truth, 103).[6]

Even though the world was heading in a downward direction and the outlook wasn't bright, however, the Church of the Nazarene still had a holiness mission to accomplish. In 1976, Stowe called on the church to stand firm in its doctrinal convictions. "Let the word go out from this Nineteenth General Assembly that the people called Nazarenes have declared their unswerving allegiance to holiness of heart and life."[7] Four years earlier, Dr. George Coulter had declared the same. While he considered the outlook bleak, it wasn't hopeless and Coulter called on the church to become more intentional in the proclamation of the holiness message.

Because of this (bleak) context, the role of the Church of the Nazarene in the world assumes greater burden and significance. Our message of heart holiness is not a narrow, sectarian view but one based upon the central teaching of the Word of God. The proclamation of "the glorious gospel of Christ" which offers justification by faith for every sinner and cleansing of the heart and divine enduement for every Christian believer is the only adequate answer to the spiritual needs of mankind. We feel confident that the joyful, aggressive, and contagious witness of Nazarenes to the reality of the Spirit-filled life is needed in this present age. We make no apology for claiming that this is our distinctive contribution as a denomination.[8] And in 1968, the Board of General Superintendents had selected "These Times . . . God Is Able,"[9] as the church's theme for that quadrennium, thus assuring the denomination that in spite of the apparently insurmountable problems that faced the world, God's redemptive purposes could yet be accomplished. The Nazarenes were still "Called unto Holiness," but it continued to be a much more modified holiness than had been the case in the early days. The message had become a "distinctive contribution" to the world at large instead of the message of redemption for the entire world.

PROBLEMS OF THE SPIRIT-FILLED LIFE

This continuing modification of the holiness doctrine is evident in the holiness books recommended in the Ministerial Course of Study in these decades. It probably would have been inconceivable to the leaders of the American-Holiness Movement at the beginning of the century that one of the books eventually recommended for study would be titled *Problems of the Spirit-filled Life* by Dr. William Deal. They might, indeed, have considered the title an oxymoron since being "Spirit-filled" was supposed to mean the end of most problems. The overall impression left by Holiness writers at the turn of the century was that the grace of entire sanctification (or being filled with the Holy Spirit) was the solution of problems and not the cause of yet more difficulties. In 1960, William Deal's book was added to the Course of Study reading list for Nazarene pastors. While it was only on the reading list from 1960 to 1964, it illustrates the continuing issue that consumed much holiness writing in these years.

Distinguishing between sin and infirmity or carnality and humanity was the problem that Deal addressed. This is not surprising since it had been one of the main problems the Holiness Movement historically had had to consider since the time of Wesley. While this problem was obviously not a new one, it was the first time an entire book had been included in the course of study that was addressed to the issue, and it represents the continuing trend to more narrowly define the province of sin and expand what could be attributed to infirmity.

After establishing in a brief first section a definition of entire sanctification that was thoroughly consistent with the Nazarenes' Article of Faith, Deal argued, in the second section of the book, for the uniqueness of every person's experience of entire sanctification. According to Deal, "The endeavor to press for uniformity of details in this experience has led to a thousand confusions and disappointments and has sometimes so discouraged believers as to cause them to give up hope of obtaining the experience."[10] He then described in a few short succeeding chapters the differences that would make each experience of entire sanctification entirely unique. Because people have different personalities and different temperaments and because people come to the experience with varying levels of spiritual maturity, no one expression of the grace of entire sanctification is normative. Those who tend to be emotional before entire sanctification would continue to be emotional afterward. The high-strung would continue to be high-strung. The staid would still be staid. There would be differences in reference to ability to perform Christian duties. After entire sanctification, some would continue to evidence competence while others would continue to struggle to perform. According to Deal, there could be no two experiences of entire sanctification alike. The obvious implication of the second part of his book was that since no experience of entire sanctification was normative, it was all but impossible to judge whether another had truly received the grace. One certainly could not discern this by mere observation alone. For example, irritability was not necessarily a sign of inbred sin; it might merely be a consequence of a temperamental personality.

This is an excuse and discard God's grace

On the other hand, there are some persons whose constitutional make-up is of a high tension, nervous type. Such persons are generally very sensitive, easily impressed, highly imaginative, and emotionally balanced so delicately that they have difficulty remaining poised. They are easily excited and tend toward quick reaction. With this type of constitution it is easy to see how some people suffer from lack of ability to always meet every situation with that perfect poise which they see in others, and for which they often long. A person of this type may sometimes be subjected to keen accusations from Satan. He will suggest that if there were perfect love in the heart there would be more perfect balance in the disposition. But this is not always true.[11]

Therefore, one should not presume to judge another person's experience. Indeed, one could not. Therefore, the benefit of the doubt should always be given to one who professed to being entirely sanctified. "The more one cultivates a sympathetic spirit and tries to understand the basic underlying causes for the behavior of another, the more likely he is to see the good and recognize much of what he once thought was evil to be merely human reaction."[12]

Most of the rest of the book was devoted to distinguishing the truly evil from the merely human. As Brockett and Taylor had done before him, Deal acknowledged that discerning within oneself whether an action was a consequence of sin or a mere expression of humanity was sometimes difficult. Some have difficulty in distinguishing between sins and mistakes, but let it be clear that "a mistake is not a sin; neither is a sin a mistake."[13]

Because it was impossible to provide a comprehensive list or description of the infirmities that the entirely sanctified still had to contend with, Deal gave a few examples that could serve to illustrate the difference between sin and mistakes. One of these distinctions that Deal believed needed to be made was between "thoughts of evil" and "evil thoughts."

> There is a difference between *thoughts of evil* as suggestions to the mind, arising either from Satan's attack or from natural circumstances by which they are often presented, and *evil thoughts* as arising from the inward heart. The former are promptly rejected. The latter is something one secretly cherishes and holds within himself.[14]

Another was the distinction between overeating on occasion and gluttony.

> One man may eat a large, hearty meal with complete freedom while another must be contented to partake sparingly because of this condition. While it most certainly is wrong to constantly overeat to the detriment of the body, it is just as certainly not sinful to overeat sometimes more or less by accident. One often does not feel he has overeaten until well afterward. This is not gluttony but poor judgment.[15]

Deal warned against depending too much on emotions for evidence of entire sanctification, and he reminded his readers that a cycle of elation and depression was perfectly natural even for entirely sanctified persons. According to Deal, the joy and peace that were to accompany entire sanctification were "not to be found in the realm of changing human emotions, but deep within the spiritual nature of man."[16]

He concluded his illustration of the difference between sins and mistakes by devoting a chapter to comparing sinful expressions of fear and anger with their merely human expressions. According to Deal, carnal fear referred exclusively to a slavish dread of God. Natural fears of sorts, therefore, were not sinful fear. Distinguishing between carnal anger and righteous indignation was a more difficult matter.

> We may describe righteous indignation as that holy zeal against unrighteousness in action or attitude on the part of another, whoever he may be. . . . The motive behind such must ever be the glory of God by our standing against that which is evil. It is a form of holy hatred against sin but it can never for an instant possess the smallest amount of hatred for the offending person or persons. It is the evil against which this righteous zeal must be manifested and not the person manifesting it.[17]   *Hate the sin Love the sinner*

Care must be taken, however, not to confuse sinful anger with anger that was simply a reaction to a surprise or sudden shock.

> Many people have difficulty in distinguishing carnal anger from natural responses to shock, insult, injury and the like and are often in bondage to this constant questioning in their minds. . . . And yet these same persons have such a clear witness to perfect love at other

times that they cannot doubt but what the work has been done in their hearts.[18]

According to Deal, reactions in entirely sanctified individuals which had the look of carnal anger were the consequence of constitutional makeup, not the consequence of sin.

He concluded the book by warning entirely sanctified believers about several dangers that they could be particularly subject to. Among the dangers were doubting their experience, not tending to their sanctification (resulting in a "leanness of soul"), worry, inordinate affections, and loss of confidence.

While this particular book was on the Ministerial Course of Study reading list for only four years, it is representative of the qualifications that were continually being made by Holiness writers in these decades. Richard Taylor, a Nazarene Theological Seminary professor, also wrote a book about entire sanctification titled *Life in the Spirit*[19] that was included in the course of study from 1968 to 1986. In this more comprehensive work on entire sanctification, there were several chapters devoted to the distinction between sin and infirmity. Taylor began a chapter titled "The Humanity of the Sanctified" with these words: "Having come this far, we should pause and look around. As glorious and satisfying as is the grace of heart holiness, it does not make angels out of us."[20] And he called on entirely sanctified believers to learn to distinguish between their own carnality and their humanity.

> We must learn to distinguish between our earthiness and sin, and then learn to let the indwelling Spirit work through our earthiness—maybe even mend some of the cracks a little. . . . When we were still in an unsanctified state, it was important that we came to understand our carnality. Now that we have been cleansed, we need to come to an understanding of our *humanity,* particularly in its relation to the sanctified life. (And we must not forget to make plenty of room for the other person's humanity as well as our own.)[21]

Taylor promised that the Holy Spirit would help one discern between that which could be attributed to sin and that which was simply a consequence of our humanity.

> You will come gradually to understand the difference between carnality and humanity. . . . In Chapter Two we talked about the "believer's failure," and in that discussion we meant sin. We described his failure to experience that love for God and man which is the New Testament standard. This failure is rooted in the carnal mind, and is a failure which may be eliminated in the grace of heart holiness. Now we seem to be talking about failure again; only this time we are calling it infirmity, or humanity. It does seem confusing, ad-

mittedly, especially when some of the personality faults may seem so similar to those which are seen in unsanctified Christians. . . . But the Spirit will help us to see that in God's sight—who alone knows the heart perfectly—there is a vast difference.[22]

Distinguishing between sin and infirmity was confusing and because of this, there was no shortage of attempts to provide distinctions. A growing casuistry characterized Nazarene discussion of human weakness. In 1960, a college level introductory textbook of Christian theology was published for use in the colleges of the denomination and was added to the course of study in 1960, where it remains to this day. Individual chapters were written by different authors from the various schools of the church with W. T. Purkiser, editor of the denomination's periodical, *Herald of Holiness,* serving as final editor. In a chapter concerning the effects of entire sanctification, Purkiser, who was author of several of the chapters, explained what entire sanctification accomplished.

"Evil concupiscence" (Col. 3:5, I Thess. 4:5)—used in the sense of a desire for that which is inherently evil, or wrong in itself—is purged away. Dispositional evils such as pride, self-will, carnal temper, envy, malice, animosity, bitterness of spirit, selfish ambition, and un-Christlikeness in attitude are cleansed away.[23]

This was consistent with what others had written concerning the sanctifying grace. Three pages later, he then distinguished between the sin that was cleansed away and the merely human that remained and that therefore needed "only" to be controlled.

One writer has listed some purely psychological drives of the human being as points at which disciplines must be applied: (1) A natural gravitation to "ease, idleness, luxury, comfort, self-liberty, and making ample provision for bodily comforts and enjoyments." (2) A tendency to be warm and enthusiastic toward certain virtues and graces, particularly those with which we are naturally well endowed, while utterly sluggish and indifferent to other virtues and graces. (3) "The human spirit is instinctively and universally in love with itself, and without being educated to it, will intuitively look out for itself, and mix up the principle of self-love in everything it does." (4) Excessive levity and foolishness: "A soul filled with God . . . is cheerful but not volatile." (5) Unevenness, fluctuation of mood and a corresponding tendency to act spasmodically.[24]

It is easy to see where this kind of distinction between sin in the unsanctified and infirmity in the entirely sanctified could lead. To those who believed that the experience of entire sanctification was essential to their salvation and who had experienced this second crisis, any "failure" subsequent to the experience of entire sanctification could by definition be attributed to the fact of a person's humanity, since all sin had been eradicated by the second work of grace. Consequently, what was sin for the unsanctified became simply personality faults in the entirely sanctified. What was considered prideful in the unsanctified was, for the entirely sanctified, the purely psychological drive of being instinctively and universally in love with oneself. What was carnal anger in the unsanctified was righteous indignation in the entirely sanctified.

Clearly, this was neither the precise meaning nor the intent of these authors. They were not writing in order to provide the entirely sanctified with rationalizations for what many considered sin. The Church of the Nazarene's particular explication of the doctrine of entire sanctification, however, with its adamant emphasis on the instantaneous eradication of the sinful nature was dramatically modified in light of the evidence of the subsequent "failures" of the sanctified. What one could expect the grace to accomplish underwent significant change.

Asbury Lowrey, whose book *Possibilities of Grace* was dropped from the Ministerial Course of Study in 1960, after being required reading since 1911, had written in 1884:

> The difference between my regenerate and sanctified state seemed to be this: 1. In regeneration my soul was alienated from sin; in sanctification it became hostile to it, and was set as a flint against it. 2. In regeneration my hopes were a mixture of assurance and fear; in sanctification my soul rested in unmixed quietness and assurance forever. Perfect love did actually cast out all fear that had torment. The physical suffering in death or other afflictions might be dreaded, but no fearful forebodings found place in my soul. 3. In regeneration the enjoyments of religion were temporary, fitful, and evanescent; in sanctification they became uniform, abiding, deep, rich, and supremely controlling. 4. In regeneration there was a constant obtrusion of worldly, ecclesiastical, or spiritual ambitions, personal to self; they preyed upon the soul and ate out the vitals of its spirituality and power; in sanctification these unholy ambitions became dead and unattractive as a faded autumn leaf.[25]

According to Nazarene Holiness writers in the last half of the 20th century, this was no longer an entirely accurate description of the entirely sanctified. According to these later Holiness writers, problems such as Lowrey had described for the simply "regenerate" could still be problems for the entirely sanctified. They just were not the consequence of sin. The doctrine as taught by teachers who were "rediscovering the deep sinfulness of man" was becoming an experience that changed definitions but not necessarily the human heart.

JOHN WESLEY'S CONCEPT OF PERFECTION

Not all were completely comfortable with this continuing expansion of the definition of infirmities. A little book titled *The Spirit of Holiness*[26] was included in the Ministerial Course of Study from 1964 to 1976. It had been written by Everett Lewis Cattell, who was president of Malone College. He had been raised a Quaker and, as such, was strongly influenced by the Holiness Movement. In the preface to this book, which argued for continued discipline in the life of the entirely sanctified, Cattell briefly described a journey that many other persons in the Holiness Movement had taken and were taking. He wrote:

As a young Christian trying to live the sanctified life, I found problems in correlating the teaching I heard with my own experience. This drove me to a deeper study of the actual teaching. Here I found that much confusion was being caused by the fact that the Holiness movement was emphasizing certain truths to the neglect or near exclusion of others. For example, the valid truth about crisis experience had been so emphasized as to leave the development of the holy life neglected. . . . By studying the writings of the really responsible leaders in the movement and particularly by going back to Wesley himself, I found the answers to these questions given, but usually tucked away out of the light of major emphasis.[27]

"Going back to Wesley himself" was what many in the Holiness Movement were doing at midcentury. Zondervan had published *The Works of Wesley* in 1958, providing those in the Wesleyan-Holiness tradition the writings of Wesley himself for the first time in over a century. In 1965, the *Wesleyan Theological Society* was formed by Leo Cox to encourage scholarly Wesleyan-Holiness research and to provide a forum for discussion of issues particularly relevant to Holiness theologians. The Church of the Nazarene began adding works of Wesley and works about Wesley to the Ministerial Course of Study in the 1950s and 1960s. John Wesley's definitive explanation of his holiness teaching, *A Plain Account of Christian Perfection,* was added to the Ministerial Course of Study for the first time in 1952. In 1964, the Church of the Nazarene recommended Leo Cox's *John Wesley's Concept of Perfection,*[28] for the course of study. This was the first time a work that dealt exclusively with an interpretation of Wesley's understanding of holiness was included in the reading list. Four years later, George Allen Turner's Ph.D. dissertation from Harvard, *The Vision Which Transforms,*[29] was also added. This biblical apologetic for a Wesleyan understanding of holiness had previously appeared in the reading list in 1952 under the title *The More Excellent Way.* In the fifth and sixth decades of the 20th century, "going back to Wesley himself" was a movement in which the Church of the Nazarene increasingly participated.

This was potentially problematic for Nazarenes, because John Wesley's writings were not entirely consistent with the holiness writings that the Church of the Nazarene had previously recommended as authoritative and with which they had long been familiar. There were significant points of divergence between Wesley's explication of entire sanctification and the denomination's understanding.

The denomination had largely understood the grace of sanctification almost entirely as an instantaneous event. John Wesley understood the term "sanctification" to refer to the entire salvific process, from justification to glorification. Entire sanctification referred strictly to that moment of complete cleansing from inbred sin. For Nazarenes, however, the two terms, "sanctification" and "entire sanctification" had become synonymous. Even when Nazarenes acknowledged the gradual aspect of the grace, it was defined so as not to compromise in any way the necessity for the instantaneous work. Leo Cox, in the conclusion of *John Wesley's Concept of Perfection,* which was on the Ministerial Course of Study from 1964 to 1968, had written, "The holiness movement of the nineteenth century in its emphasis upon the instantaneous sanctification and testimony neglected Wesley's equal insistence upon the gradual aspect."[30] Cox suggested a Wesleyan corrective to this modern holiness emphasis on the instantaneous aspect of the grace, which he considered a weakness. "A second corrective in Wesley is found in his insistence that the justified are sanctified initially and are made holy in degrees. This sanctification increases gradually as a process until the moment of entire sanctification."[31]

That Wesley understood sanctification as gradual as well as instantaneous was a fair interpretation. The book *The Heart of Wesley's Faith,* which was included in the Ministerial Course of Study from 1960 to 1968, contained an abridgment of Wesley's *Plain Account of Christian Perfection.* The first paragraph that Nazarene preachers would have read concerning the heart of Wesley's faith ended with these words:

> We are all agreed, we may be saved from all sin before death; that is, from all sinful tempers and desires. The substance then, is settled. But as to the circumstances, is the change gradual or instantaneous? It is both the one and the other. "But should we in preaching insist both on one and the other?" Certainly we should insist on the gradual change; and that earnestly and continually.[32]

Wesley's point in this paragraph was not that the gradual change should be emphasized at the expense of the instantaneous but that it should not be neglected in the emphasizing of the instantaneous.

A few pages later in that work, Wesley answered the direct question, "Is this death to sin and renewal in love gradual or instantaneous?" He wrote:

A man may be dying for some time, yet he does not, properly speaking, die till the instant the soul is separated from the body; and in that instant he lives the life of eternity. In like manner he may be dying to sin for some time, yet he is not dead to sin until sin is separated from his soul; and in that instant he lives a life full of love.[33]

For Wesley, the gradual change of sanctification was a given. Wesley's clear understanding of God's sanctifying grace was that it began at justification and continued throughout the life of the believer. As far as Wesley was concerned, what was novel was his contention that it could be instantaneous.

It need not, therefore, be affirmed over and over, and proved by forty texts of Scripture, either that most men are perfect in love at last—that there is a gradual work of God in the soul—or that, generally speaking, it is a long time, even many years, before sin is destroyed. All this we know. But we know, likewise, that God may, with man's good leave, cut short His work, in whatever degree He pleases and do the usual work of many years in a moment. He does so in many instances. And yet there is a gradual work both before and after that moment.[34]

For Nazarenes 200 years later, the instantaneous aspect of sanctification was the given. The novelty was that there was a gradual sanctifying of the believer. To Nazarenes raised on the holiness preaching and teaching of the 20th century, the revolutionary parts of *A Plain Account of Christian Perfection* were the passages that summarily insisted on sanctification as a gradual work. This gradual emphasis was what was new, and it was not entirely consistent with the holiness literature that had been previously recommended.

Another divergent aspect of Wesley's understanding of sanctification concerned its "attainability." To Holiness people of the late 19th and 20th centuries, the conditions for receiving this grace were faith and consecration and when these two conditions were met, entire sanctification was granted. There would be no need to wait nor should there be any delay. Saved and (entirely) sanctified was the expectation as soon as possible and most Nazarenes testified to receiving the grace early in their experience. Wesley's writings were not confirming of this understanding of the grace.

Q. Is [entire sanctification] given till a little before death?

A. It is not to those who expect it no sooner.

Q. But may we expect it sooner?

A. Why not? For, although we grant, (1) That the generality of believers, whom we have hitherto known, were not so sanctified till near death; (2) That few of those to whom St. Paul wrote his epistles were so at that time, nor (3) He himself at the time of writing his former epistles, yet all this does not prove that we may not be so today.[35] Again, what was a common understanding for Wesley, that the "generality of believers were not so sanctified till near death" was revolutionary to Holiness people two centuries later. Conversely, what was remarkable for Wesley, that believers might be sanctified earlier, was what was simply understood for Nazarenes. Because of this, there were passages in Wesley's *Plain Account* that would have been quite alarming to Nazarenes. At one point, Wesley was asked whether children who had been born to two entirely sanctified people wouldn't also be free from inbred sin. Wesley's reply was revealing. He didn't think it would be very likely that two entirely sanctified persons would ever be married! He answered: "It is a possible but not a probable case; I doubt whether it ever was or ever will be. But, waiving this, I answer, Sin is entailed upon me, not by immediate generation, but by my first parent."[36]

Wesley's instruction concerning how it was to be sought was also different from the Nazarenes. For Nazarenes, when one made an entire consecration and believed, one would receive the grace. This was the shorter way. Wesley taught, first of all, that the occasion of entire sanctification was up to God's sovereign will and not conditioned primarily by the desire of the seeker. He believed one must wait for the change. God dictated the when. The question then became how one waited.

> Not in careless indifference or indolent inactivity, but in vigorous universal obedience, in a zealous keeping of all the commandments, in watchfulness and painfulness, in denying ourselves and taking up our cross daily, as well as in earnest prayer and fasting and a close attendance on all the ordinances of God. And if any man dream of attaining it any other way (yea, or of keeping it when it is attained, when he has received it even in the largest measure), he deceiveth his own soul. It is true, we receive it by simple faith. But God does not, will not, give that faith unless we seek it with all diligence in the way which He hath ordained. This consideration may satisfy those who inquire why so few have received the blessing.[37]

Wesley did not equate the baptism of the Holy Spirit or Pentecost with entire sanctification. The Holy Spirit was active throughout the administration of God's grace, and he believed that the Holy Spirit was granted to every justified believer on the occasion of his or her justification. The issue as formulated by later Holiness writers was not addressed by Wesley in his definitive explanation of entire sanctification.

His description of the effects of entire sanctification was almost as promising as some of the descriptions of the Holiness writers of the late

19th century. To the question of when a person might know that he had been entirely sanctified, Wesley wrote:

A. When, after having been fully convinced of inbred sin by a far deeper and clearer conviction than that which he experienced before justification, and after having experienced a gradual mortification of it, he experiences a total death to sin, and an entire renewal in the love and image of God, so as to "rejoice evermore," to "pray without ceasing," and "in everything [to] give thanks." Not that "to feel all love and no sin" is a sufficient proof. Several have experienced this for a time before their souls were fully renewed. None, therefore, ought to believe that the work is done till there is added the testimony of the Spirit, witnessing his entire sanctification as clearly as his justification.[38]

Upon further consideration of how one might know they are entirely sanctified, Wesley replied:

A. By love, joy, peace, always abiding; by invariable long-suffering, patience, resignation; by gentleness triumphing over all provocation; by goodness, mildness, sweetness, tenderness of spirit; by fidelity, simplicity, godly sincerity; by meekness, calmness, evenness of spirit; by temperance, not only in food and sleep, but in all things natural and spiritual.

Q. 23. But what great matter is there in this? Have we not all this when we are justified?

A. What! Total resignation to the will of God, without any mixture of self-will? Gentleness without any touch of anger, even the moment we are provoked? Love to God, without the least love to the creature, but in and for God, excluding all pride? Love to man, excluding all envy, jealousy, and rash judging? Meekness, keeping the whole soul inviolably calm? And temperance in all things? Deny that any ever came up to this, if you please; but do not say all who are justified do.[39]

Wesley was skeptical of those who claimed to have been entirely sanctified if they did not evidence this fruit of the Spirit. In 1763 in London, between 300 and 400 people claimed to have been entirely sanctified. Wesley's comment concerning their claim was instructive.

[O]thers who think they have are nevertheless manifestly wanting in the fruit. How many I will not say. . . . But some are undeniably wanting in long-suffering and Christian resignation. They do not see the hand of God in whatever occurs, and cheerfully embrace it. They do not in everything give thanks and rejoice evermore. They are not happy; at least, not always happy. For sometimes they complain. They say, "This, or that is hard!" Some are wanting in gentleness. They resist evil instead of turning the other cheek. They do not receive reproach with gentleness; no, nor even reproof. Nay, they are not able to bear contradiction without the appearance, at least, of resentment . . . Some are wanting in goodness. They are not kind, mild, sweet, amiable, soft, and loving at all times, in their spirit, in their words, in their looks and air, in the whole tenor of their behavior; and that to all, high or low, rich and poor, without respect of persons; particularly to them that are out of the way, to opposers, and to those of their own household. They do not long, study, endeavor by every means, to make all about them happy. . . . Some are wanting in fidelity, a nice regard to truth, simplicity, and godly sincerity. Their love is hardly without dissimulation; something like guile is found in their mouth. . . . Some are wanting in meekness, quietness of spirit, composure, evenness of temper. They are up and down, sometimes high and sometimes low; their mind is not well balanced. . . . Some are wanting in temperance. They do not steadily use that kind and degree of food which they know, or might know, would most conduce to their health, strength, and vigor of the body. . . . Or they use neither fasting nor abstinence. . . . So far all is plain. I believe you have faith, and love, and joy, and peace . . . You are wanting either in long-suffering, gentleness, or goodness, either in fidelity, meekness, or temperance. Let us not, then, on either hand, fight about words. In the thing we clearly agree. You have not what I call Christian perfection.[40]

This too was not consistent with what was being written at midcentury about the effects of entire sanctification in the Church of the Nazarene. Wesley's evidence of the grace of entire sanctification was quite a bit more demanding than the evidence that was needed in the Church of the Nazarene. As the above paragraphs reveal, much of what Wesley considered a consequence of remaining sin was for members in this Holiness denomination simply a consequence of infirm humanity.

Wesley did address the issue of the difference between sin and infirmity. He understood that entire sanctification did not make one perfect in knowledge. He acknowledged that fallen humanity would make mistakes as a consequence of ignorance. He was the first to define sin for which persons were culpable as "voluntary transgressions of a known law."[41] Because of these infirmities, persons made perfect in love would continue to need the atoning blood of Christ.

(1) Everyone may [make a] mistake as long as he lives. (2) A mistake in opinion may occasion a mistake in practice. (3) Every such mistake is a transgression of the perfect law. Therefore, (4) Every such mistake, were it not for the Blood of atonement, would expose to eternal damnation. (5) It follows that the most perfect have contin-

ual need of the merits of Christ, even for their actual transgressions, and may say for themselves, as well as for their brethren, "Forgive us our trespasses."[42]

As Wesley's description of the grace of entire sanctification indicates, what Nazarenes in midcentury were considering mere infirmities were, according to Wesley, sin. For Wesley, sin was not defined so narrowly nor were infirmities defined so expansively.

According to Wesley, the pervasiveness of sin was such that even entirely sanctified believers whose hearts were cleansed from all sin were still absolutely dependent upon Christ's mediation and continuous infusion of grace. Amen

The holiest of men still need Christ as their Prophet, as "the light of the world." For He does not give them light but from moment to moment; the instant He withdraws, all is darkness. They still need Christ as their King. For God does not give them a stock of holiness. But unless they receive a supply every moment, nothing but unholiness will remain. They still need Christ as their Priest, to make atonement for their holy things. Even perfect holiness is acceptable to God only through Jesus Christ. . . . [T]he best of men may say, "Thou art my Light, my Holiness, my Heaven. Through my union with Thee I am full of light, of holiness, and happiness. But if I were left to myself I should be nothing but sin, darkness and hell."[43]

While entire sanctification was an act of God's grace, the conditions for receiving it and keeping it were quite demanding. Experiencing the grace of entire sanctification at any other time than just prior to death, therefore, was more exceptional than usual. Wesley's understanding of entire sanctification would have been remarkable to many Nazarenes, and his description of the state of the entirely sanctified would have been thought perhaps unattainable. According to Wesley, it almost was.

It is scarce conceivable how strait the way is wherein God leads them that follow Him; and how dependant on Him we must be. . . . As a very little dust will disorder a clock, and the least sand will obscure our sight, so the least grain of sin which is upon the heart will hinder its right motion toward God.[44]

The appeal of Wesley to many in the Holiness Movement "awed by the rediscovery of the deep sinfulness of man" was his recognition of the pervasive tenaciousness of sin, the demanding conditions required for cleansing from it, and the extraordinary nature of the life lived free from it. For Everett Lewis Cattell and others, "by going back to Wesley himself, [they] found the answers to these questions given."[45]

The Article of Faith

From 1928 to 1976, the Church of the Nazarene's Article of Faith on entire sanctification had remained unchanged. It had stated for almost half a century:

> We believe that entire sanctification is that act of God, subsequent to regeneration, by which believers are made free from original sin, or depravity, and brought into the state of entire devotement to God, and the holy obedience of love made perfect.
>
> It is wrought by the baptism of the Holy Spirit, and comprehends in one experience the cleansing of the heart from sin and the abiding, indwelling presence of the Holy Spirit, empowering the believer for life and service.
>
> Entire sanctification is provided by the blood of Jesus, is wrought instantaneously by faith, preceded by entire consecration; and to this work and state of grace the Holy Spirit bears witness.
>
> This experience is also known by various terms representing different phases of the experience, such as "Christian Perfection," "Perfect Love," "Heart Purity," "The Baptism of the Holy Spirit," "The Fulness of the Blessing," "Christian Holiness."[46]

In 1976, for the first time in almost 50 years, the denomination modified the article. They left alone what had already been written in the first four paragraphs, simply adding two qualifying paragraphs. The first paragraph added was a statement that had been a part of the Article of Faith from 1911 to 1923. In 1976, it was believed necessary to reintroduce it. It read:

> We believe that there is a marked distinction between a pure heart and a mature character. The former is obtained in an instant, the result of entire sanctification; the latter is the result of growth in grace.[47]

The second paragraph enlarged on this theme of the need for continued growth in grace. The final paragraph in the Article of Faith on entire sanctification stated:

> We believe that the grace of entire sanctification includes the impulse to grow in grace. However, this impulse must be consciously nurtured, and careful attention given to the requisites and processes of spiritual development and improvement in Christlikeness of character and personality. Without such purposeful endeavor one's witness may be impaired and the grace itself frustrated and ultimately lost.[48]

So much attention had been given to proclaiming the instantaneous nature of entire sanctification that the gradual nature of the grace had been all but abandoned. Furthermore, in the stalwart defense of the instantaneous nature of entire sanctification, there had been such redefinition of what should be considered sin over against what could be considered infirmity, the second work of grace was in danger of becoming an experience without any significant consequence. The Church of the Nazarene's act of deliberately adding to the course of study the writings of and about Wesley, even as they challenged Nazarene orthodoxy indicate—along with the addition of these two paragraphs to the Article of Faith on entire sanctification—that the denomination wanted to give more attention to the gradual growth in Christlikeness that was to accompany the grace of entire sanctification. The plain account of the distinctive doctrine of the Church of the Nazarene, which asserted the instantaneous eradication of the sinful nature by a second work of grace, was becoming anything but a plain account.

THE CREDIBILITY GAP

◆

MOTION TO REMOVE "ERADICATE"

At the 1985 General Assembly of the Church of the Nazarene, a commission appointed by the general superintendents recommended to the elected delegates of the assembly additional changes to the church's Articles of Faith. Throughout the denomination's history, there had been many such recommendations, so many in fact, that there was not a single Article of Faith agreed upon in the 1908 merger that had not been rewritten, corrected, or adjusted in some way. Prior to 1985, the last significant change to an Article of Faith had been in 1976, when the church voted to add two paragraphs to the article on "Entire Sanctification," stating the need for continued growth in grace subsequent to the second work of grace. At the 1985 General Assembly, the recommendation concerned the Article of Faith on "Original Sin" and originally was considered as a recommendation not simply to add clarifying statements to an existing Article of Faith, but to replace it with an entirely new Article of Faith.

The commission, made up of prominent church leaders and various theological professors from the denomination's educational institutions, recommended that three paragraphs be substituted for the single paragraph that comprised the existing article. Since 1928 (excepting the change in 1952 whereby the last clause became a separate sentence), the article had stated:

> We believe that original sin, or depravity, is that corruption of the nature of all the offspring of Adam, by reason of which everyone is very far gone from original righteousness, or the pure state of our first parents at the time of their creation, is averse to God, is without spiritual life, and is inclined to evil, and that continually. We further believe that original sin continues to exist with the life of the regenerate, until eradicated by the baptism with the Holy Spirit.[1]

The commission recommended to the assembly a first paragraph that would make explicit the dual nature of sin.

> We believe that sin came into the world through the disobedience of our first parents, and death by sin. We believe that sin is of two kinds: original sin or depravity, and actual or personal sin.[2]

The second and third paragraphs of the new Article of Faith continued this clarification of the difference between original sin and actual sin and then distinguished between actual sin and infirmity. The last two paragraphs of the suggested Article of Faith stated:

> We believe that original sin differs from actual sin in that it constitutes an inherited propensity to actual sin for which no one is accountable until its divinely provided remedy is neglected or rejected.
>
> We believe that actual or personal sin is a voluntary violation of a known law of God by a morally responsible person. It is therefore not to be confused with involuntary and inescapable shortcomings, infirmities, faults, mistakes, failures, or other deviations from a standard of perfect conduct which are the residual effects of the Fall. However, such innocent effects do not include attitudes or responses contrary to the spirit of Christ, which may properly be called sins of the spirit. We believe that personal sin is primarily and essentially a violation of the law of love; and that in relation to Christ sin may be defined as unbelief.[3]

The particular significance of this Article of Faith lay in the implications of this statement on the doctrine of entire sanctification. The commission, by proposing an entirely new Article of Faith on sin, was tampering with a particular understanding of the distinctive doctrine of the Church of the Nazarene. The commission, chaired by Ponder Gilliland, pastor of the prestigious Bethany, Oklahoma, First Church of the Nazarene, certainly did not believe itself to be proposing anything that was at variance with the church's traditional understanding of the doctrine. In the first paragraph of the proposed new Article of Faith, the acknowledgment that sin was of two kinds reinforced belief in the need for two works of grace. Personal sin required forgiveness. Original sin required eradication. The very first sentence of that first paragraph, which stated that sin had entered the world through the first parents reaffirmed the universality of this original sin, thus allowing for the possibility of indirectly affirming the necessity once again for a work of grace that eradicated this universal depravity. The second paragraph further distinguished between original sin and actual sin by describing original sin as an inherited propensity to sin for which persons were not responsible until they rejected the call to be entirely sanctified. The third paragraph simply addressed issues that had been consuming much of the discussion in the church concerning entire sanctification in the preceding decades. Prior to this 1985 recommended formulation, there had been no acknowledgment in the Articles of Faith of a difference between "sin" and "infirmity" and as has been noted, much confusion concerning the doctrine had been a consequence of not understanding that entire sanctification effected a Christian perfection that was fully consistent with a fallible human nature. A proper understanding of entire sanctification demanded this clear distinction, for if all infirmity was sin, then entire sanctification was an earthly impossibility.

It should be noted, however, that at the same time that the commission wanted to acknowledge this distinction between sin and infirmity, they also wanted to guard against the misuse of this distinction to consider as infirmity what should properly be considered as sin. The third paragraph of the proposed recommendation, therefore, subtly warned Nazarenes against any spirit that might be contrary to the spirit of Christ. The third paragraph thus addressed a second pressing and continuing concern of the church: if sin was simply considered infirmity, then entire sanctification would be in danger of becoming a cheap grace.

While this proposed Article of Faith was entirely consistent with the church's understanding of sin, there was a crucial omission. In the new Article of Faith, there was no mention of the remedy for this original sin, save for the undefined acknowledgment that there was a remedy. In particular, what was omitted from this new Article of Faith was the statement that "original sin continues to exist with the new life of the regenerate, until eradicated by the baptism with the Holy Spirit."[4]

As might have been expected, the recommendation to the delegates to entirely replace an existing Article of Faith generated much heated discussion. General Superintendent Eugene Stowe immediately made a motion to delete the proposed amendment and keep the original statement. Ponder W. Gilliland spoke against Stowe's motion, stating that the church needed these new articles because they clarified the truth that "regeneration mitigates the effect of our sinfulness."[5] The commission's contention concerning the existing article was that, in so emphasizing the need for original sin to be eradicated, it diminished the significance of the first work of grace. A pastor from Tennessee spoke for Stowe's motion, pleading for the wording of the founding fathers. General Superintendent V. H. Lewis also spoke against any change, arguing that to remove all reference to the Holy Spirit's eradication of original sin by the baptism of the Holy Spirit would flaw the article dangerously. Lyle Pointer, pastor of San Jose, California, First Church of the Nazarene, spoke against Stowe's motion to keep the original article and for the recommendation of the new article by arguing that the Articles of Faith should use biblical terminology and not theological terms (like "eradication"). A short recess was called, in part, to settle the delegates. Following the recess, when it became clear that the delegates, following the lead of at least two of their general superintendents, were never going to remove the original Article of Faith, Ponder Gilliland recommended adding to the original paragraph, concerning original sin continuing to exist in the life of the regenerate, the phrase "though these results are mitigated by the Holy Spirit in the life of the regenerate."[6] This was defeated. Other motions and amendments were received by the chair, and in the intensity of the discussion procedural rules governing the debate were contested and debated, forcing the committee chairman, Ponder Gilliland, and the chair of the assembly, General Superintendent Orville Jenkins, into a lengthy conference to sort out these contested procedural issues.

When debate resumed, Lyle Pointer also moved an amendment to the existing Article of Faith on original sin. He recommended, in the sentence which read, "We further believe that original sin continues to exist with the new life of the regenerate, until eradicated by the baptism with the Holy Spirit;" that "eradicated" be replaced with "cleansed" and that "baptism with the Holy Spirit" be replaced with "fullness with the Holy Spirit," so that the amended statement would then read, "[O]riginal sin continues to exist with the new life, until the heart is cleansed by the fullness with the Holy Spirit." Like the original recommendation of the commission to replace the existing article, this amendment would have also deleted reference to original sin being eradicated by a baptism with the Holy Spirit in a "personal Pentecost." The delegation, growing weary from the extended debate and not eager to discuss new amendments, summarily defeated Pointer's amendment without much discussion. After additional lively and intense debate concerning this particular Article of Faith, prompting one delegate to move that the entire matter be tabled indefinitely because of the apparent irresolution of the matter, the delegates of the 1985 21st General Assembly finally adopted an Article of Faith on original sin that retained the original paragraph without change while adding the three paragraphs that had been recommended to replace the existing one. At the end of the day, the Church of the Nazarene's Article of Faith on sin, titled "Sin, Original and Personal," was four paragraphs long and slightly redundant. Now one of the longest Articles of Faith, it distinguished between original and actual sin, between actual sin and infirmity, warned against confusing sin with infirmity, and most importantly, still stated that original sin was eradicated by a baptism with the Holy Spirit.

This effort to remove "eradicate" and "baptism with the Holy Spirit" from the Article of Faith on sin was not the first time these particular terms had been called into question concerning what was accomplished by entire sanctification, nor was the discussion on the floor of the assembly the first time debate over the appropriateness of this specific terminology had taken place. The 1985 General Assembly debate over the Article of Faith on sin was evidence of a dynamic discussion that had been ongoing in the denomination for approximately 15 years and had only in the years immediately preceding that 21st General Assembly become divisive and potentially problematic for the church. The issues were not new to many of the delegates and participants in the discussion. They had come to that assembly prepared to "discuss." When the commission proposed replacing the

Article of Faith and when Lyle Pointer proposed amending the existing Article of Faith, both of which would have deleted the word "eradication" and the phrase "baptism with the Holy Spirit," they were representing a well-defined movement within the Church of the Nazarene to understand entire sanctification in a way that, according to those with the more traditional understanding, would undermine the distinctive doctrine of the Church of the Nazarene. When the majority of the delegates defeated Pointer's amendment and voted to add the new Article of Faith to the old Article of Faith, instead of replacing it, they were representing a movement within the Church of the Nazarene trying to understand entire sanctification in a way that, according to those who proposed the change, would eventually mean its permanent irrelevancy.[7]

AN EXPERIENCE BEYOND CONVERSION

The event that initiated the kind of earnest debate in evidence at the 21st General Assembly, more than any other single event, was the publication of a book written by Mildred Bangs Wynkoop, a 67-year-old theology professor from Trevecca Nazarene College in Nashville, Tennessee. In 1973, Beacon Hill Press of Kansas City, an arm of the Nazarene Publishing House, published *A Theology of Love* which was, according to a book review in the Nazarene Theological Seminary's monthly publication, a milestone in Wesleyan publication history. According to the *Seminary Tower:*

> As a sustained theological treatment of the fundamental dynamism of Wesley's thought, it deserves to be placed with such scholarly works as those of Turner and Lindstrom, among non-Nazarenes; and with Wiley's *Christian Theology* and Timothy Smith's *Called Unto Holiness,* among works by Nazarenes.[9]

Another reviewer wrote that *A Theology of Love* was "one of the most important books ever published by Beacon Hill Press of Kansas City . . . for here is the first *modern* theology of holiness."[10] Promoted by the publishing house as an "opus" on holiness theology,[11] it was perceived as the first truly creative holiness theology in decades. While not added to the Ministerial Course of Study as required reading until 1986, anyone interested in contemporary discussion of holiness theology was familiar with her book. The *Seminary Tower* was correct in its assessment that it was a milestone, for, independent of whether or not her book deserved to be placed alongside Turner's *The Vision Which Transforms,* Lindstrom's *Wesley and Sanctification,* Wiley's *Christian Theology,* or Smith's *Called unto Holiness,* it was this book that called into question the relevance of the "traditional" understanding of the doctrine of entire sanctification.

One of the reasons the book was initially hailed by so many was because it acknowledged without apology the difficulty of believing the promise of entire sanctification as it had been defined at midcentury. The understanding of entire sanctification prior to the publication of *A Theology of Love* was that entire sanctification was a second work of grace in which the sinful nature was entirely eradicated, thus enabling persons to live without sin. The apparent distance between the promise of entire sanctification and the experience of those who claimed to have received the grace is what prompted many Holiness professors in these midcentury years to define sin more narrowly and define infirmity more expansively. Wynkoop, in the third chapter of *A Theology of Love,* called this apparent irreconciliation between the promise of entire sanctification and the facts of human experience "The Credibility Gap."[12] She wrote:

> Our problem is a credibility gap. Of all the credibility gaps in contemporary life, none is more real and serious than that which exists between the Christian, and particularly Wesleyan, doctrine and everyday human life. The absolute of holiness theology may satisfy the mind but the imperfection of the human self seems to deny all that the perfection of Christian doctrine affirms. . . . This has created a vast and disturbing dualism between idea and life, between profession and practice. Such a dualism fosters either bewildered dishonesty (in the interest of loyalty) or abject discouragement. The ultimate result is rejection of the Christian message as itself unrealistic and unbelievable if not actually false.[13]

She then highlighted some of the practical questions that the doctrine of entire sanctification was prompting among Nazarenes and which were generating much confused discussion.

> Wesleyans speak of a second work of grace or a second crisis or blessing in the Christian life. What is the significance of *two* special moments among the many in life? Why two, not one or three or 100? How is one recognized from the other or how does one distinguish the first from the second? If a Christian loses one "blessing," which one does he lose, and what happens to the other, and how would one know when he had recovered what was lost? Does God withhold some measure of grace from the first experience that is later given in the second? Or does He solve only part of the sin problem in each "work of grace"?
>
> Is one fully saved when he is regenerated or only partially saved? If God does not save completely, couldn't He if He would? And if He could, why does He not do so in the new birth? If one is wholly saved in the new birth, why must he have another special moment to prepare him for heaven? And, back of these, why a *crisis* experience? And why is there any mathematical designation in reference to it? What is crisis? Process? The relation between the two? What is perfection? Cleansing? Love? Faith? Sanctification?[14]

Wynkoop's solution to this problem of the "credibility gap" and her response to these questions was more radical than any suggested to date. Instead of finessing definitions, she proposed nothing less than a restructuring of the conceptual framework within which holiness theologians had worked. She believed that this new conceptual framework could be applied to the writings of John Wesley himself, and in particular, she believed this "relational hermeneutic" was more adequate for, what she called, John Wesley's "theology of love."

Wynkoop believed that the American-Holiness Movement had significantly departed from classical Wesleyan theology. By going back to Wesley himself and by adopting this conceptual framework, the credibility gap could be overcome and the questions that were being asked would not necessarily have answers but would be understood as the wrong questions entirely. According to Wynkoop, the reason it was difficult to believe the doctrine of entire sanctification was because the American-Holiness Movement had uncritically adopted a fundamentally wrong ontology, an ontology which could not be faithful to the theology of John Wesley.

According to Wynkoop, there were three major conceptual adjustments that needed to be made. The first concerned an understanding of the nature of persons. Wynkoop called for the rejection of a "Greek" definition of person, in which person was understood as being comprised of a divine soul trapped in a material and thus evil body. This understanding demanded a soteriology that was necessarily escapist and one that was fundamentally antithetical to classical Wesleyan theology. According to Wynkoop, this "pagan" dualism had been uncritically adopted by the American-Holiness Movement and had resulted in an unbiblical denigration of human nature. This was what had led, in part, to the artificial distinctions that were being made in the Holiness Movement between infirmity and sin. She believed that a return to a "Hebrew" definition of person as a unity (and therefore as not essentially evil) would erase some of the confusions surrounding the doctrine of entire sanctification.

The second and perhaps most important conceptual adjustment that needed to be made was intrinsically related to the first. It concerned the Nazarenes' understanding of the nature of sin. Wynkoop called for a rejection of what she called the *substantial* concept of sin and the adoption of a *relational* view.[15] According to Wynkoop, the Holiness Movement had erred when it conceived of sin in terms of a kind of substance inhering somewhere within the person, thus needing to be "eradicated" in a second work of grace. Much of the confusion in the Holiness Movement was a consequence of this inappropriate and unbiblical concept. Wynkoop believed that sin was better understood as a relational term. It did not describe anything. It was rather best understood as a wrong relation) and she insisted that this definition of sin was more faithful to John Wesley's definition. "Sin-less-ness" therefore simply consisted in being in right relation to God.

The third conceptual adjustment that Wynkoop recommended concerned the definition of salvation. She contrasted what she called the "magical" versus the "moral" interpretation of salvation. According to Wynkoop, the "dualistic" concept of persons coupled with a "substantive" definition of sin led to a "magical" understanding of salvation.

> This means that a sub-rational, psychological mutation defines cleansing from sin. The problem here is that men come to expect a substance alteration of the soul in salvation which occurs below the level of rational life and which, apart from personal involvement, changes the impulsive reactions of the self.[16]

According to Wynkoop, salvation should be understood principally as a matter of ethical relationship. Salvation was not to be understood as something that happens to man; salvation was a consequence of being in a right relationship with God (and others) contingent on and determined by love. This she believed was a truly "Wesleyan" understanding of salvation.

To Wesley, sanctification was an ethical relationship, never a moralism, never an emotion or a deliverance from emotions, never a magical elimination of a thing ("like a sore tooth") or the addition of something, even the "addition" of the Holy Spirit. The direction of one's attention and "aim" was not toward an examination of one's emotional states, or the quantity of one's religious acts and obeyed rules. Religion to Wesley was in the quality and object of one's love.[17]

This "relational" and thoroughly "moral" understanding of salvation was reflected in her definitions of sin and holiness. According to Wynkoop, sin was simply the description of the estranged relationship between God and man. In a chapter titled "Sin and Holiness," she stated this repeatedly. "God seeks our love and gives His love without measure. Sin is simply the absence of this relationship because man has repudiated it."[18] Two pages later, she wrote again, "First of all, sin is a rupture of fellowship with God."[19] And on the very next page, she reiterated the point; "Sin is love, but love gone astray. . . . Men find themselves locked by their own love into an orbit about a center. Sin is love locked into a false center, the self. . . . Sin is the distortion of love."[20]

Conversely, holiness was simply the description of a completely restored relationship between God and man.

> Wesleyan theology rejects the concept of original holiness as an impersonal goodness, in favor of a more biblical idea of holiness which stresses a right personal relationship to God. Holiness, or morality, is never a quality of impersonal substance but the way one reacts to God and to persons. To understand this is to help correct

the idea that sin has substance or is a thing which can be—or cannot be—removed as a diseased part of the body. Holiness is not metaphysically conditioned substance, but a proper relationship to God by the Holy Spirit.[21]

As she had with her definition of sin, she stated this definition of holiness repeatedly. In the chapter on "Sin and Holiness," she wrote: "Holiness is love: pure love, personal, mutual love between God and man, and between man and man in God's love."[22] Two pages later she wrote: "Holiness consists of this unobstructed personal communion and, deep, personal fellowship with God."[23] And on the very next page, she reiterated her point. "Holiness is fullness of mutual love, great or small, limited by the person's capacity at any given time but nonetheless full, clean, whole love."[24]

According to Wynkoop, estrangement from God, which she defined as the essence of sin, and communion with God, which she defined as holiness, were contingent on a person's obedience. "Holiness and sin are, thus, two kinds of relationship to God, one positive, the other negative, but both active because it is the person, forced to decision, choosing the right or wrong object of his love."[25] Salvation therefore was contingent on the choice of a freely acting agent. At one point she equated holiness with moral integrity. "Holiness is moral integrity, and sin is the lack of moral integrity."[26] So fundamental was this existential decision to her definition of salvation that she seemed to suggest that persons were absolutely responsible concerning their condition.

We need also to note that no man is ever given any comfort by the suggestion that since he is "in sin" and under the bondage of sin, and deceived, and his mind is darkened and his will perverted, he is absolved from responsibility regarding it. Never can it be found in scripture that a man sins because he cannot help it, and therefore can excuse himself.[27]

She balanced this emphasis on the power of the human will by reminding her readers of the doctrine of prevenient grace, which Wesley believed countered a person's sinful inclination. She even felt compelled to write at several points, "This position is not Pelagianism,"[28] but the emphasis throughout *A Theology of Love,* in view of her exclusively relational view of salvation, was not so much on the grace of God in the salvation process as on the moral responsibility of persons for their salvation. According to Wynkoop,

Every step in grace is taken in sharp conscious awareness, and clear rational insight, and the most deliberate moral decisiveness. Consciousness is not bypassed, submerged, or violated. All the powers of the personality converge with full rational responsibility upon these moments, to which the Holy Spirit carefully and imperiously draws us. Nor is there any relaxation of this moral responsibility within the Christian life—rather an ever deepening capacity for it.[29]

This "relational" theology led to quite different emphases when applied specifically to the distinctive doctrine of entire sanctification, and Wynkoop did not hesitate to correct what she considered the flawed traditional descriptions of the grace. First of all and perhaps most obviously, Wynkoop rejected terms like "eradication" and "sinful nature," and she called for very specific definitions of biblical terms like "cleansed," as in "cleansed from all sin."[30] To make the point that sin was not something that needed to be removed as the term "eradication" suggested, she referred to a question that John Wesley had been asked by one his preachers concerning how it was that Christ could *continue* to cleanse from sin if, in entire sanctification, a person was cleansed from all sin. Wynkoop surmised:

> Perhaps the preacher supposed that sin was a sort of substance in the soul that could be *removed* and after it has been removed the soul becomes and remains pure. In other words, purity to him, was an entity or rather a characteristic inherent in an entity capable of self-existence. His comment is a significant commentary on one of the prevailing views of what the soul is and how grace acts in respect of it. At least the language, if unguarded, permits the interpretation that the soul and sin are "things" which one has or may get free from.[31]

Sin was not a thing that could be eradicated by a second work of grace. It was descriptive of an estranged relationship. Conversely, freedom from sin, therefore, or purity, was descriptive of a harmonious relationship. Specifically, Wynkoop defined a pure heart as a heart that, as Kierkegaard had written, willed one thing.[32] Wynkoop wrote:

> A clean heart is one whose deepest purpose has been centered in Christ. . . . Purity or cleansing is a moral relationship to God and man, not a quality in the substance of the soul. . . . It is not an independent real which can maintain its character apart from this relationship. . . . A clean heart is a single heart, which is love, which is fellowship. . . . Single-heartedness is its fundamental characteristic.

A person whose entire heart was centered in Christ could be said to be entirely sanctified. The emphasis in *A Theology of Love* was not so much on the grace of God effecting any real change in a person. Rather, the emphasis was more on the purity of a person's consecration which would lead to unhindered communion with God. When one willed Christ without reservation or duplicity, one could be considered entirely sanctified by virtue of the purity of the subsequent relationship with God.

This definition had challenging implications for other aspects of the doctrine. If there was no such thing as inbred sin that needed eradicating by a second work of grace, then there was no *essential* need for two works of grace. This Wynkoop admitted. Some persons could be so spiritually intuitive concerning the state of their own heart that they could be entirely sanctified and thus brought into a pure relationship with God at the moment of their conversion. "It must always be held possible that the spiritual insight of some individuals is great enough, at that moment [of conversion], to make the total human commitment which moral experience requires."[34] For the most part, however, two works of grace were needed because of the need for moral development subsequent to the first work of grace. "There may be justly two crucial moments identified, not because God has structured salvation that way, but because He has structured man as a moral creature."[35] In other words, because of the ordinary process of human development, it was very difficult to make the kind of full commitment or consecration necessary for entire sanctification at the beginning of a relationship with God. According to Wynkoop, the acknowledgment of sin and the search for pardon was the first step in this thoroughly moral relationship, but it usually took some time before the need for a full commitment could be realized, and it usually required some spiritual and moral development before an entire consecration could even be possible. Referring to the process of sanctification, which included the first and second definitive moments, Wynkoop wrote:

> The crisis and process refer to our own side of this covenant. It is a crisis in life when we make our commitment and are accepted of God. Within this sacred fellowship we develop and grow according to the laws of spiritual life. The full, personal commitment to Christ, crucifixion with Christ, and the Holy Spirit's indwelling are by their very nature climactic and abrupt. It may take some time to align our central self to God's will, but when it is done a crisis . . . has properly occurred. It is a crucial and formative act and has repercussions in all of life.[36]

This definition of salvation as a relationship to God contingent on the existential decision of an absolutely free and responsible person[37] that usually manifested itself in two crisis experiences led Wynkoop to deny any essential distinction between the first crisis of justification and the second crisis of entire sanctification. Both crises were sanctifying and the difference between the two was simply a difference between degrees of commitment. Wynkoop referred to Wesley to support her understanding of the relationship between the two works of grace. According to Wynkoop:

> Wesley's concept of justification is very high—so high indeed that it may seem to some that he is confusing it with sanctification. BUT THIS IS JUST THE POINT. Wesley insisted that sanctification began in justification,—not only is Christ *for* us, but He is *in* us. This

lifts the whole redemption enterprise to a new level of meaning. Something begins in justification that has no ceiling. It ushers the new Christian into a relationship that entails a new way of life. . . . Justification and sanctification are not two *kinds* of grace, but two *dimensions* of the experience of God's love and grace.[38]

She quoted several excerpts from Wesley's works to support this contention that sanctification began in justification.

> Q. 7. "Is every man, as soon as he believes, a new creature, sanctified, pure in heart? Has he then a new heart? Does Christ dwell therein? And is he a temple of the Holy Ghost?"
>
> A. "All these things may be affirmed of every believer, in a true sense. Let us not therefore contradict those who maintain it. Why should we contend about words?" (*Works*, VIII, 291).[39]
>
> I believe it [the new birth] to be an inward thing; a change from inward wickedness to inward goodness; an entire change of our inmost nature from the image of the devil (wherein we were born) to the image of God, a change from the love of the creature to the love of the Creator; from earthly and sensual, to heavenly and holy affections;—in a word, a change from the tempers of the spirit of darkness to those of the angels of God in heaven (*Works*, I. 225).

This was new. While Nazarenes had long recognized that the first work of grace could be considered an "initial sanctification," the emphasis throughout the denomination's history had been on the marvelous effects of the *second* work of grace. Justification was popularly understood as a relatively minor preface to the truly significant work of God, which was, of course, entire sanctification. While John Wesley had cautioned against this depreciation of justification,[40] it was very difficult to do particularly when the reason for the denomination's being was the preservation and propagation of the doctrine of entire sanctification. Wynkoop, however, heeded Wesley's warning. Throughout *A Theology in Love,* she described the first work of grace in terms that had been previously reserved for the second.

> When a person is "saved" he is wholly saved. God, by His grace . . . saves the whole man. Involving a personal act and a Person acting and a person reacting to God's personal action, salvation is complete and extends to the whole of the person's being . . . God does not partially save and then fully save . . . Sin is not partially destroyed at one time and fully destroyed at another, nor is a second work of grace for the purpose of correcting the defects of the first. At least there is no biblical warrant for this kind of explanation. The *"second crisis" is . . . not different in degree, from the first.*[41]

It sounded like Wynkoop was suggesting that sin was entirely destroyed in the life of the believer in the first work of grace. This would not be correct since Wynkoop had rejected that kind of substantive language. Sin wasn't "destroyed" in the first work of grace because there wasn't anything needing to be destroyed. "Sin" was not a *thing,* not an ontological entity in its own right. Salvation was a quality of relationship. What this did mean, however, was that the initial restoration of that relationship was the most significant moment of grace. Wynkoop's "corrective" emphasis on the first moment of salvation had the effect, as far as traditional Nazarenes were concerned, of depreciating the second. This was not her intent. She believed she had fully justified the need for a second crisis. It, too, was just not based on any*thing* needing to be destroyed. The second pivotal crisis, which Nazarenes had called entire sanctification and they had previously understood as a work of grace that eradicated the sinful nature, was, as far as Wynkoop was concerned, simply a consequence of the nature of spiritual maturation, which (one hoped) would result in an eventual entire consecration.

Perhaps the most challenging implication of her reconceptualization of the doctrine of entire sanctification concerned the doctrine of the baptism of the Holy Spirit. The denomination's Article of Faith on sin stated that "original sin continues to exist with the new life of the regenerate, until eradicated by *the baptism with the Holy Spirit.*"[42] According to Wynkoop, and contrary to the Nazarenes' traditional understanding, entire sanctification was not effected by the baptism with the Holy Spirit. The occasion of the believer's reception of the Holy Spirit was the *first* work of grace. "We cannot divide the Holy Spirit up so that we receive a part of Him at one time and more of Him at another time. The Holy Spirit is a person and comes as a Person and He relates himself to persons. When one is saved, the Holy Spirit comes to him."[43]

Wynkoop appealed to 19th-century Holiness professor Daniel Steele concerning this "novel" understanding of the baptism of the Holy Spirit. Steele had written, in *Steele's Answers*[44] that John Wesley never referred to entire sanctification as the baptism with the Holy Spirit.

"The baptism of (or with) the Spirit," and "fullness of the Spirit," are not phrases used by [Wesley], probably because there is an emotional fullness of a temporary nature, not going down to the very roots of the moral nature. Nor did he use "receiving the Holy Spirit," because in a sense of entire sanctification" the phrase is not scriptural and not quite proper; for they all received the Holy Ghost when they were justified.[45]

Wynkoop also declared that the understanding that the baptism of the Holy Spirit was the occasion of entire sanctification could not be supported by scripture.

In the interest of clarity, it is well to note that Jesus, in John 17, did not indicate the manner in which sanctification would take place. He did not equate it with the coming of the Holy Spirit; in fact the Holy Spirit is not mentioned in the prayer. Though theology is inclined to relate them, it is of interest to note that *so far as any specific scripture* is concerned, the Pentecostal experience is not said to be an answer to Jesus' prayer in John 17. . . . In fact never is sanctification, as such, directly identified with the coming of the Spirit on that day.[46]

Thus, according to Wynkoop, entire sanctification did not eradicate the sinful nature. Entire sanctification was not essentially different from initial sanctification. Entire sanctification was a probable but not necessary crisis in the salvation process. Entire sanctification was not the occasion of the baptism with the Holy Spirit.

For most Nazarenes in 1973, this was all quite revolutionary, and it is perhaps a testament to the difficulties that the traditional understanding of the doctrine was encountering that Wynkoop's work was received and published by the denomination's publishing house at all. Granted, she did write,

> Wesleyan theology asserts: (1) that sanctification is a "this-life" experience, (2) that it is a relationship to God logically distinct from and morally of quite a different dimension than "justification," (3) that it follows regeneration, (4) that it is crisis-oriented, and (5) that in a proper sense it can be called a "second crisis."[47]

Yet her explication of the distinctive doctrine of the Church of the Nazarene was considerably removed from the church's traditional understanding. While her intent was to provide a more adequate conceptual framework for the doctrine and therefore "justify" it for a contemporary audience, her definitions tended to undermine the doctrine's distinctiveness. Perhaps a sentence from one of the last pages of *A Theology of Love* will highlight this depreciation. Recommending a name for entire sanctification, she wrote: "If one could allow a rather general expression for the sake of putting up a signpost, "an experience beyond conversion" would be a useful designation."[48]

The Debate on the Baptism with the Holy Spirit

Mildred Bangs Wynkoop's *A Theology of Love* was not the only challenge to the traditional Nazarene understanding of the doctrine of entire sanctification in the seventh and eighth decades of the century. Her book might be considered the first Wesleyan theology formulated by a respected Nazarene theologian that deviated from the typical American-Holiness explication, but she was certainly not alone in her critique of Nazarene "orthodoxy." As has already been noted, many in the Church of the Nazarene had been "rediscovering John Wesley" and noticing the variances between his and the denomination's understanding of entire sanctification. *The Heart of Wesley's Faith,* which contained John Wesley's *A Plain Account of Christian Perfection,* had become required reading in the Ministerial Course of Study in 1960. Leo Cox's *John Wesley's Concept of Perfection* was recommended in 1964 and George Allen Turner's *The Vision Which Transforms* was added in 1968. The issue that became, more than any other, a source of considerable conflict and debate concerned the doctrine of the baptism with the Holy Spirit. Nazarene orthodoxy had stated that the baptism of the Holy Spirit was the moment of entire sanctification. This understanding of Pentecost as the occasion of the disciples' entire sanctification provided biblical justification for the interpretation of the doctrine as an instantaneous second work of grace subsequent to justification. However, as Wynkoop had noted in *A Theology of Love*, this was not Wesley's understanding of the baptism of the Holy Spirit. Wesley considered that every believer had received the Holy Spirit upon conversion. Leo Cox had written a decade before Wynkoop:

> According to Wesley one was not yet a Christian if he had not received the Holy Spirit. A Christian is one who is "anointed with the Holy Ghost, and with power." . . . In 1744 he believed that no one has salvation until he receives the Holy Ghost. . . . This teaching of Wesley may appear strange to some who insist that the Holy Spirit is given subsequent to regeneration at the time of a "second blessing," but in this concept Wesley is at one with most Reformed teaching.[49]

George Allen Turner briefly acknowledged the same. "John and Charles said or wrote little about the baptism in the Holy Spirit. This emphasis is relatively recent. It is not easy to find Wesleyan writers devoting much space to it or associating it with entire sanctification."[50]

The *Wesleyan Theological Journal* became a forum for the debate, publishing over 15 articles on the matter between 1973 and 1982. In the 1979 spring and fall issues, Alex R. G. Deasley, J. Kenneth Grider, and Mildred Bangs Wynkoop, all professors at Nazarene Theological Seminary at the time, and George Allen Turner of Asbury Theological Seminary were among the nine scholars who submitted articles to the journal, defending either the classical "Wesleyan" interpretation or the "Nazarene" position. Theologians in the Church of the Nazarene were significantly divided over the issue.

Hoping to clarify the issues among Nazarenes, Dr. Rob Staples read a paper summarizing the current debate at a breakfast meeting of Nazarene seminary faculty in March of 1979. At the time, Staples was a theology professor at Nazarene Theological Seminary along with Mildred Bangs Wynkoop. He had formerly been a professor of theology at Bethany Nazarene College and was an alumnus of Trevecca Nazarene College. In this 39-page paper, Staples restated what was becoming common knowledge in the denomination: that Wesley did not equate entire sanctification with the baptism with the Holy Spirit. Rather, according to the most recent holiness scholarship, this equation of entire sanctification with the baptism of the Holy Spirit was an American addition to Wesley's doctrine coming primarily from outside the Wesleyan tradition via Charles G. Finney and New School Presbyterianism. After 23 pages of historical review, Staples then expounded on some implications of the debate for the Church of the Nazarene. He referred to the Articles of Faith as being inconsistent with the classical "Wesleyan" understanding of the baptism with the Holy Spirit and stated:

> When one considers the historical situation in which the Articles were framed, and the immediate religious soil from which the Church of the Nazarene sprang, it is perhaps indisputable that what the statements were meant to convey is the position of the nineteenth century holiness movement in which entire sanctification is described as the baptism with the Holy Spirit. There is no evidence, however, that any divergence from Wesley was intended . . . That they were apparently wrong in this assumption presents a dilemma for a growing number of Wesleyan scholars in general, and Nazarene scholars in particular, who are convinced that sound exegesis does not support the view which equates Spirit baptism with entire sanctification. Rather, these exegetes believe that Spirit baptism in the New Testament generally, and in Luke-Acts particularly, is initiatory in its meaning. . . . They are convinced that Wesley's position on this issue was more biblical than that of the American holiness movement of the nineteenth century which, according to Timothy Smith, was turned into its present direction by Oberlin evangelist Charles G. Finney.[51]

The problem, as Staples well knew, was that this "more biblical Wesleyan position" was inconsistent with the Church of the Nazarene's Articles of Faith, and this was particularly problematic for professors in the denomination's colleges and seminary. Yet he contended that fidelity to biblical truth took priority over fidelity to a denomination's "creed." According to Staples, "Creeds are but the church's human articulation of the message of the Bible. . . . The church must keep alert to the priority of the gospel over the creeds. The church's demand for loyalty to the creeds must basically be a demand for loyalty to the *kerygma*."[52]

Staples proposed two solutions in that breakfast meeting. The first solution to the dilemma could be found in an attempt on the part of church leaders to change the Articles of Faith of the denomination, though he believed that such an attempt at that particular time in the church's history would be divisive and counterproductive. He instead issued, in the spirit of John Wesley, a call for a tolerant attitude among persons of divergent beliefs. "Attitudinally, we must draw upon Wesley's 'Catholic Spirit,' and reaffirm that when we cannot think alike we may still love alike, and when we are not of one opinion we still are of one heart."[53]

The third part of his paper was a call for a "holistic approach" to the baptism with the Spirit. Here Staples suggested that the denomination follow John Fletcher's lead in not restricting the number of baptisms of the Holy Spirit. Staples quoted from an article in the *Wesleyan Theological Journal* by David Cubie titled, *"Perfection in Wesley and Fletcher."*

> Fletcher teaches that the baptism with the Holy Spirit is repeated in a succession of events beginning with the new birth and concluding with glory. Though crisis is present in "a Baptism with the Holy Spirit," what is occurring in most lives is a series of crises, i.e., of baptisms until perfection is attained. Thus Fletcher would ask not whether a believer had received his baptism, but whether he or she had "received the Comforter in his fullness." Christian perfection is not defined by or identical with an experience. One cannot say, I have been baptized with the Holy Spirit; therefore my heart is perfect in love. Instead, for Fletcher, each baptism is a divine effusion cleansing the heart as far as faith is able to receive, usually necessitating further baptism until the believer is perfected in love.[54]

Staples believed that the divergent interpretations of the baptism with the Holy Spirit could be accommodated within this "holistic" approach. Those who believed that the first work of grace was the occasion of the baptism with the Holy Spirit were correct, and those who believed that the second work of grace was the occasion for the baptism with the Holy Spirit were correct also.

For the most part, Staples's paper lay unnoticed until the church's latest commissioned systematic theology raised the same issue over the proper interpretation of the baptism with the Holy Spirit. H. Ray Dunning, chairman of the Department of Religion and Philosophy at Trevecca Nazarene College, had been asked by the Board of General Superintendents in the fall of 1979 to write a contemporary one-volume systematic theology to replace H. Orton Wiley's three volume set, which had been in use now for almost half a century. The church had considered simply updating Wiley's *Christian Theology,* but Dr. Westlake Purkiser, professor at Nazarene Theological Seminary, after considering the matter for almost a year, recommended that Wiley's work remain as it was. In addition to recommending Dunning, the Board of General Superintendents also recommended that an editorial board be appointed to work with Dunning to provide limited "oversight" of the project. The recommendation of an editorial board to oversee this "official" theology reflected the concern on the part of some that Dunning's systematic theology be truly representative of the denomination's historic position on the doctrine of entire sanctification. Two weeks after Dunning accepted the assignment, General Superintendent Dr. William M. Greathouse, who had been president of Trevecca Nazarene College and president of Nazarene Theological Seminary before being elected general superintendent, wrote a letter in February of 1980 to M. A. (Bud) Lunn, manager of the Nazarene Publishing House, acknowledging that Dunning would be forced to address this contentious and potentially divisive issue.

> Naturally, there are sensitive areas where Ray {Dunning} will need to enter into deep consultation with the committee. It is becoming increasingly evident that the modern holiness movement which developed in the nineteenth century incorporated within its theological position a number of non-Wesleyan elements. Among these are Phoebe Palmer's "altar theology" as well as a new view of the baptism of the Holy Spirit developed by New School Presbyterian Charles G. Finney. The latter issue is especially sensitive, as you well know. Ray is sensitized at these points as well as others. I believe he has the intellectual and spiritual maturity to produce a work that will be irenic. I predict, however, that there will be some interesting discussions along the way since there are varying points of view on the advisory committee.[55]

"I predict . . . that there will be some interesting discussions along the way" would turn out to be a great understatement, for Dunning, in his church-commissioned systematic theology, did not identify the baptism of the Holy Spirit with entire sanctification, just as Wynkoop and Staples had not. In the letter to Lunn, Dr. Greathouse concluded by expressing the same hope that Staples had expressed, namely that an inclusive interpretation of the Articles of Faith would be able to accommodate a view of entire sanctification that diverged from the historic position.

> Perhaps I feel more strongly than some others that John Wesley was a true reformer whose insights and understandings are more truly scriptural than some of the later advocates of holiness. At the same time, I am absolutely sure that the Articles of Faith of the Church of the Nazarene were intentionally framed with enough breadth to bind all holiness advocates and witnesses together even though their private views at minor points may happen to differ.[56]

Others were not so "absolutely sure" that the Articles of Faith of the Church of the Nazarene were framed with enough breadth to accommodate these alternative understandings of the distinctive doctrine. While Greathouse would have liked to consider these variations of understanding "minor points," many others did not, and Dr. Rob Staples's paper, presented at a breakfast club for Nazarene Theological Seminary professors, became the focal point of this divisive issue.

The problem was becoming more than just an academic issue debated by Holiness scholars in academic journals and at obscure breakfast clubs. It was becoming a denominational issue because increasingly pastors trained in the denomination's schools under some of these professors were no longer preaching the traditional doctrine. Furthermore, they were not afraid to acknowledge to their district superintendents their disagreement with the Article of Faith statement on entire sanctification. Dr. Greathouse, in a June 22, 1982, letter to Dr. Dunning, mentioned the problem.

> A district superintendent in this area has three men up for license who have said they do not agree with the statement in our Article that entire sanctification is "wrought by the baptism with the Holy Spirit." They acknowledge they came to this view in Rob's (Staples) classes. The superintendent has met with Rob, who gave him his (breakfast club) paper. I am to meet with the superintendent next week. So this is already becoming an issue.[57]

That a Nazarene Theological Seminary professor was teaching doctrine not perceived to be in conformity to the denomination's stated doctrinal position was a problem. Granted, Staples wasn't alone. The occasion, however, upon which the doctrinal issue came to a head was over whether or not the Nazarene Theological Seminary Board of Trustees should grant tenure to Dr. Rob Staples. In short, if Staples's position, that entire sanctification was not *"the* baptism with the Holy Spirit," could not be accommodated by the denomination's Articles of Faith, then the Board of Trustees would be justified in *not* granting tenure to Dr. Staples. If Staples's position could be accommodated by the Articles of Faith, then the board would be obligated to grant it.

In 1983, the Board of Trustees of the seminary appealed to the Board of General Superintendents for an interpretation of the Articles of Faith as they related to Staples's interpretation. In particular, they wanted to know if Dr. Staples's position (that entire sanctification was not the only occasion of the baptism of the Holy Spirit) would be an acceptable interpretation of the Articles of Faith (which stated that entire sanctification was "wrought by the baptism with the Holy Spirit").[58] Clearly, this was a matter that transcended the granting of tenure to a single seminary professor. The denomination had already published Wynkoop's *A Theology of Love* with great fanfare 10 years earlier and Wynkoop had not equated the baptism with the Holy Spirit and entire sanctification. Dr. Dunning was in the process of writing a commissioned systematic theology that would also be perceived as at odds with the denomination's Articles of Faith. Dr. Greathouse, past president of one of the denomination's colleges and its graduate school seminary and currently a presiding general superintendent, was clearly sympathetic to Wynkoop's, Staples's, and Dunning's views concerning the matter.[59] While the focus was acutely on Staples, the implication of the general superintendents' ruling was far-reaching, which is perhaps why the Board of Trustees handed the matter over to them.

In the fall of 1983, Dr. Staples sent his breakfast club paper with a 16-page addendum to the Board of General Superintendents. In this addendum, Staples brought to the attention of the general superintendents that Alex R. G. Deasley, professor of New Testament at the seminary, had written in an article in the *Wesleyan Theological Journal* that H. Orton Wiley devoted only a single page to the baptism of the Holy Spirit and that "the structure of his argument for entire sanctification is not affected by it in the least degree."[60] He also informed the general superintendents that prior to 1923, the *Manual* in its Article of Faith on "Entire Sanctification" "did not contain the Spirit-baptism language which is found in the present form of the Article."[61] He referred to the Deasley article again to support his holistic interpretation of the baptism of the Holy Spirit. Staples wrote:

> Whereas Fletcher held that "many baptisms of the Spirit" may be necessary to bring about entire sanctification, Deasley makes Spirit-baptism the all-embracing category, with regeneration and entire sanctification being different aspects or phases of Spirit-baptism. From the standpoint of current biblical scholarship, Deasley's view doubtless has more to commend it. But both Deasley's view and Fletcher's are in harmony with the Nazarene Articles of Faith in which it is declared that entire sanctification is "wrought by" the baptism with the Holy Spirit."[62]

On March 2, 1984, Dr. William Greathouse, secretary of the Board of General Superintendents, sent a letter to Dr. Paul Cunningham, chairman of the Board of Trustees of Nazarene Theological Seminary, to inform him of their ruling. They agreed with Dr. Staples. Dr. Greathouse wrote, in part:

> As you requested, Dr. Rob Staples sent copies of his paper to each member of our Board, to which he appended a rather detailed clarification of his personal position on sensitive issues, in particular his view of the relationship of Pentecost to the entire sanctification of the apostles. It is the consensus of the Board that Dr. Staples' view is in accord with our interpretation of Article X.
>
> After thoughtful consideration and discussion of these issues, the Board of General Superintendents voted to communicate to the Board of Trustees of Nazarene Theological Seminary, through you as chairman, the action:
>
> The Board of General Superintendents rules that Article X of the Nazarene "Articles of Faith" is an adequate articulation of the bibli-

cal doctrine of entire sanctification as understood by historic Methodism and the modern holiness movement, recognizing as it does "various terms representing its different phases, such as "Christian perfection," "perfect love," "heart purity," "the baptism with the Holy Spirit," "the fullness of the blessing" and "Christian holiness."

We reaffirm the historic position of the Church of the Nazarene that the apostles, previously converted, were entirely sanctified by the baptism with the Holy Spirit on the Day of Pentecost and remain for us models of Christian holiness.[63]

Dr. Staples was subsequently granted tenure by the Nazarene Theological Seminary Board of Trustees. Not everyone, however, was pleased with the general superintendents' ruling. The Article of Faith on entire sanctification, as Dr. Staples had made clear in his paper, had been historically understood as stating that entire sanctification was *the* baptism with the Holy Spirit and not *a* baptism with the Holy Spirit. The ruling by the Board of General Superintendents reflected a more elastic interpretation of the doctrine than had ever been given before. The chairman of the Board of Trustees of the seminary, Dr. Paul Cunningham, wrote to Dr. Staples about the general superintendents' decision and indicated his perplexity concerning it.

Among other things, he mentioned to Staples that Wiley did in fact state that the baptism with the Spirit was entire sanctification.[64] Expressing the grave concern that was on many minds at the time, Cunningham wrote: "It is difficult for me to understand how our pastors in the making, and the constituents to whom they will ultimately minister can accept our distinctive doctrine of entire sanctification when it is preached on a multiple choice basis."[65]

In any event, the denomination now had a theological "ruling" that permitted a broad understanding of the doctrine of entire sanctification. According to the most official decision the denomination had at its disposal, entire sanctification was *the* occasion of the baptism of the Holy Spirit and thus quite a distinct work of grace. But entire sanctification was also *an* occasion of *a* baptism with the Holy Spirit, and thus not *that* distinct. Both were acceptable interpretations of the Articles of Faith. However, with this ruling, the distinctive doctrine of the Church of the Nazarene was continuing to become less and less "distinct."

A "SUBVERSIVE" THEOLOGY

In 1980, when Dr. H. Ray Dunning accepted the commission to write a systematic theology to replace Wiley's, he had no idea the intensity of the conflict his theology was going to generate in the denomination nor did he know that some would consider it nothing less than "subversive" to the holiness theology of the Church of the Nazarene.[66] It was eventually published as *Grace, Faith and Holiness: A Wesleyan Systematic Theology* by Beacon Hill Press of Kansas City in 1988 and added to the Ministerial Course of Study in 1990, but for a time there was a question whether it would be published by the Nazarene Publishing House at all. That it was finally approved to be published was in part due to the fact that the commission for the work was changed. When the project had first been conceived, it was thought that Dunning would write a systematic theology to replace Wiley's and become the standard holiness theology of the Church of the Nazarene. This is the implication of the official letter Dunning received from the manager of the Nazarene Publishing House, M. A. (Bud) Lunn.

> Perhaps you have heard by now that you have been approved by the Board of General Superintendents to author a new single volume systematic theology. Possibly it would have to be a two-volume set, but our current thinking is only one. At the time we published our biblical theology, *God, Man and Salvation,* we promised that Board of General Superintendents we would eventually develop a new systematic theology.[67]

This was the understanding of at least one of the members of the editorial board appointed to "oversee" Dunning's work. Richard Taylor, professor emeritus of Nazarene Theological Seminary and editor of the *Beacon Dictionary of Theology,* wrote to Dr. John Knight, a fellow editorial board member and general superintendent of the denomination:

> My general understanding was that Ray Dunning was to prepare a systematic theology for primary use in the Church of the Nazarene, as a suitable training guide for Nazarene students and candidates for the ministry; also an available reference or study work for interested laymen. In some measure at least it was to replace Wiley as the "official" Nazarene theological statement.[68]

According to Taylor, however, Dunning's theology was not representative of the doctrine of the Church of the Nazarene and therefore should not be published. In that same letter, he informed Dr. Knight that:

> Any systematic theology which supposedly expounds the doctrine of the Church of the Nazarene must be the interface of the full unabridged Articles of Faith. I do not mean that these Articles must dictate the format of the work, but that the work must be faithful to the doctrinal positions which are the official positions of the *Manual.* We have no right to approve for the study of candidates for the ministry or for use in Nazarene colleges any textbook which deviates from these positions. Only the General Assembly, backed by the Districts, has authority to change our doctrinal positions. To endorse a

textbook which in any significant point departed from the *Manual* or shifted the center of gravity from traditional, mainline Wesleyanism to a new or aberrant center would be impermissible as an act and disastrous in its consequences, not the least of which would be to *officially* render our Creedal Statement a dead letter.[69]

After writing about several of his specific concerns, Taylor recommended that it be published as a private monograph, as Wynkoop's theology had been, rather than as an official Nazarene textbook.

When the project was published by the Nazarene Publishing House, it was *not* presented as the "official" theology of the Church of the Nazarene, but as a *representative* theology of the Church of the Nazarene. This "compromise" was recommended by W. T. Purkiser, another one of the editorial board members. In 1986, after Dunning had completed his work and two years before it was published, the issues had become so contentious and irreconcilable that this seemed the only avenue available for its publication. At the end of a letter in which Purkiser pointed out some of the difficulties he was having with the book, he wrote to General Superintendent Dr. John Knight:

> I want to raise one question that this committee cannot really answer. That is whether or not we have outgrown the need for and possibility of an "official theology." I doubt seriously that anyone can do now what H. Orton Wiley did 45 years ago. Our church is getting more and more pluralistic all the time, and we are able to tolerate different points of view on non-essential matters. Perhaps there is room for more than one theology in the church.[70]

When it was published, the foreword, signed by the general superintendents, defended the work and declared that it was consistent with the doctrinal positions of the Church of the Nazarene.

> The Book Committee serving Nazarene Publishing House, with the approval of the Board of General Superintendents, commissioned Dr. H. Ray Dunning to produce a systematic theology in the Wesleyan tradition that is true to the doctrinal standards of the Church of the Nazarene and at the same time is aware of, and dialogues with, contemporary thought theologically, philosophically, psychologically, and culturally.[71]

The foreword also acknowledged, however, that Dunning's theology was not going to please everyone.

> In a work of this magnitude not every affirmation will solicit full agreement from all readers. But the fundamental declarations of faith are biblically and doctrinally sound and consistent with the *Wesleyan* tradition. Dr. Phineas F. Bresee's words serve us well at this point: "In essentials unity, in nonessentials liberty, and in all things charity."[72]

Dr. H. Ray Dunning's systematic theology was different. He intended it to be. In the preface, Dunning wrote: "The method herein proposed is considerably different from the way systematic theology has been pursued in the Wesleyan tradition."[73] While the foreword by the general superintendents declared it to be "a theology in the Wesleyan tradition that [was] true to the doctrinal standards of the Church of the Nazarene," its presuppositions and emphases were such that it could easily be (and to some, justifiably) interpreted as divergent. That it could be understood as faithful to the doctrines of the denomination was due to the kind of interpretations of the Articles of Faith that had accommodated Staples's view of the baptism with the Holy Spirit and due in no small part to the fact that Dunning's work was a sophisticated theology with highly nuanced definitions and subtle articulations. One of the criticisms leveled at the book by some of the editorial board members was that it was too specialized. He wrote as a theologian with theologians in mind.

As Wynkoop had a decade earlier, Dunning adopted a "relational model of ontology in contrast to substantial modes of thought."[74] According to Dunning, a person's essence was constituted primarily by their relation to God. Man qua man did not exist and it was this essential relation to God that defined a person's being. According to Dunning, failure to recognize persons as intrinsically related beings had given rise to all kinds of confusions and had proven theologically inadequate, particularly for a comprehensible explication of the doctrine of entire sanctification. "Substantial modes of describing man's state of being in sin makes entire sanctification difficult if not impossible to fit logically into a theological conceptuality."[75] He called for the rejection of much of the language that had traditionally been used to explain the doctrines of the church. "I feel we must abandon the (substantial) terminology in order to fully clear ourselves from the implications it carries to the modern reader."[76] Neither did he hesitate to assert that a "fixation" on a particular historical formulation of doctrine resulted in irrelevance and even perversion of the doctrine.

> This perversion always takes place when some historically conditioned formulation of the Christian faith is crystallized and held onto as the final statement as in the case of . . . any theologian of the holiness movement sanctifying the 19th-century formulations."[77]

He credited the traditional formulations of holiness doctrine with creating what Wynkoop had coined "the credibility gap."

> The result of applying non-personal explanations to personal life is not only less than helpful in any practical way but also creates what Mildred Bangs Wynkoop has termed a "credibility gap." This is a gap between doctrine and life that ultimately causes skepticism concerning the real practicality of theological analyses.[78]

According to Dunning, a "relational model of ontology" would make viable again a doctrine of a real sanctification and, in particular, make the doctrine of freedom from sin an actually comprehensible possibility. This would be due primarily to his relational definition of sin. Dunning wrote on the first page of the fourth section of his systematic theology, titled "The Doctrines of God the Savior," in the chapter on "Man the Sinner," that:

> Sin does not exist independently of man. It is furthermore not to be regarded as some flawed or defective part of human nature. . . . So we must not so much speak about sin as about man as sinner. W. T. Purkiser states that sin "is best defined not as a thing, an entity or quantity having ontic status, but as the moral condition of a personal being."[79]

According to Dunning, sin as an act was whatever violated the relationship between God and man[80] and sin as "original" was understood as the loss of the pre-Fall relation between God and man. Thus, "sin [was] not the result of man's creaturehood or in any sense the result of forces or factors beyond his control. It [was] the consequence of the exercise of his God-given gift of freedom."[81] Dunning did not, however, reduce his definition of sin to simply privation of relationship. He did acknowledge a positive perversion of human "nature" that resulted from the Fall. "There is a positive aspect in the sense that man in his natural state as it is now is corrupt in every aspect of his being."[82] But he insisted that this sinful state of being must always be comprehended relationally, defined essentially as his lost relation to God.[83]

Since sin was not an inevitable condition of a person's creatureliness and since it did not have ontic status, then there was the possibility for persons to be "cleansed" from sin. As had Wynkoop, so did Dunning define holiness as single-minded devotion to Christ. "Mildred Bangs Wynkoop is correct in defining sin as 'love locked into a false center, the self,' and holiness as 'love locked into the True Center, Jesus Christ our Lord.'"[84] Right relatedness was the essence of holiness.

> [Wesley] learned that the essence of piety was inward and intentional. "Purity of intention" was the phrase he used to speak of what he learned from (Jeremy) Taylor. This paved the way for his recognition that while man can never be restored to the image of God in any legal sense . . . he can be perfectly related to Him in terms of love. . . . Consequently, when he was asked what Christian perfection or entire sanctification meant, he always replied, "It is loving God with the whole heart, soul, mind, and strength," and "our neighbor as ourselves." While in our fallen condition we can never achieve the level of perfect performance and be restored to the image of God in its un-

tarnished splendor, we may, by grace, stand in perfect relation to Him through the "expulsive power of a new affection."[85]

This definition of holiness as right relationship resulted in some different emphases when it came to the specific understanding of sanctification. In the space of two and a half pages, Dunning made five unequivocal theological pronouncements concerning sanctification, all of which, while fairly representing a "Wesleyan" understanding of the doctrine, did not fully represent the American-Holiness Movement's formulation. He prefaced these five pronouncements by distinguishing between "ceremonial" sanctification, in which a person or a thing is *rendered* sacred by its relation to God, and the "ethical" use of the term, in which a person is *actually* made righteous. Considering sanctification in the ethical sense led Dunning to his first "exegetically derived theological proposition": "Sanctification is logically subsequent to justification."[86] Since justification was a relative change while sanctification implied a real change in the condition or "nature" of persons, sanctification had to be logically subsequent to justification. To this everyone in the Holiness Movement agreed. The next pronouncement, however, was a bit more controversial. In light of the ceremonial use of the term "sanctification," Dunning stated his second theological proposition: "All believers are sanctified."[87] Furthermore, since "ceremonial" sanctification cannot be absolutely distinguished from the "ethical," Dunning posited a third theological proposition similar to the second. According to Dunning, justification and sanctification, while logically distinct were chronologically simultaneous."[88] "Saved and sanctified" happened at the same time! This was revolutionary and demanded an immediate clarification. "That is, at the moment of justification, in that same instant, the process of sanctification begins, although it is not a completed work. . . ."[89]

Because the moment of justification inaugurated the process of sanctification, Dunning, as Wynkoop had, placed more emphasis on the radical nature of the change of the first work of grace than on the second. Dunning quoted Wesley's description of the new birth as

> that great change which God works in the soul when He brings it into life; when He raises it from the death of sin to the life of righteousness. It is the change wrought in the whole soul by the almighty Spirit of God when it is "created anew in Christ Jesus"; when it is "renewed after the image of God in righteousness and true holiness"; when the love of the world is changed into the love of God; pride into humility; passion into meekness; hatred, envy, malice, into a sincere, tender, disinterested love for all mankind.[90]

Forty pages later, when writing of sanctification, Dunning again quoted one of Wesley's lengthy descriptions of conversion or the first work of grace.

> There is as great a change wrought in our souls when we are born of the Spirit, as was wrought in our bodies when we are born of a woman. There is, in that hour, a general change from inward sinfulness, to inward holiness. The love of the creature is changed to the love of the Creator; the love of the world into the love of God. Earthly desires, the desire of the flesh, the desire of the eyes, and the pride of life, are, in that instant, changed by the mighty power of God, into heavenly desires. . . . Pride and haughtiness subside into lowliness of heart, as do anger, with all turbulent and unruly passions, into calmness, meekness, and gentleness. In a word, the earthly, sensual, devilish mind, gives place to "the mind that was in Christ Jesus."[91]

These sounded like descriptions that had previously been reserved for the second work of grace or entire sanctification. Dunning was insistent, however, on the first work of grace, which had previously been considered primarily as justification, as being sanctifying.

> What Wesley consistently does is apply his generic definitions of sanctification to regeneration, showing that he understands it to be a particular expression of the work of the Spirit in restoring man to the image of God, a real change involving true holiness.[92]

His fourth unequivocal theological proposition concerned the baptism with the Holy Spirit. Regarding the activity of the Holy Spirit, Dunning wrote: "All believers, being sanctified by the Holy Spirit, are recipients of the Spirit."[93] This interpretation of the doctrine of the Holy Spirit was consistent with what Wynkoop had written in her "personal monograph" but it was also what had almost cost Dr. Rob Staples his tenure at Nazarene Theological Seminary, had the general superintendents not provided an interpretation of the Articles of Faith that accommodated this understanding. Dunning's pronouncement, however, in a commissioned "Nazarene" systematic theology, which described the activity of the Holy Spirit in terms that had also previously been strictly reserved for the moment of "entire" sanctification was even more "undermining" of the denomination's historical understanding. His last theological proposition concerned the content of the sanctified life. "Sanctification in the New Testament is oriented toward Jesus Christ."[94] That is, the goal of sanctification was Christlikeness.

Dunning elaborated on this fourth theological proposition in his section on the Holy Spirit in a chapter titled "The Christian Experience of the Holy Spirit." He cautioned against using the early Christian experiences of the Holy Spirit as found in the Book of Acts as a paradigm for later believers. "It is not Luke's primary intention to provide a normative or normal pattern of individual experience. Obviously, there are implications to be drawn here, but to make this an exegetical principle will lead to mass confusion."[95] However, it could be understood from the biblical evidence that the gift of the Holy Spirit to the disciples on the day of Pentecost was sanctifying.

> Those who received the Spirit in His fullness understood that not only were they being given a special kind of power to carry on Jesus' mission in the world, but they also were being transformed into a new existence that involved a through-and-through sanctification of their natures.[96]

He even went so far as to identify the Day of Pentecost with the occasion of entire sanctification for *some* of the believers who received the Holy Spirit on that day.

> For those who had lived with Jesus and come through the 40-day training session about what had happened and what was about to happen, it doubtless led them to the full dispensation of the Spirit (Fletcher), and their baptism with the Spirit resulted in full or entire sanctification.[97]

The baptism with the Holy Spirit was not to be exclusively identified with entire sanctification, however, because the extent of the Holy Spirit's work was contingent on the faith and understanding of the recipient. "We are suggesting that both the measure and character of the Spirit's work was the result of the understanding faith of those who appropriated Him at any point in their experience."[98] Thus, there can be many "baptisms" with the Holy Spirit. The baptism with the Holy Spirit that would result in an experience of entire sanctification would be determined by the believer. "The result of the Spirit's filling is correlative to the recipient's understanding and appropriating faith."[99]

Dunning's doctrine of the Holy Spirit and his identifying justification as concomitant with sanctification led him to emphasize the continuity of the salvation process more than the crises. It should be stated that he did recognize a moment in the sanctifying process which could be identified as a second crisis experience known as entire sanctification.

> Wesley interprets the Christian life as a process of developing love that moves along in part by way of definable stages. Love is instilled in the heart in regeneration. From that point on, there is a gradual development that knows no finis, not even death. But there is an instantaneous moment in the process that may be called perfect love, or entire sanctification, perfect only in the sense of being unmixed.[100]

Dunning's focus, as Wynkoop's had been, was on the process of sanctification that began in regeneration. As Wynkoop had done, Dunning also did not distinguish any qualitative difference between the two works of grace. Referring again to Wesley, Dunning wrote: "It is unequivocal that

Wesley equated regeneration with the first movement of sanctifying grace in the soul. Although it was complete in a moment, it was not qualitatively different from the subsequent working of grace."[101]

He so stressed the continuity of the sanctifying process that he came close to suggesting that the second crisis was inconspicuous. Dunning quoted Lindstrom's analysis of Wesley to make this point.

What then, from this point of view is the difference between new birth and perfect sanctification? Love has already been instilled into the heart of man at new birth. From then on there is a gradual development. This is thought to continue even after the stage of perfect sanctification until the very moment of death—indeed after death too. There is therefore, Wesley thinks, no perfection of degrees, i.e. no perfection of concluded development. The distinction between new birth and entire sanctification seems therefore to be nothing more than a difference of degree in a continuous development.[102]

Dunning's comment immediately following Lindstrom's analysis of Wesley is instructive. He wrote:

(Renewing man in the image of God) commences at the dawn of spiritual life and continues—ideally—in an uninterrupted progression throughout all finite existence. Therefore one should never ask the question, "At what point in the Christian life does this occur?" It is occurring from the beginning on.[103]

Dunning's definition of entire sanctification in terms of intention or motive, along with his emphasis on the process of sanctification, precluded the kinds of specific descriptions of the life of the entirely sanctified that previous holiness writers had written. There were no glorious portrayals of the life of the entirely sanctified to be distinguished from the "merely" saved in either Wynkoop or Dunning. Dunning described entire sanctification as Wesley (and Wynkoop) had. "When [Wesley] was asked what . . . entire sanctification meant, he always replied, 'It is the loving God with the whole heart, soul, mind, and strength,' and 'our neighbor as ourselves.'"[104] And Dunning was quick to note that this did not imply any kind of perfectionism.

While in our fallen condition we can never achieve the level of perfect performance and be restored to the image of God in its untarnished splendor, we may, by grace, stand in perfect relation to Him through the "expulsive power of a new affection" (Thomas Chalmers). And from that point, man can seek ever more perfectly to reflect God's character in his character and personality until the beauty of Jesus is more and more seen in and through his life.[105]

This sanctification process that began with justification and included along the way an experience of entire sanctification resulted in the continuous renewal of persons in the image of God. This "renewal" or "restoration" Dunning defined relationally—in terms of freedom. There were four fundamental freedoms: freedom for God, freedom for other persons, freedom from the earth, and freedom from self-domination.[106] He understood "freedom for God" to mean living in the presence of God, obedient to God, and evidencing various aspects of His love, such as joy, peace, patience, etc.[107] "Freedom for the other person" meant disinterested love for that other.[108] He defined "freedom from the earth" primarily as stewardship and "freedom from self-domination" as submission to God.[109]

This renewal in the image of God, however, was not completed by a second work of grace. It could be said that it certainly furthered the restoration but the renewal was a lifelong process, regardless of when one's intention became "pure" or when one was "entirely sanctified." Thus, it is perhaps understandable that Dunning's theology was perceived by some as a radical departure from the traditional Nazarene explications of the doctrine, as divergent from the Articles of Faith and subversive to the historic understanding of the doctrine. Indeed, what might be considered remarkable is not that the general superintendents of the Church of the Nazarene would have to acknowledge that not every affirmation would solicit full agreement from all readers but that *Grace, Faith, and Holiness* could be considered true to the doctrinal standards of the church.

The Theological Formulation

The same year that Mildred Bangs Wynkoop's *A Theology of Love* was added to the Ministerial Course of Study and four years before H. Ray Dunning's *Grace, Faith, and Holiness* was added, the first and third volumes of a three volume set titled *Exploring Christian Holiness* were included as recommended readings. According to the preface, the set was intended to be a comprehensive and definitive summation of holiness doctrine.[110] The first volume was written by W. T. Purkiser and was a survey of the biblical foundations. The second volume, coauthored by Paul M. Bassett and William M. Greathouse, traced the historical development of the doctrine but was not included in the course of study. The third volume, published in 1985, was written by Richard S. Taylor and was titled *The Theological Formulation*. "The" theological formulation was written by Taylor at the same time that he was serving on the editorial board overseeing Dunning's *Grace, Faith, and Holiness* and thus heavily involved in the serious debate with Dunning over whether or not his systematic theology was in harmony with the Articles of Faith of the denomination. Because Taylor's understanding of entire sanctification was representative of the more traditionally understood historical formulation of the doctrine, Taylor directly challenged in his work positions that Wynkoop and Dunning held.[111] The introduction clearly indicated the direction his work was going to take.

> If holiness is to be experienced as a privilege of grace . . . its centrality in the plan of salvation must be shown and the way made clear. . . . For this reason . . . holiness has been approached, not as an ideal to be praised, but as a relationship with God and a state of soul to be enjoyed. The key is not time but faith . . . Holiness is an experience of the heart available—indeed, obligatory—now.[112]

He refuted the relational understanding of sin and salvation, calling it heretical. After briefly describing the substantive and relational approaches, he wrote:

> To pit the relational against the substantive, as if a theologian had to be one or the other is foolish, futile and even heretical. It is heretical because a denial of an inherited sinful bent, not the product of one's own choices but the product of the Fall, is Pelagianism, pure and simple, and needs to be labeled as such. And furthermore, it is certainly not Wesleyan. Authentic, normative Wesleyanism has always insisted that there was in fallen human nature a real predisposition and subvolitional sinfulness that needed a real cleansing. This cornerstone of Wesleyanism must not be suppressed or compromised.[113]

Wynkoop and Dunning would of course reject Taylor's charge of Pelagianism. They did not believe their restatement of the doctrine in relational terms resulted in a denial of an inherited sinful bent. They would also reject Taylor's charge that relational theology was anti-Wesleyan. On the contrary, they believed that their explication of the doctrine was more true to Wesley than the traditional Nazarene formulation. But in Taylor's mind, this reconceptualization of holiness doctrine couldn't be more wrong.

Against Wynkoop and Dunning, Taylor believed that there was a qualitative difference between initial sanctification and entire sanctification. Saved and sanctified were not to be identified in any way. To try to comprehend the second work of grace in the first, as Wynkoop and Dunning had done, was not true to the holiness tradition. Taylor appealed to Wiley concerning the matter.

> To expand either "conversion" or "new birth" to include *full* salvation is to tend to obscure the radical difference between the first work as a *birth* and the second work of grace as a *correction* and *restoration*. Wiley warns against overloading regeneration. We "are not to infer," he says, "that because the new life is a holy life, that the simple growth and unfolding of this life will 'bring the soul to entire sanctification.' Failure to discriminate here, leads inevitably to the 'growth theory' of sanctification. Sanctification is an act of cleansing

and unless inbred sin be removed, there can be no fullness of life, no perfection in love. In a strict sense, regeneration is not purification."[114]

Taylor also insisted that entire sanctification was *the* baptism with the Holy Spirit. Lest there be no mistake, the chapter in which he wrote specifically of the second work of grace was titled, "The Baptism with the Spirit: Entire Sanctification."[115] And while he acknowledged that there was a sense in which the Holy Spirit was imparted in the first work of grace, he insisted that "if believers are ever to be filled with the Spirit, they must consciously choose to receive the Spirit in His sanctifying office."[116]

This baptism with the Holy Spirit, which resulted in a person being entirely sanctified, was always conspicuous and revolutionary. There was always a marked change that occurred when one was entirely sanctified.

> As hunger [of the saved believer] deepens, there will develop a major crisis of confrontation with God, issuing in total surrender and the infilling with the Holy Spirit. This will be the second major change. After this will come released power and freedom, more rapid progress, new learning and advanced discoveries, increased strength, knowledge, and usefulness.[117]

Taylor went so far as to suggest that an emphasis on sanctification as a gradual process instead of as an instantaneous second crisis experience was due to sin.

> While it is a mark of the carnal mind to prefer gradual processes to crises, gradualness alone is not compatible with *(a)* the unitary nature of indwelling sin, which demands punctiliar action; *(b)* either the will of God that we be holy now, or the power of God to make us holy now; *(c)* the nature of faith, which is the conditional factor in our sanctification; *(d)* the hunger and thirst after righteousness experienced by a convicted believer who yearns for deliverance now; *(e)* the challenge and expectation of immediacy that permeates the New Testament.[118]

Taylor intentionally distinguished his understanding of the doctrine from Wynkoop's and Dunning's. According to Taylor, his own explication of entire sanctification was as the Articles of Faith of the Church of the Nazarene had stated it to be. It was an act of God, subsequent to regeneration, by which believers were made free from original sin and it was wrought by the baptism with the Holy Spirit.

Thus, in 1986, the Nazarene Publishing House was publishing and, in 1990, the Ministerial Course of Study was recommending divergent interpretations of the distinctive doctrine of entire sanctification. One interpretation emphasized the instantaneous crisis while the other emphasized the gradual process. One interpretation declared entire sanctification to be a consequence of the baptism with the Holy Spirit while the other declared it to be just one of many baptisms of the Holy Spirit. One interpretation believed the second work of grace "cleansed" or "eradicated" the sinful nature, thus allowing for a real change between the saved and the entirely sanctified. The other believed no such eradication was even possible, and thus believed the second work of grace to be qualitatively indistinguishable from the first and not even always necessary as a second work.

As a result, beginning with the publication in 1973 of *A Theology of Love,* there were competing explanations of the distinctive doctrine of entire sanctification in a denomination that had historically understood its primary reason for being to consist in the preservation and propagation of that distinctive doctrine. "The Credibility Gap," which Wynkoop had so aptly called the inability to accept the doctrine of entire sanctification as it had been traditionally formulated, had created a different kind of credibility gap for the denomination. The question was no longer simply a matter of the proper formulation of the doctrine so that it might be acceptable to "a generation awed by its rediscovery of the deep sinfulness of man." In light of the two divergent and apparently irreconcilable explications of the doctrine of entire sanctification within the denomination itself, as evidenced by the heated debate at the 1985 General Assembly, the question in the last decades of the 20th century was whether or not the Church of the Nazarene had a coherent and cogent doctrine of holiness at all.

8
"WE ARE A HOLINESS PEOPLE"

◆

WHY THE HOLINESS MOVEMENT DIED

In March of 1999, *God's Revivalist*, an independent holiness periodical, published an article by Richard S. Taylor titled "Why the Holiness Movement Died." It was widely circulated in the Church of the Nazarene and expressed the sentiments of many within (and without) the denomination. According to Taylor, in spite of his and many others' best efforts to preserve the message as traditionally articulated, the doctrine of entire sanctification as a second work of grace, subsequent to regeneration, which eradicated the sinful nature, was becoming extinct. In the article itself, Taylor conceded that the Holiness Movement was not actually dead and that his title was more rhetorical flourish than a reflection of the actual state of the Holiness Movement. While he quoted a statement made in a recent annual meeting of the Christian Holiness Association that the Holiness Movement was dead, Taylor did not completely agree with that assessment.[1] He did believe, however, that the holiness message was in serious decline and in imminent danger of dying. He believed this strongly enough to go public with his concerns, in spite of recommendations by some within the Church of the Nazarene not to have the article published.

According to Taylor, there were many reasons for the decline. The first and most basic reason was that the holiness message itself was not one that fallen creatures wanted to hear. Sinful people were inherently depraved and therefore predisposed to reject the doctrine. "Obtaining the experience [of entire sanctification] is humbling and costly. Few people are willing to pay the price."[2] He acknowledged that the extravagant claims made for the second blessing were often unrealistic and, therefore, undermined the doctrine. He suggested that another reason for the decline was the hypocrisy of those who claimed to have been entirely sanctified. "Now we must at this point shamefacedly confess that a further contributing factor in the demise of the holiness movement was the shabby demonstration of holiness on the part of so many of its professors."[3] He suggested that the influences of pastoral counseling and the church growth movement on the pastors of the denomination distracted them from their first obligation of preaching the message of heart holiness. Along with these was the general neglect on the part of pastors and others to read holiness literature.

There was plenty of blame to go around, and Taylor did not slight either the professors in the denomination's academic institutions or their works. According to Taylor, there was a group of teachers with earned doctorates from "liberal" schools who had come back to teach in holiness academic institutions and, without malice necessarily, contributed to the demise of the doctrine. *"But the damage and terrible drift has been perpetrated by the [newly doctored] who bring their new liberal ideas about the Bible and doctrine with them and stay, quietly undermining. It is very subtle, very suave, and very gradual—but the damage is done."*[4]

His final volley was leveled at the single book published by the Nazarene Publishing House in 1973 that was proclaimed by many within the Church of the Nazarene as a landmark Wesleyan publication. According to Richard Taylor, Mildred Bangs Wynkoop's *A Theology of Love* bore much of the blame for the current state of the Holiness Movement.

> While I will doubtless be taken to task for the critique I am about to make, the gravity of the issues and the welfare of what is left of the holiness movement compels me to do so. I believe that a major contributing cause of the staggering of the holiness ranks has been *The Theology of Love* by Mildred Wynkoop.[5]

As has already been noted, the problem with Wynkoop's theology, according to many in the denomination, was that her relational understanding of holiness tended to undermine the Nazarene distinctives concerning the second work of grace. Nevertheless,

> Scores of young preachers were captivated by this remarkable woman and followed her as a Pied Piper, with the result that the message of a clear, knowable experience of entire sanctification which cleansed the carnal mind was muted if not blunted altogether, and a whole generation has been paralyzed as holiness preachers.[6]

Taylor concluded this indicting article with a call to return to the traditional proclamation of entire sanctification as a real change in the nature of persons effected by the baptism with the Holy Spirit subsequent to regeneration. This was the only recourse if the Holiness Movement was to escape dying out altogether.

It should be noted that his was not the only voice calling for a return to the traditional formulation of the doctrine. J. Kenneth Grider, a Nazarene Theological Seminary professor, had been in the process of writing a holiness theology for publication by the Nazarene Publishing House when Dunning was commissioned to write one to replace Wiley's. Grider sought to have his finished and published before Dunning's and thus preempt Dunning's particular formulation, but the publishing house would not publish Grider's work until after Dunning's had been published. Grider's theology, titled *A Wesleyan-Holiness Theology*, was finally published in 1994, a full six years after Dunning's work, and represented the more traditional theological formulation of holiness doctrine. The first paragraph of Grider's chapter on entire sanctification stated unequivocally his understanding. "This second work of grace is obtained by faith, is subsequent to regeneration, is occasioned by the baptism with the Holy Spirit, and constitutes a cleansing away of Adamic depravity and an empowerment for witnessing and for the holy life."[7] His explanation of entire sanctification took up a full fifth of his systematic theology and was more in line with Wiley's formulation and particularly critical of Wynkoop's.

Another voice critical of a "relational" formulation of entire sanctification was Donald S. Metz's, a theology professor at MidAmerica Nazarene College. Metz had published a holiness textbook in 1971, titled *Studies in Biblical Holiness,* which became one of the recommended readings in the course of study for ministers beginning in 1976. Metz had written his work at the same time that Wynkoop had been writing *A Theology of Love.* Metz's work, however, identified entire sanctification with the baptism with the Holy Spirit and as an instantaneous crisis experience subsequent to regeneration that cleansed one from all sin.

> *Holiness* may be said to refer to a state of personal spiritual life resulting from the baptism with the Holy Spirit, involving freedom from voluntary sin, purity of conscious intention and motivation, the practice of personal Christian ethics, and complete devotement to God.[8]

Twenty-two years after *Studies in Biblical Holiness* was published, Metz himself published a book in 1994 titled *Some Crucial Issues in the Church of the Nazarene.* In this work, Metz called attention to the divisive debate within the church over the correct formulation of the distinctive doctrine of the church.

> In the last decades of the twentieth century, it is evident there is "a profound disagreement within the denomination" on doctrinal and other essential matters. Several generations of Nazarenes have traveled the royal road of holiness emphasizing Christ-like dynamics, sacrificial service, enthusiastic fellowship, and historic Wesleyan doctrine. Now there is increasing pressure from articulate academicians, pragmatic pastors and vocal laypersons to modify the historic doctrines and reshape the traditional mission which served as the foundation of the denomination's heritage.[9]

As Taylor would do in 1999, Metz called for a return to the traditional formulation of the doctrine of entire sanctification. He quoted the "Union Statement" in the 1907 *Manual of the Church of the Nazarene* to remind his readers of the denomination's historic calling.

> 'These persons were convinced that they were called of God unto holiness, to teach others the doctrine, and to lead them into the experiences of entire sanctification. They were convinced, both by

the teachings of the Holy Scriptures and by their own experiences, that entire sanctification necessarily implies a second work of Divine grace to be received by faith in Christ, and wrought by the Holy Spirit.' The above statement of mission, forged in 1907, precisely defined the mission of the Church of the Nazarene. In the decades since 1907, this mission statement has been officially ratified by elected delegates, it has been proclaimed from the pulpits of the Church, it has been taught in the church's schools, it has been explored and examined in literature, and it has been experienced by hosts of believers. At the end of the twentieth century, the mission of the Church of the Nazarene seems to be somewhat clouded or confused.[10] Metz then issued a warning to the church. "If a church rejects its historic mission . . . that church is in fact embalming itself for burial or tranquilizing itself into deadening formality."[11] Bold Statement

Of course, not everyone agreed with Taylor's or Metz's analysis that the Church of the Nazarene was forsaking the distinctive doctrine or that an alternative interpretation of entire sanctification was a significant reason for the decline of the Holiness Movement. Dunning and Wynkoop certainly did not see their work as "subversive" of the mission of the church or as undermining of the Wesleyan-Holiness movement in general. On the contrary, they believed themselves to be "saving" the doctrine from certain extinction by providing a more truly Welseyan formulation and, in the process, a more relevant and more comprehensible explanation. Regardless of the particular position taken by the participants in the debate as to the reason for the increasing incredibility of the doctrine, however, the truth was that at the end of the 20th century, there was no substantial agreement in the denomination over what it meant to be "entirely sanctified." The Church of the Nazarene no longer had a precisely articulated definition of their distinctive doctrine, the doctrine that at one time had been their sole reason for being.

HOLINESS IS A CORE VALUE

Denominational leaders were certainly not unresponsive to this unusual situation of their church being without shared theological definition of their destinctive doctrine. In the spring of 1999, for the first time in the denomination's history, the general superintendents of the Church of the Nazarene printed a mission statement titled "Core Values." This little booklet was sent to every pastor in the denomination and was included as an insert in the denomination's periodical, Holiness Today. It declared that the Church of the Nazarene had been historically defined by three primary values, and it declared that the church was still defined by these values. The second of the three "core values" was titled "Holiness," and it asserted without apology that Nazarenes were indeed a "holiness people." This highly edited work, with contributions from Dr. Ron Benefiel, president of Nazarene Theological Seminary; Dr. Jim Bond, general superintendent; Wes Tracy, professor at NTS and former editor of the *Herald of Holiness;* and Dr. Carl Leth, pastor of Detroit First Church of the Nazarene, acknowledged that sanctification included both a crisis moment and then a process that would last a lifetime. In any event, it unequivocally affirmed the church's continuing commitment to holiness.

We believe that God uniquely entered our world through the incarnation of His only Son, Jesus of Nazareth, the historic God-man. Jesus came to renew the image of God in us, enabling us to become a holy people. We believe that holiness in the life of the believer is the result of both a crisis experience and a lifelong process. Following regeneration, the Spirit of our Lord draws us by grace to the full consecration of our lives to Him. Then, in the divine act of entire sanctification, also called the baptism with the Holy Spirit, He cleanses us from original sin and indwells us with His holy presence. He perfects us in love, enables us to live in moral uprightness, and empowers us to serve. . . . Having had the divine image restored in us in God's act of entire sanctification, we acknowledge that we have not yet arrived spiritually; our lifelong goal is Christlikeness in every word, thought, and deed. By continued yieldedness, obedience, and faith, we believe that we are "being transformed in his [Christ's] likeness with ever-increasing glory" (2 Corinthians 3:18).[12]

These core values, "Christian, Holiness, Missional," even informed the quadrennial address given by the general superintendents at the 25th General Assembly of the Church of the Nazarene. In June of 2001, in the RCA Dome in Indianapolis, Dr. Paul Cunningham forcefully reminded and instructed the church of its theological identity. Recognizing the need for a reaffirmation of the distinctive doctrine of the Church of the Nazarene, Dr. Cunningham quoted the entire 10th Article of Faith on "entire sanctification." Following his reading of that defining article, Dr. Cunningham declared:

This throbbing, biblical doctrine had languished on the fringes of Christianity for a time, but God raised up servants like the Wesley brothers, John Fletcher, and others who recognized the biblical teaching of Christian perfection and a second, definite work of God's amazing grace.

It is born of a relationship with Jesus that is nurtured and grows as we become seekers after the mind of Christ. There is a hunger to be like Jesus—so much so that when He reveals to us that we have been born with a flawed nature that only the Holy Spirit can change, we say yes to Jesus by making a complete consecration to God of everything we are or ever will be and rejoice as He purifies our hearts by faith.[13]

A few minutes later, he reiterated the need for preservation of the church's holiness identity by reading the "Agreed Statement of Belief" from the denomination's *Manual* and then he issued a warning and a challenge.

> The Board of General Superintendents, without equivocation, declares our continued commitment to our historical doctrines as stated in the Articles of Faith. . . . These foundational beliefs are essential to Christian experience and remain requirements for membership in the Church of the Nazarene. . . . The Board of General Superintendents also remains committed to propagating the biblical message of Christian holiness. A denomination of our age must beware of the damage . . . of historical drift. We can never take for granted that our religion departments or our pulpits are forever safe from doctrinal dilution. . . . Due diligence concerning these matters must be exerted by our administrators and boards of trustees at our colleges, universities, seminaries, Bible colleges, and all other instructional institutions, as well as by Boards of Credentials worldwide.[14]

There was no mistaking the general superintendents' commitment to the doctrine of entire sanctification, even if there wasn't complete agreement in the church at large concerning the proper formulation of the doctrine. It was still the church's reason for being. It was still its central core value. And in the second year of the new millennium, with the church approaching its centennial anniversary, the Church of the Nazarene was not about to abandon the call to holiness.

THEOLOGY CONFERENCES ADDRESS THE ISSUE.

Two weeks before the 25th General Assembly, in which Dr. Cuningham called for faithfulness to the distinctive doctrine of the church, General Superintendent Jim Bond gave the keynote address at the "Faith, Living and Learning Conference" at Mt. Vernon Nazarene College, in Mt. Vernon, Ohio. This conference was a quadrennial gathering of Nazarene educators from the United States and Canada, and Dr. Bond took this occasion to confront the issue of theological ambiguity concerning the doctrine of entire sanctification. In this straightforward address, which received a standing ovation from those attending, Dr. Bond appealed to the educators for help in resolving the current dilemma. He did not mince words.

> We Nazarenes believe with Wesley that "this doctrine is the grand depositum which God has lodged with the people called Methodists (and Nazarenes); and for the sake of propagating this

chiefly he appears to have raised us up." Question—Do we yet believe this? Do we embrace it with conviction and commitment? Do
we view it as our "reason for being" on the campuses of all our educational institutions? I am not being accusatory. I am baring my soul.
I believe that we are in a struggle for the soul of our denomination
and that struggle is being waged throughout the church at all levels
and around the world. . . . We have a situation that requires thoughtful dialogue among our best and brightest people who love God and
have great affection for His Church, particularly the Church of the
Nazarene—people who will make the commitment to see us through
these current dilemmas that we might ultimately impact people and
cultures around the world where we are located with the liberating
holiness message.[15]

He distributed the "Core Values Booklet" and used the three core
values as the outline of the remainder of his address. His particular concern was that the church was not emphasizing enough the "secondness"
of sanctification. He was afraid that with so much emphasis on process,
that we would become theologically indistinct from other traditions that,
while agreeing to the process of sanctification, did not believe that one
could actually be made holy. After expressing his particular concern, he
closed his address with a plea.

My friends, I appeal to you—stay with us! We need you! Help
us work through our dilemmas! Help us refocus on our unique mission. Embracing the call means embracing the Church—blemishes,
defects, and imperfections all! And vowing by God's grace to remain
in the church, always seeking to be positive, constructive and redemptive! Thanks for permitting a churchman to share some thoughts
on the role of Nazarene higher education in the fulfillment of the denomination's calling and mission.[16]

Nine months later, many of these educators were given an opportunity to help the church "work through (these) dilemmas." Nazarene Theological Seminary had hosted periodic theology conferences in the United
States, but in April of 2002, under the leadership of Dr. Ron Benefiel and
Dr. Jerry Lambert, who was director of the Department of Education, it
was decided that the next theology conference ought to be international.
Called the "Global Theology Conference," approximately 300 persons
from all over the world gathered at the Nazarene Seminary in Guatemala
City, Guatemala, to discuss the church's particular mission and identity.
General superintendents, college presidents, religion professors, district
superintendents, missionaries, pastors, and graduate students were invited.
Papers on historical identity, mission, holiness doctrine, and eschatology
were presented, but the issue that compelled most attention and around

which all others revolved concerned the particular doctrine of entire sanctification. Dr. Bond presented a paper titled "What About the 'Secondness'
of Entire Sanctification" in which he enlarged on his concern first presented at the Faith, Learning and Living Conference. He wrote:

> Intuitively, I perceive that our current emphasis is on process to
> the neglect of crisis. . . . Are we willing to disregard this theological
> distinctive? If so, it is a major departure from our understanding and
> proclamation over the past 100 years. . . . It is time for us to reaffirm
> this important aspect of our theology and restate it in the most plau-
> sible manner.[17]

Dr. Henry Spaulding, professor of theology at Trevecca Nazarene
University, presented a paper with the rhetorical title "Does Holiness Theology Have a Future?" While acknowledging the identity crisis within the
holiness tradition, he wrote that it was his deepest conviction that holiness
theology most certainly did. Dr. Roger Hahn, dean of Nazarene Theological Seminary, reminded the conference not to forget in the current debate
over entire sanctification that holiness understood as "cleansing, purity,
and separation from the world were significant parts of the previous generations' understanding of holiness."[18] On the last day of the conference,
Dr. Thomas Noble, professor at Nazarene Theological Seminary, presented
an endnote paper in which he suggested that instead of focusing on the
"secondness" of entire sanctification, we might do better to consider entire sanctification as simply "subsequent" to regeneration, a word he reminded the conferees appears in the 10th Article of Faith on "entire sanctification." Those attending the conference were divided into small groups,
and the majority of time was spent, not listening to papers, but in discussion about the mission and identity of the church. In the response to the
papers and in the discussions, it was very clear that there was indeed a
lack of agreement among the participants concerning how best to understand and articulate a doctrine of holiness. In the last plenary session, in
which participants could speak to the summary papers, it was decidedly
evident there was not much consensus. However, what was also very
clear in the three-day conference was the intense desire on the part of all
to address the church's theological ambiguity. What was very clear was
that this theological identity crisis was no small matter to those conferees.
Indeed, what they were united on was the need to confront and resolve
the theological issue.[19]

Holiness unto the Lord

The "Core Values Booklet," which was first published in 1999, sent
to all the pastors of the denomination, included as an insert in the periodical *Holiness Today*, which declared "We are a Holiness People," and

which was becoming central in the church's self-identity, concluded on a very optimistic note. The editors of this booklet wrote on its last page:

> At the turn of the 21st century, the future of this denomination has never been brighter! Many believe that we were raised up, not for the 20th century, but for the 21st century. . . . This affirmation is grounded in our Wesleyan-Holiness heritage with its radical optimism of grace. We believe that human nature, and ultimately society, can be radically and permanently changed by the grace of God. We have an irrepressible confidence in this message of hope, which flows from the heart of our holy God.[20]

This confidence, that "human nature, and ultimately society, [could] be radically and permanently changed," is precisely what the first Nazarenes eagerly embraced without question. Early in the century, Nazarenes had believed that the grace of entire sanctification would so transform human nature that persons would be almost angelic in their dispositions and behaviors and this personal transformation would have the inevitable effect of transforming the world. The union of the fractious holiness groups was evidence of the promise of holiness and a sure sign of things to come. However, as the century wore on, this "radical" optimism, which was reflective of an optimistic American culture at large, faded a bit and apologists for the traditional articulation of the doctrine of entire sanctification adjusted definitions in light of this new "theological realism."

In response to this growing awareness of the "deep sinfulness of man," many holiness theologians at midcentury enlarged their definition of infirmity and restricted their definition of sin. In brief, according to theologians like Brockett, Purkiser, and Taylor, sin "properly so called" was nothing short of an intentionally premeditated and fully willful act of conscious disobedience. Anything less was defined as "infirmity" and therefore inevitable. They continued to insist on the possibility of a complete eradication of inbred sin effected by the baptism with the Holy Spirit. To these holiness writers at midcentury, the sin that needed eradicating was very narrowly defined and what was left, by definition, had to be considered infirmity.

A later school of holiness authors, like Wynkoop and Dunning, responded to the increasing incredibility of the revised formulation of the doctrine in light of the "deep sinfulness of man" by also changing definitions. For these apologists, nothing less than an entire restatement of the doctrine would suffice to restore it to credibility. Rejecting the traditional language of the denomination, they wrote of entire sanctification as a quality of relationship. This reconceptualization of the doctrine of holiness, however, necessarily led to divergent emphases. Sanctification was understood more as a lifelong process instead of as an instantaneous work. Its most decisive moment was the first work of grace and not the second. It was in the first work of grace and not the second that the baptism of the Holy Spirit occurred. Glorious descriptions of what was accomplished by the second work of grace were therefore precluded. There was no essential difference between an earnest Christian who had not been entirely sanctified and one who had. Entire sanctification was simply an "experience beyond conversion," a part of the process along the way to full salvation.

The problem with these redefinitions for the denomination was that they effectively emasculated the promise of entire sanctification, at least as it had been understood at the beginning of the century. The promise of a gloriously transformed human nature, so vividly proclaimed by late 19th-century authors, was for the most part missing at the end of the 20th century. In its place was either a doctrine of entire sanctification that left persons, while not strictly sinful, still very much infirmed, or a doctrine that acknowledged that a gloriously transformed human nature was the result of a lifelong process that included an experience of entire sanctification. The question for the Church of the Nazarene at the dawn of the new millennium is how to understand this promise of freedom from sin as an amazing work of God's grace in the believer's life while acknowledging the reality of the deep sinfulness of humankind.

As was stated above, the editors of the "Core Values Booklet," consistent with the proclamation of the earliest proponents of holiness, profess great optimism. The last paragraph on the last page of the church's most recent mission statement reads:

> P. F. Bresee was fond of saying, "The sun never sets in the morning." It is still morning in the Church of the Nazarene, and the sun never sets on our denomination around the world. We are radically optimistic about impacting our 21st-century world with the Holiness message! With clarity of vision, total commitment, and firm faith, we view this new century as our day of greatest opportunity for making Christlike disciples of all nations.[21]

There are reasons for this "radical optimism." It is evident that the Church of the Nazarene is not ignoring this lack of theological precision concerning the doctrine of entire sanctification. It is evident that many in the denomination are wrestling with and attempting to articulate a formulation that is faithful to the Bible, experience, and the historic faith. It is very evident that the church still believes in the promise of holiness. The Church of the Nazarene still affirms the possibility of human nature being "radically and permanently changed by the grace of God." Indeed, in spite of the theological ambiguity of their distinctive doctrine, Nazarenes authentically and with great zeal, still sing:

"Called unto holiness," Church of our God,
Purchase of Jesus, redeemed by His blood;
Called from the world and its idols to flee,
Called from the bondage of sin to be free.

"Called unto holiness," children of light,
Walking with Jesus in garments of white;
Raiment unsullied, nor tarnished with sin;
God's Holy Spirit abiding within.

"Called unto holiness," praise His dear name!
This blessed secret to faith now made plain:
Not our own righteousness, but Christ within,
Living, and reigning, and saving from sin.

Refrain:
"Holiness unto the Lord" is our watchword and song;
"Holiness unto the Lord" as we're marching along.
Sing it, shout it, loud and long:
"Holiness unto the Lord" now and forever.[22]

EPILOGUE

LIBERTY MEMORIAL RESTORED

On May 25th, 2002, there was another great gathering at the Liberty Memorial in Kansas City. Eighty-one years after the dedication of the land for the Liberty Memorial, in which the five allied commanders of World War I attended, the Liberty Memorial was rededicated, with the Chairman of the Joint Chiefs of Staff, General Richard B. Myers, presiding. The governor of the State of Missouri, the mayor of Kansas City, members of Congress from Missouri and Kansas all attended. Twenty-five thousand people turned out for the occasion, including three veterans from World War I: Paul Sunderland, age 106; Frank Robb, age 104; and Jacob Sunderland, age 103.

The closing of the monument in 1994 had come as a shock to many of the people of Kansas City, and a movement to restore the monument began not long after its closing. In 1998, the citizens of Kansas City voted to approve a sales tax to help raise the 60 million dollars needed to restore the monument. Restoration began in the spring of 2000. Decks were refurbished, stairways fortified, broken stones replaced, the entire limestone exterior was cleaned, murals restored, and the sphinxes were patched. Once again, the Liberty Memorial, one of Kansas City's most recognizable landmarks and the only major memorial and museum in the United States dedicated to the "Great War," was open to the public and was once again a worthy tribute to those who served their country in World War I.

In his remarks to the crowd that had gathered on Memorial Day 2002, General Richard Myers had this to say:

> The Liberty Memorial is not only a symbol of the struggle and sacrifices made by those who fought in World War One. It also stands as a symbol of what it takes to preserve liberty and our freedoms. As one Irish patriot put it, "Eternal vigilance is the price of liberty." Unfortunately, this beautiful memorial gradually fell into disrepair over time, left to the elements without a sustained effort of support and care and so, too, can our hard fought liberties wither away over time if we do not remain eternally vigilant. . . . Tonight, the torch atop the Liberty Memorial will be relit. In my view, this flame really never went out, for it has always burned and continues to glow within the hearts of patriots across this great Nation. It is our duty as citizens to live our lives each and every day in celebration of

what these men and their fallen comrades fought so valiantly for over 80 years ago. This beautiful memorial is a lasting and durable legacy to pass on to future generations of Americans. It will still take vigilance and hard work to preserve this memorial and to preserve our liberty, but I know that each of us is up to the challenge.[1]

APPENDIX 1

THE ARTICLES OF FAITH OF THE CHURCH OF THE NAZARENE 1905—2001

A Fuller Statement of Belief
1905-1932

As Christians associated together for Christian discipline (*fellowship and service* instead of *Christian discipline:* 1907-1932) in the (*Pentecostal* included: 1907-1915) Church of the Nazarene, that there may be with us, no harmful and divisive differences of belief, to the injury of any or the disturbance of the harmony and peace of the Church; but that there may be with all "the same mind and the same judgment," so that "with one mind and one voice we may glorify God," edify His people and give Christian testimony to the world, we formulate the following enlarged statement of doctrine:

Preamble
1932—2001

In order that we may preserve our God-given heritage, the faith once delivered to the saints, especially the doctrine and experience of sanctification as a second work of grace, and also that we may co-operate effectually with other branches of the Church of Jesus Christ in advancing God's kingdom (*among men*: omitted 1997), we, the ministers and laymembers of the Church of the Nazarene, in accordance with the principles of constitutional legislation established among us, do hereby ordain, adopt and set forth as the fundamental law or constitution of the Church of the Nazarene, the Articles of Faith, the General rules, and the Articles of Organization and Government, here following, to-wit:

God
1905-1923

We believe in one (*unoriginated*: 1905-1907 only), eternally existent, infinite God, Sovereign of the Universe. That He only is God, holy in nature, character and purpose, creative and administrative. *That He only is God, creative and administrative, holy in nature, character and purpose.* (This sentence substituted for previous sentence: 1911) That He, as God, is Triune in essential being, revealed as Father, Son and Holy Spirit.

I. Of the Triune God
1923—2001

We believe in one eternally existent, infinite God, Sovereign of the universe; that He only is God, creative and administrative, holy in nature, attributes and purpose; that He, as God, is Triune in essential being, revealed as Father, Son and Holy Spirit.

Christ
1905-1911

The eternally existant [sic] Son, the second Personality of the Adorable Trinity, is essentially divine. As the divine Son He became incarnate by the Holy Spirit, being born of the Virgin Mary, thus joining to Himself inseparably the divinely begotten human Son of man, called Jesus. So that two whole and perfect natures, that is to say, the God-head and manhood are thus joined in one person, very God and very man.

Christ
1911-1923

The eternally existent Son, the second Person of the Adorable Trinity, is divine. As the Son of God, He became incarnate by the Holy Spirit, being born of the Virgin Mary, thus uniting with Himself inseparably the divinely begotten (added *human*: 1911 only) Son of Man, called Jesus. So that two whole and perfect natures, that is to say, the Godhead and manhood are thus united in one person, very God and very man.

II. Of Christ, the Son of God
1923-1928

The eternally existent Son, the Second Person of the adorable Trinity, is Divine. As the Son of God, He became incarnate by the Holy Spirit, being born of the Virgin Mary, thus uniting with Himself inseparably the divinely begotten Son of Man, called Jesus. So that two whole and perfect natures—that is to say, the Godhead and manhood—are thus united in one person, very God and very man.

We believe that Christ truly rose again from the dead, and took again His body, with all things appertaining to the perfection of man's nature, wherewith He ascended into heaven, and there is engaged in intercession at the right hand of the Father until He shall come again.

II. Jesus Christ
1928—2001

We believe in Jesus Christ, the second person of the Triune Godhead;

that He was eternally one with the Father; that He became incarnate by the Holy Spirit and was born of the Virgin Mary, so that two whole and perfect natures, that is to say the Godhead and manhood, are thus united in one person very God and very man.

We believe that Jesus Christ died for our sins, and that He truly arose again from the dead, and took again His body, together with all things appertaining to the perfection of man's nature, wherewith He ascended into heaven, and is there engaged in intercession for us.

The Holy Spirit
1905-1908

We believe in the Holy Spirit, the third Personality of the God-head ever present and efficiently active in and with the Church of Christ, sanctifying believers, convincing the world of sin, and leading into the truth as it is in Jesus.

The Holy Spirit
1908

We believe in the Holy Spirit, the third Personality of the God-head ever present and efficiently active in and with the Church of Christ, convincing the world of sin, sanctifying believers, and leading into the truth as it is in Jesus.

(III. added: 1923) The Holy Spirit
1911—2001

We believe in the Holy Spirit, the third Person of the (*Triune*: added 1928) Godhead, (*that He is*: added 1932) ever present and efficiently active in and with the Church of Christ, convincing the world of sin, (*regenerating those who repent*: added 1915, *and believe*: added 1923), sanctifying believers, and guiding into all the truth as it is in Jesus.

The Holy Scriptures
1905-1911

By the Holy Scriptures we understand the canonical books of the Old and New Testaments, given by Divine inspiration, containing (*revealing*: 1907) the will of God concerning us in all things necessary to our salvation; so that whatever is not contained therein, nor can be proved thereby, is not to be enjoined as an article of faith.

(IV. added 1923) The Holy Scriptures
1911-1928

By the Holy Scriptures we understand the (*sixty six* added: 1915) books of the Old and New Testaments, given by Divine inspiration, revealing the will of God concerning us in all things necessary to our salvation; so that whatever is not contained therein is not to be enjoined as an article of faith.

IV. The Holy Scriptures
1928—2001

We believe in the plenary inspiration of the Holy Scriptures, by which we understand the sixty-six books of the Old and New Testaments, given by divine inspiration, inerrantly revealing the will of God concerning us in all things necessary to our salvation; so that whatever is not contained therein is not to be enjoined as an article of faith.

The Old Testament
1905-1907

The Old Testament is not contrary to the New; for both in the Old and New Testaments, everlasting life is offered to mankind through Christ, who is the only Mediator between God and man. Wherefore, they are not to be heard, who feign that the fathers did look only for transitory promises. Although the law given from God by Moses, as touching ceremonies and rites, doth not bind Christians nor ought the civil precepts thereof, of necessity, be received in any commonwealth; yet notwithstanding, no Christian, whatsoever, is free from the obedience of the commandments which are called moral.

(XII. added 1923) The Second Coming of Christ
(Article moved in 1923 to follow "Entire Sanctification")
1907-1928

We believe that the Lord Jesus Christ will return to judge the quick and the dead; that we that are alive at His coming shall not precede them that are asleep in Christ Jesus, but that, if we are abiding in Him, we shall be caught up with the resurrected (*risen* instead of *resurrected*: 1915) saints to meet the Lord in the air, so that we shall ever be with the Lord; and that we are to comfort one another with these words.

We do not, however, regard the numerous theories that gather around this Bible Doctrine as essential to salvation, and so we concede full liberty of belief among the members of the Pentecostal Church of the Nazarene. (last paragraph a footnote: 1915-1923)

XI. (XV: 1989) The Second Coming of Christ
1928—2001

We believe that the Lord Jesus Christ will come again; that we who are alive at His coming shall not precede them that are asleep in Christ Jesus; but that, if we are abiding in Him, we shall be caught up with the risen saints to meet the Lord in the air, so that we shall ever be with the Lord.

Original Sin
1907-1911

Original Sin is that corruption of the nature of all who are engendered as the offspring of Adam, whereby everyone is very far gone from original righteousness, and is inclined to evil, and that continually. In the Scriptures it is designated as "The Carnal Mind," our "Old Man," "the flesh," "Sin that dwelleth in me," etc. It cannot be pardoned, and continues to exist with the new life of the regenerate until eradicated and destroyed by the baptism with the Holy Spirit.

Inherited Depravity
1905-1911

Since the sin and fall of Adam, all are without spiritual life, and by natural impulse and disposition are averse to God and holiness and inclined to sin. It is not possible that any should turn and prepare themselves by their own natural ability, to faith and calling upon God, or the doing of good works, acceptable and pleasing to Him, without the enabling Spirit and grace of God which are freely proffered to all men through our Lord Jesus Christ.

(V. added 1923) Original Sin—Depravity
1911-1928

Original sin, or depravity, is that corruption of the nature of all the offspring of Adam, by reason of which everyone is very far gone from original righteousness, (*or the pure state of our first parents at the time of their creation*: added 1923) is averse to God, is without spiritual life, and is inclined to evil, and that continually. In the Scriptures it is designated as "the carnal Mind,' our "old man," "the flesh," "sin that dwelleth in me," etc. It continues to exist with the new life of the regenerate until eradicated and destroyed by the baptism with the Holy Spirit.

It is not possible that any should turn and prepare himself by his own natural ability to faith and calling upon God, or the doing of good works, acceptable and pleasing to Him, without the enabling Spirit and grace of God which are freely proffered to all men through our Lord Jesus Christ. (last paragraph dropped in 1923)

V. Original Sin, or Depravity
1928-1985

We believe that original sin, or depravity, is that corruption of the nature of all the offspring of Adam, by reason of which everyone is very far gone from original righteousness, or the pure state of our first parents at the time of their creation, is averse to God, is without spiritual life, and is inclined to evil, and that continually; and that it (*We further believe that original sin* instead of *and that it*: added 1952) continues to exist with the new life of the regenerate, until eradicated and destroyed by the baptism with the Holy Spirit.

V. Sin, Original and Personal
1985—2001

We believe that sin came into the world through the disobedience of our first parents, and death by sin. We believe that sin is of two kinds: original sin or depravity, and actual or personal sin.

We believe that original sin, or depravity is that corruption of the nature of all the offspring of Adam by reason of which everyone is very far gone from original righteousness or the pure state of our first parents at the time of their creation, is averse to God, is without spiritual life, and inclined to evil, and that continually. We further believe that original sin continues to exist with the new life of the regenerate, until eradicated (replaced the word *eradicated* with the phrase *the heart is fully cleansed* in 2001) by the baptism with the Holy Spirit.

We believe that original sin differs from actual sin in that it constitutes an inherited propensity to actual sin for which no one is accountable until its divinely provided remedy is neglected or rejected.

We believe that actual or personal sin is a voluntary violation of a known law of God by a morally responsible person. It is therefore not to be confused with involuntary and inescapable shortcomings, infirmities, faults, mistakes, failures, or other deviations from a standard of perfect conduct which are the residual effects of the Fall. However, such innocent effects do not include attitudes or responses contrary to the spirit of Christ, which may be properly called sins of the spirit. We believe that personal sin is primarily and essentially a violation of the law of love; and that in relation to Christ sin may be defined as unbelief.

VI. Atonement
1923-1928

We believe that the atonement made by Jesus Christ through the shedding of His own blood for the remission of sins and the cleansing of the heart from all original sin, is the only ground of salvation, and is provided for every individual.

VI. Atonement
1928—2001

We believe that Jesus Christ, by His sufferings, by the shedding of His own blood, and by His meritorious death (dropped the word *meritorious* in 2001) on the cross, made a full atonement for all human sin, and that this atonement is the only ground of salvation, and that it is sufficient for every individual of Adam's race. The Atonement is graciously efficacious for the salvation of the irresponsible and for children in innocency but is efficacious for the salvation of those who reach the age of responsibility only when they repent and believe.

VII. Free Will
1923-1928

The condition of man after the fall of Adam is such that he can not turn and prepare himself, by his own natural strength and works, to faith, and calling upon God; wherefore we have no power to do good works, pleasing and acceptable to God, without the grace of God by Christ assisting us.

VII. Free Agency *(changed to Prevenient Grace in 2001)*
1928—2001

We believe that man's (*the human race's* instead of *man's:* 1993) creation in Godlikeness included the ability to choose between right and wrong, and that thus he (*human beings:* 1993) was (*were*) made morally responsible; that through the fall of Adam he (*they*) became depraved so that he (*they*) can not now turn and prepare himself (*themselves*) by his (*their*) own natural strength and works to faith and calling upon God; but (*we also believe that:* 1952-1989) the grace of God through Jesus Christ is freely bestowed upon all men (*people*), enabling all who will to turn from sin to righteousness, believe on Jesus Christ for pardon and cleansing from sin, and follow good works pleasing and acceptable in His sight.

We believe that man (all persons)*, though in the possession of the experience of regeneration and entire sanctification, may fall from grace and apostatize, and, unless he* (they) *repent of his* (their) *sin, be hopelessly and eternally lost.* (last paragraph: 1936—2001)

(VIII. added 1923) Repentance
1905-1928

Repentance is a sincere and thorough change of the mind in regard to sin, involving a sense of the personal guilt and a voluntary turning from sin. (1907 and following)

"*God commandeth all men everywhere to repent.*" (previous sentence 1905-1911 only) Repentance from (*all*: 1905-1915 only) sin and toward God is demanded of all, who, by act or attitude, have become sinners against or before Him; ability of will to repent being possessed by all who know their guiltiness as sinners.

To all who will to repent, the Spirit of God gives the gracious help of penitence of heart and hope of mercy that they may believingly receive Christ as Lord and Savior unto pardon and spiritual life.

Antinomian teaching to the effect that regeneration is precedent to repentance is unscriptural, inconsistent and most injurious to those who receive it, occasioning with many delay, if not fatal neglect of the repentance demanded of all sinners, and without which no sinner can be saved. (last paragraph 1905-1911 only)

VIII. Repentance
1928—2001

We believe that repentance, which is a sincere and thorough change of the mind in regard to sin, involving a sense of personal guilt and a voluntary turning away from sin, is demanded of all who have by act or purpose become sinners against God. The Spirit of God gives to all who will repent the gracious help of penitence of heart and hope of mercy, that they may believe unto pardon and spiritual life.

Justification
1905-1911

Justification is that gracious and judicial act of God by which He grants full pardon and release from all the guilt and penalty of sins committed, to all who believingly receive Jesus Christ as Savior and Lord.

(IX. added 1923) Justification
1911-1928

Justification is that gracious and judicial act of God by which He grants full pardon of all guilt and complete release from penalty of sins committed, to all who believingly receive Jesus Christ as Savior and Lord. To all such He also grants acceptance as righteous through the merits of Jesus Christ.

Regeneration
1905-1907

Regeneration is the spiritual quickening of the moral nature, and the giving of the distinctively spiritual life, by the gracious work of God, whereby the repentant believer is made capable of the obedience of faith and love.

(X. added 1923) Regeneration
1907-1928

Regeneration is the new birth of the soul, through the gracious work of God, whereby the moral nature of the repentant believer is spiritually quickened and given a distinctively spiritual life, capable of obedience, faith and love. *This work of regeneration is simultaneous with justification.* (last sentence added 1919-1923)

IX. Justification, Regeneration, and Adoption
1928—2001

We believe that justification is that gracious and judicial act of God, by which He grants full pardon of all guilt and complete release from penalty of sins committed, and acceptance as righteous, to all who believingly receive Jesus Christ as Lord and Savior.

We believe that regeneration, or the new birth, is that gracious work of God, whereby the moral nature of the repentant believer is spiritually quickened and given a distinctively spiritual life, capable of faith, love, and obedience.

We believe that adoption is that gracious act of God by which the justified and regenerated believer is constituted a son of God.

(*We believe that*: added 1952) Justification, regeneration, and adoption are simultaneous in the experience of seekers after God and are obtained upon the condition of faith, preceded by repentance; and to this work and state of grace the Holy Spirit bears witness.

Sanctification
1905-1907

Entire sanctification is that work of God, subsequent to justification, by which regenerate believers are made free from inbred sin, and brought into the state of entire devotement to God, and the holy obedience of love made perfect. It is provided through the meritorious blood of Jesus, and wrought by the gracious agency of the Holy Spirit, by a definite act of appropriating faith, upon a full and final consecration of the believer, and to this work and state of grace the Holy Spirit bears witness.

Christian Perfection
1905-1907

Christian perfection is the state of grace implying full deliverance from sin through pardon, regeneration and sanctification, and the indwelling of the Holy Spirit in His fulness, ever prompting to obedience, service and worship.

Sanctification
1907-1911

Entire sanctification is that act of God, subsequent to justification, by which regenerate believers are made free from inbred sin, and brought into the state of entire devotement to God, and the holy obedience of love made perfect. It is provided through the meritorious blood of Jesus, and wrought upon the full and final consecration of the believer, and a definite act of appropriating faith, by the gracious agency of the Holy Spirit, and to this work and state of grace the Holy Spirit bears witness.

This experience is also known by various terms representing different phases of the experience, such as "Christian Perfection," "Perfect Love," "Heart Purity," "The Baptism with the Holy Spirit," "The fulness of the blessing," "Christian Holiness," etc.

(XI. Entire added 1923) Sanctification
1911-1928

Entire sanctification is that act of God, subsequent to conversion, by which regenerate believers are made free from inbred sin, and brought into the state of entire devotement to God, and the holy obedience of love made perfect. It is provided through the blood of Jesus, and is wrought immediately by the gracious agency of the Holy Spirit, upon the full and final consecration of the believer, and a definite act of appropriating faith; and to this work and state of grace the Holy Spirit bears witness.

This experience is also known by various terms representing different phases of the experience, such as "Christian Perfection," "Perfect Love," "Heart Purity," "The Baptism with the Holy Spirit," "The fulness of the blessing," "Christian Holiness," etc.

There is a marked distinction between a perfect heart and a perfect character. The former is obtained in an instant, but the latter is the result of growth in grace. It is one thing to have the heart all yielded to God and occupied by Him; it is quite another thing to have the entire character, in every detail, harmonize with His Spirit, and the life becomes conformable to His image. (last two paragraphs were a footnote: 1915-1928)

X. *Entire Sanctification*
1928—2001

We believe that entire sanctification is that act of God, subsequent to regeneration, by which believers are made free from original sin, or depravity, and brought into the state of entire devotement to God, and the holy obedience of love made perfect.

It is wrought by the baptism of the Holy Spirit, and comprehends in one experience the cleansing of the heart from sin and the abiding, indwelling presence of the Holy Spirit, empowering the believer for life and service.

Entire sanctification is provided by the blood of Jesus, is wrought instantaneously by faith, preceded by entire consecration; and to this work and state of grace the Holy Spirit bears witness.

This experience is also known by various terms representing different phases of the experience, such as "Christian Perfection," "Perfect Love," "Heart Purity," "The Baptism with the Holy Spirit," "The Fulness of the Blessing," "Christian Holiness."

We believe that there is a marked distinction between a pure heart and a mature character. The former is obtained in an instant, the result of entire sanctification; the latter is the result of growth in grace.

We believe that the grace of entire sanctification includes the impulse to grow in grace. However, this impulse must be consciously nurtured, and careful attention given to the requisites and processes of spiritual development and improvement in Christlikeness of character and personality. Without such purposeful endeavor one's witness may be impaired and the grace itself frustrated and ultimately lost. (last two paragraphs: added 1976)

XI. *The Church*
1989—2001

We believe in the Church, the community that confesses Jesus Christ as Lord, the covenant people of God made new in Christ, the body of Christ called together by the Holy Spirit through the Word.

God calls the Church to express its life in the unity and fellowship of the Spirit; in worship through the preaching of the Word, observance of the sacraments, and ministry in His name; by obedience to Christ and mutual accountability.

The mission of the Church in the world is to continue the redemptive work of Christ in the power of the Spirit through holy living, evangelism, discipleship, and service.

The Church is a historical reality, which organizes itself in culturally conditioned forms; exists both as local congregations and as a universal body; sets apart persons called of God for specific ministries. God calls the Church to live under His rule in anticipation of the consummation at the coming of our Lord Jesus Christ.

Resurrection
1919-1923

"We shall not all sleep, but we shall all be changed, in a moment, in the twinkling of an eye, at the last trump; for the trumpet shall sound, and the dead shall be raised incorruptible, and we shall be changed" (I Cor. 15:51,52).

"Marvel not at this: for the hour is coming, in the which all that are in the graves shall hear his voice, "And shall come forth; they that have done good, unto the resurrection of life; and they that have done evil, unto the resurrection of damnation" (John 5:28,29).

XIII. Resurrection
1923-1928

The Scriptures say concerning this glorious consummation of the walk and warfare of the children of God: "We shall not all sleep, but we shall all be changed, in a moment, in the twinkling of an eye, at the last trump; for the trumpet shall sound, and the dead shall be raised incorruptible, and we shall be changed" (I Cor. 15:51,52). "But I would not have you to be ignorant, brethren, concerning them which are asleep, that ye sorrow not, even as others which have no hope. For if we believe that Jesus died and rose again, even so them also which sleep in Jesus will God bring with Him. For this we say unto you by the word of the Lord, that we which are alive and remain unto the coming of the Lord shall not prevent [precede] them which are asleep. For the Lord himself shall descend from heaven with a shout, with the voice of the archangel, and with the trump of God; and the dead in Christ shall rise first; then we which are alive and remain shall be caught up together with them in the clouds, to meet the Lord in the air; and so shall we ever be with the Lord. Wherefore comfort one another with these words." (I Thessalonians 4:13-18). "Marvel not at this: for the hour is coming, in the which all that are in the graves shall hear his voice, and shall come forth; they that have done good, unto the resurrection of life; and they that have done evil, unto the resurrection of damnation" (John 5:28,29).

Destiny
1905-1911

Concerning all who savingly believe in and obediently follow Jesus Christ our Lord, it is revealed that everlasting and glorious life with rewards of grace in heaven are assured. The fuller rewards and the greater glories being reserved until the resurrection of the saints and the day of judgment. Equally certain is it that persistence in sin, and the rejection of Christ and salvation by grace divine, will involve everlasting condemnation, punishment and misery for the willfully wicked and unrepentant sinner.

(XIV. added 1923) Destiny
1911-1928

Concerning all who savingly believe in and obediently follow Jesus Christ our Lord, everlasting and glorious life with rewards of grace in heaven are assured. The fuller rewards and the greater glories are reserved until the resurrection of the saints and the day of judgment. It is equally certain that persistence in sin, and the rejection of Christ and salvation will involve everlasting punishment and misery for the finally impenitent sinner.

XII. (XVI: 1989) Resurrection, Judgment, and Destiny
1928—2001

We believe in the resurrection of the dead, that the bodies both of the just and of the unjust shall be raised to life and united with their spirits—"they that have done good, unto the resurrection of life; and they that have done evil, unto the resurrection of damnation."

We believe in future judgment in which every man shall appear before God to be judged according to his deeds in this life.

We believe that glorious and everlasting life is assured to all who savingly believe in, and obediently follow, Jesus Christ our Lord; and that the finally impenitent shall suffer eternally in hell.

Baptism
1905-1907

Baptism, by the ordination of Christ, is to be administered to repentant believers as declarative of their faith in Him as their Savior, for the remission of sins unto salvation, and the full purpose of obedience in holiness and righteousness. Baptism being the seal of the New Testament, young children may be baptized upon request of parents or guardians, who shall give assurance for them of necessary and Christian teaching.

Whenever a person through conscientious scruples becomes desirous of again receiving the ordinance of baptism, it may be administered.

Baptism may be administered by sprinkling, pouring or immersion according to the choice of the applicant.

(XV. added 1923) Baptism
1907-1928

Christian Baptism is a sacrament, or ordinance, signifying one's acceptance of the benefits of the Atonement of Jesus Christ.

It is to be administered by ordained ministers of the Gospel to believers as declarative of their faith in Him as their Savior, and full purpose of obedience in holiness and righteousness.

Baptism, being the seal (*symbol* instead of *seal*: 1923) of the New Testament, young children may be baptized upon request of parents or guardians who shall give assurance for them of necessary Christian teaching.

Baptism may be administered by sprinkling, pouring or immersion, according to the choice of the applicant.

In case a preacher, when requested to administer baptism in a mode which he deems unscriptural, has conscientious scruples against so administering the ordinance, he shall not be required to do so, but shall see to it that the candidate for baptism shall be baptized in the mode desired by the applicant. (last paragraph was a footnote in 1915-1923)

XIII. (XII: 1989) Baptism
1928—2001

We believe that Christian baptism (*commanded by our Lord*; added 1985) is a sacrament signifying acceptance of the benefits of the Atonement of Jesus Christ, to be administered to believers, as (*and* instead of *as*: 1985) declarative of their faith in Jesus Christ as their Savior, and full purpose of obedience in holiness and righteousness.

Baptism, being the symbol of the New Testament, (*new covenant* instead of *New Testament*: 1985) young children may be baptized, upon request of parents or guardians who shall give assurance for them of necessary Christian teaching.

Baptism may be administered by sprinkling, pouring, or immersion, according to the choice of the applicant.

(XVI. added 1923) The Lord's Supper
1905-1928

The memorial and communion supper instituted by our Lord and Savior is essentially a New Covenant ordinance. It is declarative of His sacrificial death through the merits of which we, as believers, have life and salvation and promise of all spiritual blessing in heavenly places.

It is distinctly for those who are prepared for reverent appreciation of its significance, and by it, they do show forth the Lord's death till His coming again. Being the Communion feast only those who have faith in Christ and love for the saints should be called to participate therein.

Of the obligation to partake of the privileges of this sacrament, as often as we may be providentially permitted, there can be no doubt.

XIV. (XIII: 1989) The Lord's Supper
1928—2001

We believe that the Memorial and Communion supper instituted by our Lord and Savior Jesus Christ, is essentially a New Testament sacrament, declarative of His sacrificial death, through the merits of which believers have life and salvation, and promise of all spiritual blessings in Christ. It is distinctly for those who are prepared for reverent appreciation of its significance, and by it they show forth the Lord's death till He come again. Being the Communion feast, only those who have faith in Christ and love for the saints should be called to participate therein.

Divine Healing
1907-1908

The harmony and unity of holiness people is absolutely essential, and while we recognize that God heals with and without means, we hold that no one has the right to take such an extreme position as may result in the death of any person without medical attention.

XV. (XIV: 1989) Divine Healing
1928-1997

We believe in the Bible doctrine of divine healing and urge our people to seek to offer the prayer of faith for the healing of the sick. Providential means and agencies when deemed necessary should not be refused.

XIV. Divine Healing
1997—2001

We believe in the Bible doctrine of divine healing and urge our people to seek to offer the prayer of faith for the healing of the sick. We also believe God heals through the means of medical science.

The Church

(These statements on "The Church" preceded the Articles of Faith until 1915 at which time they were moved to follow the Articles of Faith)

The General Church
1905—2001

The Church of God is composed of and includes all spiritually regenerate persons, whose names are written in heaven.

The Churches Severally
1905—2001

The churches severally are to be composed of such regenerate persons as by providential permission, and by the leadings of the Spirit, become associated together for holy fellowship and ministries.

The (Pentecostal added: 1908-1915) Church of the Nazarene
1905-1928

We seek holy Christian fellowship, the conversion of sinners, the entire sanctification of believers and their upbuilding in holiness, together with the preaching of the Gospel to every creature. We also seek the simplicity and Pentecostal power manifest in the Primitive New Testament Church.

The Church of the Nazarene
1928—2001

The Church of the Nazarene is composed of those persons who have voluntarily associated themselves together according to the doctrines and polity of said church, and who seek holy Christian fellowship, the conversion of sinners, the entire sanctification of believers, their upbuilding in holiness, and the simplicity and spiritual power manifest in the primitive New Testament Church, together with the preaching of the gospel to every creature.

Agreed Statement of Belief
1905—2001

Recognizing that the right and privilege of persons to church membership rests upon the fact of their being regenerate, we would require only such avowals of belief as are essential to Christian experience.

Whatever is thus essential lies at the very basis of their association and fellowship in the church, which there can be no failure to believe without forfeiting Christian life itself, and thus the right of all church affiliation. That which is not essential to life in Christ Jesus may be left to the individual liberty of Christian thought. (previous paragraph omitted in 1928)

We, therefore, deem belief in the following brief statements sufficient.

1st. In one God—The Father, Son and Holy Spirit.

2nd. In the Divine inspiration of the Holy Scriptures, as found in the Old and New Testaments, and that they contain all truth necessary to faith and Christian living. (1905-1928)

(2) In the plenary inspiration of the Old and New Testament Scrip-

tures, and that they contain all truth necessary to faith and Christian living. (1928-1952)

2. That the Old and New Testament Scriptures, given by the plenary inspiration, contain all truth necessary to faith and Christian living. (1952—2001)

3rd. That man is born with a fallen nature, and is, therefore, inclined to evil, and that continually.

4th. That the finally impenitent are hopelessly and eternally lost.

5th. That the atonement through Christ is universal and that whosoever repents and believes on the Lord Jesus Christ is therefore saved from the condemnation and dominion of sin. (1905-1911)

Fifth. That the atonement through Christ is for the whole human race, and that whosoever repents and believes on the Lord Jesus Christ is justified and regenerated and saved from the dominion of sin. (1911—2001)

6th. That believers are to be sanctified wholly, subsequent to justification (*conversion* instead of *justification*: 1911-1928; *regeneration* instead of *conversion*: 1928-2001), through faith in the Lord Jesus Christ.

7th. That the Holy Spirit bears witness to justification by faith (*the new birth* instead of *justification by faith*: 1911-2001), and also to the (*further work of*: 1905-1915) entire sanctification of believers.

8th. In the resurrection of the dead and final judgment. (1905 only)
8th. In the return of our Lord, in the resurrection of the dead, and in the final judgment.

8. That our Lord will return, the dead will be raised, and the final judgment will take place. (1952—2001)

APPENDIX 2

REPRESENTATIVE BOOKS IN THE MINISTERIAL COURSE OF STUDY

Author	Title	Years in the Course of Study
Angell	Psychology	1928
Arthur	Tongue of Fire	1919, 1923, 1928, 1932, 1936, 1940, 1944, 1948, 1952, 1956, 1960
Beacon Bible Commentary		1968, 1972, 1976, 1979, 1981, 1983, 1986, 1988, 1990, 1991, 1993, 1995
Binney	Theological Compendium	1911, 1915, 1919, 1923, 1928, 1932
Bounds	Preacher and Prayer	1908, 1911, 1915, 1919, 1923, 1928, 1932, 1936, 1940, 1944, 1948, 1952, 1956, 1960, 1964
	Power through Prayer	1976, 1979, 1981, 1986, 1988
Brannon	It's Altar Time	1990, 1991, 1993, 1995
Bresee	Sermons on Isaiah	1928
Brickley	Man of the Morning	1960, 1964, 1968, 1972, 1976, 1979, 1981, 1983, 1986, 1988, 1990, 1991, 1993, 1995
Brockett	Scriptural Freedom from Sin	1940, 1944, 1948, 1952, 1956
Brown	Meaning of Sanctification	1948, 1952, 1956
Bunyan	Pilgrim's Progress	1986, 1988, 1990, 1991, 1993, 1995
Campbell	Witness to Holiness	1936, 1940, 1944
Cattell	The Spirit of Holiness	1964, 1968, 1972
Chadwick	The Way to Pentecost	1940, 1948, 1952, 1956, 1960, 1964
	The Call to Christian Perfection	1944
Chambers	An Invisible Partnership	1928, 1932, 1936
Chapman	History of the Church of the Nazarene	1932, 1936
	Holiness Triumphant	1948
	The Preaching Ministry	1948, 1952, 1956
	The Terminology of Holiness	1948, 1952, 1956, 1960, 1964, 1968, 1972
Collett	All About the Bible	1908, 1919, 1923, 1928, 1932, 1936, 1940
Corlett	The Meaning of Holiness	1944, 1948, 1952
	Spirit-Filled	1948, 1952

203

Cox	*John Wesley's Concept of Perfection*	1964
	Psychology	1976, 1979, 1981, 1986, 1988
Deal	*Problems of the Spirit-Filled Life*	1960
Dewey	*Psychology*	1911, 1919
Dieter	*The Holiness Revival of the 19th Century*	1991, 1993, 1995
Dunnam	*Dynamic Process of Spiritual Formation*	1986, 1988, 1990, 1991, 1993, 1995
Dunning	*Grace, Faith, and Holiness*	1990, 1991, 1993, 1995
Earle	*Know Your New Testament*	1944, 1948, 1952
	Exploring the New Testament	1960, 1964, 1968, 1972, 1976, 1979, 1981, 1986, 1988
Ellyson	*Compendium*	1908, 1923, 1928, 1932
	Doctrinal Studies	1936, 1940
Fisher	*History of the Christian Church*	1919
Fisher	*Why I Am a Nazarene*	1960, 1964, 1968, 1972, 1976, 1979, 1981, 1983
Fitchett	*Wesley and His Century*	1911, 1915, 1919, 1923
Fletcher	*Checks to Antinomianism*	1948, 1952, 1956
Foster	*Christian Purity*	1911, 1915
Girvin	*A Prince in Israel*	1919, 1923, 1928, 1932, 1936, 1986, 1988, 1990, 1991, 1993, 1995
Goodwin	*The Secret Place of Prayer*	1928, 1932, 1936
Gordon	*Quiet Talks on Prayer*	1908, 1911
Gould	*The Precious Blood of Christ*	1960, 1964
Greathouse	*Fullness of the Spirit*	1986, 1988, 1990, 1991, 1993, 1995
Greathouse/Bassett		
	Exploring Christian Holiness II	1986, 1988, 1990, 1991, 1993, 1995
Greathouse/Dunning		1986, 1988, 1990, 1991, 1993, 1995
	Introduction to Wesleyan Theology	
Harper	*The Story of Ourselves*	1952, 1956, 1960, 1964, 1968, 1972, 1976, 1979, 1981
Herald of Holiness		1915, 1919, 1923, 1928, 1932, 1936, 1940
Hills	*Holiness and Power*	1911, 1915, 1919, 1923, 1928, 1932, 1936, 1940, 1948, 1952, 1956, 1960, 1964
	Homiletics and Pastoral Theology	1928, 1932, 1936

	Fundamental Theology	1932, 1936
Hinson	*The Power of Holy Habits*	1995
Hopkins	*Evidences of Christianity*	1915
Howard	*Newness of Life*	1986, 1988, 1990, 1991, 1993, 1995
	So Who's Perfect?	1986, 1988, 1990, 1991, 1993, 1995
Hurst	*History of the Christian Church*	1911, 1915, 1923, 1928, 1932, 1936, 1940
Jessop	*Foundations of Doctrine*	1940, 1944, 1948, 1952, 1956
Johnson	*Christian Excellence*	1986, 1988, 1990, 1991, 1993, 1995
Jowett	*The Preacher—His Life and Work*	1915, 1919, 1923, 1928, 1932, 1936, 1940
Kinlaw	*Preaching in the Spirit*	1986, 1988, 1990, 1991, 1993, 1995
Latourette	*Christianity through the Ages*	1976, 1979, 1981
Lewis	*Mere Christianity*	1986, 1988, 1990, 1991, 1993, 1995
Lowry	*Possibilities of Grace*	1911, 1915,1919, 1923, 1928, 1932, 1936, 1948, 1952, 1956
Lyons	*Holiness in Everyday Life*	1995
Maloney	*Wholeness and Holiness*	1986, 1988, 1990, 1991, 1993
McDonald	*Life of John S. Inskip*	1911, 1915
	New Testament Standard/ Piety	1911, 1915
McKinley	*Where Two Creeds Meet*	1960, 1964
Mead	*Handbook of Denominations*	1952, 1956, 1960, 1964, 1968, 1972
Metz	*Studies in Biblical Holiness*	1976, 1979, 1981, 1983, 1986, 1988, 1990, 1991, 1993, 1995
Miley	*Systematic Theology*	1911, 1915, 1919, 1923, 1928
Mitchell	*Great Holiness Classics II*	1986, 1988, 1990, 1991, 1993, 1995
Morgan	*Intro to Psychology*	1940, 1944
Morrison	*Our Lost Estate*	1932, 1936
Murray	*With Christ in the School of Prayer*	1940, 1944
Outler	*The Wesleyan Theological Heritage*	1995
Parrott	*Softly and Tenderly*	1990, 1991, 1993, 1995
Peck	*The Central Idea of Christianity*	1948, 1952, 1956
Preacher's Magazine		1928, 1932, 1936, 1940
Purkiser	*Know Your Old Testament*	1948, 1952
	Conflicting Concepts of Holiness	1956, 1960, 1968, 1972, 1986, 1988, 1990, 1991, 1993, 1995
	Security, the False and the True	1956, 1960, 1964

	Exploring our Christian Faith	1960, 1964, 1968, 1972, 1976, 1979, 1981, 1983, 1986, 1988, 1990, 1991, 1993, 1995
	Exploring the Old Testament	1960, 1964, 1968, 1972, 1976, 1979, 1981, 1986, 1988
	Beliefs That Matter Most	1968, 1972, 1976, 1979, 1981, 1983
	God, Man, and Salvation	1976, 1979, 1981, 1983, 1986, 1988, 1990, 1991, 1993, 1995
	Called unto Holiness II	1986, 1988, 1990, 1991, 1993, 1995
	Exploring Christian Holiness I	1986, 1988, 1990, 1991, 1993, 1995
	Gifts of the Spirit	1986, 1988, 1990, 1991, 1993, 1995
	These Earthen Vessels	1986, 1988, 1990, 1991, 1993
Qualben	*Church History*	1952, 1956, 1960, 1964, 1968, 1972
Ralston	*Elements of Divinity*	1919, 1923, 1928, 1932, 1936
Redford	*The Rise of the Church of the Nazarene*	1948, 1952, 1956, 1960, 1968, 1972, 1976, 1979, 1981, 1983
Ruth	*Entire Sanctification*	1908
Simpson	*Lectures on Preaching*	1908, 1911, 1915, 1919, 1923
Smith	*Certainties of Faith*	1960
Smith	*Called unto Holiness*	1964, 1968, 1972, 1976, 1979, 1981, 1983, 1986, 1988, 1990, 1991, 1993, 1995
	Revivalism and Social Reform	1986, 1988, 1990
Steele	*The Gospel of the Comforter*	1908, 1911, 1915, 1919, 1923, 1928, 1932, 1960, 1964, 1968, 1972
Stewart	*Heralds of God*	1948, 1952, 1956, 1960, 1964
	Life and Teaching of Jesus Christ	1960, 1964, 1986, 1988
Stuber	*How We Got Our Denominations*	1948
Taylor, R.	*A Right Conception of Sin*	1940, 1944, 1948, 1952, 1956, 1960, 1964, 1968, 1972, 1976, 1979, 1981, 1983, 1986, 1988, 1990, 1991, 1993, 1995
	Holiness, the Finished Foundation	1964
	Life in the Spirit	1968, 1972, 1976, 1979, 1981, 1983
	Preaching Holiness Today	1968, 1972, 1976, 1979, 1981, 1983, 1991, 1993, 1995
	Exploring Christian Holiness III	1986, 1988, 1990, 1991, 1993, 1995
	Preaching Biblical Holiness	1990
Telford	*Life of Wesley*	1928, 1932, 1936, 1940

Tracy	*When Adam Clarke Preached*	1986, 1988, 1990, 1991, 1993
Turner	*The More Excellent Way*	1952
	The Vision Which Transforms	1968, 1972, 1976, 1979, 1981, 1983, 1986, 1988, 1990, 1991, 1993, 1995
Upham	*The Interior Life*	1948, 1952, 1956, 1960, 1964
Wakefield	*Systematic Theology*	1908
Walker	*Philosophy of the Plan of Salvation*	1908, 1911
	Sanctify Them	1936
Wesley	*Five Sermons*	1908, 1911
	Ten Sermons	1915, 1919, 1923, 1928
	Plain Account	1952, 1956, 1968, 1972, 1976, 1979, 1981, 1983
White	*Essential Christian Beliefs*	1944, 1948, 1960, 1964
	Five Cardinal Elements in Sanctification	1952, 1960
	Eradication Defined, Explained . . .	1956, 1960, 1964
Wiley	*Christian Theology Vols. 1-2*	1940
	Christian Theology Vols. 1-3	1944, 1948, 1952, 1956, 1960, 1964, 1968, 1972, 1976, 1979, 1981, 1983
	Introduction to Christian Theology	1944, 1948, 1952, 1956, 1960, 1976, 1979, 1981, 1983, 1986, 1988, 1990, 1991, 1993, 1995
	Epistle to the Hebrews	1960, 1964
	Christian Theology Vol. II	1986, 1988, 1990, 1991, 1993, 1995
Wilkes	*The Dynamic of Faith*	1948, 1952, 1956, 1960, 1964
	The Dynamic of Redemption	1948, 1952, 1956
	The Dynamic of Service	1948, 1952, 1956, 1960, 1964
Williams	*Temptation*	1923, 1928, 1932, 1936
	Sanctification	1928, 1932, 1936
	Relationships in Life	1940, 1952, 1956
Williamson	*Labor of Love*	1944, 1948, 1952, 1956, 1960, 1964
	Preaching Scriptural Holiness	1956, 1960, 1964
Winchester	*Christian Life and Ministry*	1932, 1936, 1940, 1944, 1948, 1952, 1956
	Crisis Experiences in the Greek NT	1956
Wood	*Christian Perfection as Taught by John Wesley*	1919, 1923, 1928
	Perfect Love	1919, 1923, 1928, 1944, 1948, 1952, 1956, 1960, 1964, 1968, 1972

	Purity and Maturity	1944
Wood	*John Wesley, the Burning Heart*	1976, 1979, 1981, 1983, 1986, 1988, 1990, 1991, 1993
Woodworth	*Psychology*	1932, 1936
Wynkoop	*Foundations of Wesleyan-Arminian Theology*	1976, 1979, 1981, 1983
	Theology of Love	1986, 1988, 1990, 1991, 1993, 1995

NOTES

Chapter 1

1. *Manual, Church of the Nazarene* (Kansas City: Nazarene Publishing House, 1919), 21.

2. H. Ray Dunning, ed. *The Second Coming: A Wesleyan Approach to the Doctrine of Last Things* (Kansas City: Beacon Hill Press of Kansas City, 1995), 166.

3. Melvin Easterday Dieter, *The Holiness Revival of the Nineteenth Century* (Metuchen, N.J.: The Scarecrow Press, Inc., 1980), 40.

4. Ibid., 5.

5. Timothy Smith, *Called unto Holiness* (Kansas City: Nazarene Publishing House, 1962), 12.

6. Proceedings of the First Annual General Assembly: 1907, 43-45.

7. *Holiness Evangel* (October 14, 1908), 7.

8. L. D. Peavey, *The Beulah Christian* (October 24, 1908), 3.

9. E. A. Girvin, *Phineas F. Bresee: A Prince in Israel* (Kansas City: Nazarene Publishing House, 1916), 411-12.

10. Ibid., 413-14.

11. Vinson Synan, *The Holiness-Pentecostal Movement in the United States* (Grand Rapids: William B. Eerdmans Publishing Company, 1971), 22.

12. Ibid., 30.

13. Edward Bellamy, *Looking Backward* (New York: Penguin Books, 1986), 85.

14. Ibid., 68.

15. Ibid., 111.

16. Ibid., 82.

17. Charles M. Sheldon, *In His Steps: What Would Jesus Do?* (Chicago: Thompson and Thomas), 300-301.

18. Cliftone E. Olmstead, *History of Religion in the United States* (Englewood Cliffs, N.J.: Prentice-Hall Inc., 1960), 504.

19. Walter Rauschenbusch, *Christianizing the Social Order* (New York: The Macmillan Company, 1913), 155.

20. Martin Marty, *The Righteous Empire: The Protestant Experience in America* (New York: The Dial Press, 1970), 189.

21. Ibid., 229.

22. Ibid., 195.

23. *The Liberty Memorial, Perpetuating the American Ideal* (Kansas City: The Liberty Memorial, 1941), 3.

24. Liberty Memorial Brochure.

25. Revelation 6:8; Isaiah 60:18; Micah 6:8; Psalm 67:6.

26. P. F. Bresee, the considered founder of the denomination, had died in 1915, just two months after the last General Assembly, as had W. C. Wilson, who had just been elected general superintendent. E. F. Walker, a third general superintendent who had been in failing health at the time of his election in 1915 died in 1918. The church therefore came to the assembly without three of the four general superintendents that had been elected in the last. Timothy Smith, in chapter 12 of *Called unto Holiness*

(Kansas City: Nazarene Publishing House, 1962), writes of the "tumultuous" years 1915 to 1919 as being a time of serious conflict in the church in part precipitated by the passing of these strong leaders.

27. *Manual, Church of the Nazarene* (Kansas City: Nazarene Publishing House, 1919), 9-10.

28. Proceedings of the Fifth General Assembly of the Pentecostal Church of the Nazarene, 65.

29. Ibid., 69.

30. Smith, *Called unto Holiness,* 351.

31. H. Ray Dunning, *Grace, Faith and Holiness: A Wesleyan Systematic Theology* (Kansas City: Beacon Hill Press, 1988), 479n.

32. In 1976 the General Assembly adopted an additional paragraph to the article of faith on sanctification. It reads: "We believe that there is a marked distinction between a pure heart and a mature character. The former is obtained in an instant, the result of entire sanctification; the latter is the result of growth in grace. We believe that the grace of entire sanctification includes the impulse to grow in grace. However, this impulse must be consciously nurtured, and careful attention given to the requisites and processes of spiritual development and improvement in Christlikeness of character and personality. Without such purposeful endeavor one's witness may be impaired and the grace itself frustrated and ultimately lost." See Appendix 1 for the changes in the Articles of Faith from 1905—2001.

Chapter 2

1. *Manual, Pentecostal Church of the Nazarene* (Kansas City: Nazarene Publishing House, 1908), 67.

2. *Manual, Church of the Nazarene* (Kansas City: Nazarene Publishing House, 1997), 252-53.

3. Quoted in Dieter, *The Holiness Revival of the Nineteenth Century,* 241.

4. J. A. Wood, *Purity and Maturity* (Boston: The Christian Witness Company, 1899), 47.

5. Smith, *Called unto Holiness,* 37.

6. Stan Ingersol, "Christian Baptism and the Early Nazarenes: The Sources that Shaped a Pluralistic Baptismal Tradition." *Wesleyan Theological Journal* 25 (spring 1990): 161-80.

7. H. Ray Dunning, "Nazarene Ethics as Seen in a Historical, Theological, and Sociological Context" (Ph.D. diss., Vanderbilt University, 1969).

8. *Manual, Pentecostal Church of the Nazarene,* 26.

9. Ibid., 28-29.

10. For a representative selection of authors and titles from 1908 to 1995, see Appendix 2.

11. Wood, *Purity and Maturity,* 9.

12. Ibid., 236-37.

13. Ibid., 129.

14. Ibid., 25.

15. Ibid., 49.

16. Ibid., 29.

17. Ibid., 17.

18. Ibid., 100.

19. Ibid., 81.

20. Ibid., 17.

21. Ibid., 159.

22. For an extensive treatment of sanctification as the eradication of sin, see Leroy Lindsey, Jr.'s 1996 Ph.D. dissertation from Drew University, "Radical Remedy: The Eradication of Sin and Related Terminology in Wesleyan-Holiness Thought, 1875—1925."

23. Donald Dayton, "The Doctrine of the Baptism of the Holy Spirit: Its Emergence and Significance." *Wesleyan Theological Journal* 13 (spring 1978): 118.

24. Ibid., 121.

25. *Manual, Pentecostal Church of the Nazarene,* 1908, 26.

26. Richard Taylor, *Leading Wesleyan Thinkers* (Kansas City: Beacon Hill Press of Kansas City, 1985), 253.

27. Daniel Steele, *Gospel of the Comforter* (Salem, Ohio: Schmul Publishing Company, Inc., 1960), 32-33.

28. Ibid., 32, 34-35.

29. Ibid., 151-52.

30. Ibid., 99.

31. Ibid., 100-101.

32. Ibid., 62.

33. Ibid., 138-39.

34. *Manual, Pentecostal Church of the Nazarene,* 1908, 28-29.

35. Taylor, *Leading Wesleyan Thinkers,* 335.

36. A. M. Hills, *Holiness and Power* (Cincinnati, Ohio: Revivalist Office, 1897), 18.

37. S. B. Shaw, ed. *Echoes of the General Holiness Assembly* (New York: Garland Publishing, Inc., 1984), 10-11.

38. Hills, *Holiness and Power,* 120.

39. *And the very God of peace sanctify you wholly; and I pray God your whole spirit and soul and body be preserved blameless unto the coming of our Lord Jesus Christ* (KJV).

40. Hills, *Holiness and Power,* 128.

41. Ibid., 85.

42. Ibid., 91-92.

43. Ibid., 146-47.

44. Ibid., 221.

45. Ibid., 236.

46. Ibid., 242.

47. Ibid., 246.

48. Ibid., 237.

49. *I am crucified with Christ: nevertheless I live; yet not I, but Christ liveth in me: and the life which I now live in the flesh I live by the faith of the Son of God, who loved me, and gave himself for me* (KJV).

50. Hills, *Holiness and Power,* 284.

51. *Whatsoever toucheth the altar shall be holy. . . . for whether is greater, the gift, or the altar that sanctifieth the gift?* (KJV).

52. Phoebe Palmer, *Faith and Its Effects* (New York: Published for the author at 200 Mulberry St., 1854), 242.

53. Ibid., 52.

54. Hills, *Holiness and Power*, 265-66.

55. Steele, *Gospel of the Comforter*, 84.

56. Wood, *Purity and Maturity*, 177.

57. *Manual, Pentecostal Church of the Nazarene*, 1908, 28.

58. Hills, *Holiness and Power*, 259.

59. Ibid., 265.

60. Ibid., 279.

61. Ibid., 275.

62. Steele, *Gospel of the Comforter*, 100-101.

63. Wood, *Purity and Maturity*, 175.

64. *Manual, Pentecostal Church of the Nazarene*, 1908, 28.

65. Ibid., 29.

66. Asbury Lowrey, *Possibilities of Grace* (Chicago: The Christian Witness Company, 1884), 11.

67. Ibid., 202.

68. Ibid., 447.

69. Hills, *Holiness and Power*, 30.

70. Steele, *Gospel of the Comforter*, 184.

71. Wood, *Purity and Maturity*, 204-5.

72. Lowrey, *Possibilities of Grace*, 451.

73. Ibid., 270.

74. Ibid., 353.

75. Ibid., 306.

76. Ibid., 311.

77. Ibid., 53.

78. Ibid., 239.

79. Ibid., 106-7.

80. Ibid., 39.

81. Ibid., 277.

82. Ibid., 131.

83. Ibid., 331.

84. Ibid., 63.

85. Ibid., 245.

86. Ibid., 426.

87. Ibid., 217.

88. Ibid., 224.

89. Ibid., 240.

90. Quoted in Ibid., 14.

91. Wood, *Purity and Maturity*, 202.

92. Ibid.

93. Steele, *Gospel of the Comforter*, 221.

94. Ibid., 119.

95. *But the fruit of the Spirit is love, joy, peace, patience, kindness, goodness, faithfulness, gentleness and self-control. Against such things there is no law* (NIV).

96. Hills, *Holiness and Power*, 298.

97. Ibid., 302.

98. Ibid., 303.

99. Ibid., 308.

100. Ibid., 320.

101. Haldor Lillenas, *Worship in Song Hymnal* (Kansas City: Lillenas Publishing Company, 1972), 430.

Chapter 3

1. Martin Marty, *The Noise of the Conflict,* vol. 2 of *Modern American Religion* (Chicago: University of Chicago Press, 1997), 3-4.

2. Ibid., 9.

3. Smith, *Called unto Holiness,* 289.

4. Ibid.

5. Vinson Synan, *The Holiness-Pentecostal Movement,* 106.

6. H. Orton Wiley, "The Tongues Movement in History," *The Preacher's Magazine* (March 1926): 3.

7. Ernest R. Sandeen, *The Roots of Fundamentalism British and American Millenarianism 1800-1930* (Chicago: University of Chicago Press, 1970), 192.

8. "Fundamentalism," *The Westminster Dictionary of Church History,* 1971 ed.

9. George M. Marsden, *Fundamentalism and American Culture* (Oxford: Oxford University Press, 1980), 171.

10. Paul Merritt Bassett, "The Fundamentalist Leavening of the Holiness Movement, 1914-1940 The Church of the Nazarene: A Case Study," *Wesleyan Theological Journal* 13 (Spring 1978): 65.

11. George M. Marsden, *Understanding Evangelicalism and Fundamentalism* (Grand Rapids: William B. Eerdmans Publishing Company, 1991), 70.

12. Proceedings of the Sixth General Assembly: 1923, 183.

13. Proceedings of the Seventh General Assembly: 1928, 49.

14. Ibid., 52.

15. Proceedings of the Eighth General Assembly: 1932, 183-84.

16. *Manual, Church of the Nazarene,* 1923, 22.

17. *Manual, Church of the Nazarene,* 1928, 22.

18. Bassett, "The Fundamentalist Leavening," 75.

19. H. Orton Wiley, *Christian Theology* (Kansas City: Beacon Hill Press, 1940), 1:3.

20. John Miley, *Systematic Theology* (Peabody, Mass.: Hendrickson Publishers, 1989), 2:369.

21. Ibid., 2:369.

22. Ibid., 2:370.

23. Ibid., 2:365.

24. Ibid., 2:365.

25. Daniel Steele, John Wood, and Asbury Lowrey are among the holiness writers Miley quoted in this section on sanctification.

26. Miley, *Systematic Theology,* 379 *(emphasis mine).*

27. Ibid., 2:371.

28. H. Ray Dunning, "Nazarene Ethics," 45.

29. Wiley, *Christian Theology,* 1:3.

30. Ibid., 1:5.

31. Robert E. Chiles, *Theological Transition in American Methodism: 1790—1935* (Nashville: Abingdon Press, 1965), 187.

Notes

214

32. Ibid., 175.

33. Miley, *Systematic Theology,* 2:274.

34. Ibid., 2:280.

35. Ibid., 2:296.

36. Ibid., 2:305.

37. Ibid.

38. Ibid., 2:304.

39. L. Paul Gresham, *Waves Against Gibraltar: A Memoir of Dr. A. M. Hills, 1848—1935* (Bethany, Okla.: Southern Nazarene University Press, 1992), 152.

40. Ibid., 162.

41. Letter from Orval Nease to Dr. Wiley, September 24, 1932, Nazarene Archives.

42. Letter from Charles E. Thomson to Dr. Wiley, July 11, 1932, Nazarene Archives.

43. *Manual, Pentecostal Church of the Nazarene,* 1908, 22.

44. Smith, *Called unto Holiness,* 309.

45. We do not, however, regard the numerous theories that gather around this Bible Doctrine as essential to salvation, and so we concede full liberty of belief among the members of the Pentecostal Church of the Nazarene (*Manual, Pentecostal Church of the Nazarene,* 1908, 26).

46. A. M. Hills, *Fundamental Christian Theology* (Pasadena, Calif.: C. J. Kinne, 1932), 566.

47. Hills, *Fundamental Christian Theology,* 560.

48. H. Orton Wiley, *Herald of Holiness,* July 2, 1951.

49. S. S. White, *Herald of Holiness,* Feb. 26, 1958.

50. See Paul Bassett, "Fundamentalist Leavening," 80.

51. Hills, *Fundamental Christian Theology,* 230.

52. Ibid.

53. Ibid., 233.

54. Ibid., 234.

55. Ibid.

56. Ibid.

57. Ibid.

58. *Manual, Pentecostal Church of the Nazarene,* 1908, 22-23.

59. Ibid., 23.

60. *Manual, Pentecostal Church of the Nazarene,* 1911, 19-20.

61. 09. Of Original or Birth-Sin. Original sin standeth not in the following of Adam as the Pelagians do vainly talk, but it is the fault and corruption of the nature of every man, that naturally is engendered of the offspring of Adam, whereby man is very far gone from original righteousness and is of his own nature enclined to evil, so that the flesh lusteth always contrary to the spirit, and therefore in every person born into this world, it deserveth God's wrath and damnation . . . 10. Of Free Will. The condition of man after the fall of Adam is such that he cannot turn and prepare himself by his own natural strength and good works to faith and calling upon God; wherefore we have no power to do good works pleasant and acceptable to God, without the grace of God by Christ preventing us, that we may have a good will, and working with us, when we have that good will. (The Thirty-nine Articles, 1571)

62. 7. Of Original or Birth Sin. Original sin standeth not in the following of Adam

(as the Pelagians do vainly talk,) but it is the corruption of the nature of every man, that naturally is engendered of the offspring of Adam, whereby man is very far gone from original righteousness, and of his own nature inclined to evil, and that continually. 8. Of Free Will. The condition of man after the fall of Adam is such that he cannot turn and prepare himself, by his own natural strength and works, to faith and calling upon God; wherefore we have no power to do good works, pleasant and acceptable to God; without the grace of God by Christ preventing us, that we may have a good will, and working with us, when we have that good will. (Methodist Articles of Religion, 1784)

63. *Manual, Church of the Nazarene,* 1923, 23.

64. Smith, *Called unto Holiness,* 320.

65. *Manual, Church of the Nazarene,* 1928, 23.

Chapter 4

1. H. Orton Wiley, *Christian Theology* (Kansas City: Beacon Hill Press of Kansas City, 1940), 1:3.

2. Ibid.

3. Mark A. Noll, *Between Faith and Criticism: Evangelicals, Scholarship, and the Bible in America* (San Francisco: Harper and Row, 1986), 209, 213.

4. "H. Orton Wiley," *Handbook of Evangelical Theologians,* 1993 ed.

5. Wiley, *Christian Theology,* 1:175.

6. Ibid., 1:176.

7. Ibid., 1:182.

8. Ibid., 1:184.

9. Ibid., 1:212 *(emphasis mine).*

10. *Manual, Church of the Nazarene,* 1928, 22 *(emphasis mine).*

11. Wiley, *Christian Theology,* 2:303.

12. Ibid., 2:334-78.

13. The doctrine of predestination is set forth in the Westminster Confession of Faith as follows: "By the decree of God for the manifestation of His glory, some men and angels are predestinated unto everlasting life, and others foreordained to everlasting death. These men and angels, thus predestinated and foreordained, are particularly and unchangeably designated; and their number is so certain and definite that it cannot be either increased or diminished. Those of mankind that are predestinated unto life, God, before the foundation of the world was laid, according to His eternal and immutable purpose, and the secret counsel and good pleasure of His will, hath chosen in Christ unto everlasting glory, out of His mere free grace and love, without any foresight of faith and good works, or perseverance in either of them, or any other thing in the creature, as conditions or causes moving Him thereto, and all to the praise of His glorious grace. As God hath appointed the elect unto glory, so hath He, by the eternal and free purpose of His will, foreordained all the means thereunto. Wherefore, they who are elected being fallen in Adam, are redeemed by Christ; are effectually called unto faith in Christ by His Spirit working in due season; are justified, adopted, sanctified and kept by His power through faith unto salvation. Neither are any other redeemed by Christ, effectually called, justified, adopted, sanctified, and saved, but the elect only. The rest of mankind God was pleased, according to the unsearchable counsel of His own will, whereby He extendeth or withholdeth mercy as He pleaseth, for the glory of His Sovereign power over His creatures, to pass by, and to ordain to dishonor and wrath for their sin, to the praise of His glorious justice." Quoted in Ibid., 2:350.

14. The doctrine of the Remonstrants is set forth in five propositions. These are known as the "Five Points of Controversy between the disciples of Arminius and Calvin." They are given by Mosheim as follows: 1. "That God, from all eternity, determined to bestow salvation on those who, as He foresaw, would persevere unto the end in their faith in Jesus Christ, and to inflict everlasting punishment on those who should continue in their unbelief, and resist, to the end of life, His divine succors. 2. That Jesus Christ, by His death and suffering, made an atonement for the sins of mankind in general, and of every individual in particular; that, however, none but those who believe in Him can be partakers of that divine benefit. 3. That true faith cannot proceed from the exercise of our natural faculties and powers, or from the force and operation of free will, since man, in consequence of his natural corruption, is incapable of thinking or doing any good thing; and that therefore it is necessary to his conversion and salvation that he be regenerated and renewed by the operation of the Holy Ghost, which is the gift of God through Jesus Christ. 4. That this divine grace or energy of the Holy Ghost, which heals the disorders of a corrupt nature, begins, advances, and brings to perfection everything that can be called good in man; and that, consequently, all good works, without exception, are to be attributed to God alone, and to the operation of His grace; that, nevertheless this grace does not force the man to act against his inclination, but may be resisted and rendered ineffectual by the perverse will of the impenitent sinner. 5. That they who are united to Christ by faith are thereby furnished with abundant strength and succor sufficient to enable them to triumph over the seductions of Satan and the allurements of sin; nevertheless they may, by the neglect of these succors, fall from grace, and, dying in such a state, may finally perish. This point was started at first doubtfully, but afterward positively as a settled doctrine." Quoted in Ibid., 2:351.

15. Ibid., 2:353.

16. Ibid., 2:357.

17. Proof texts is his word. Under the heading, THE SCRIPTURAL BASIS OF THE DOCTRINE, Wiley wrote: "[We] must limit this study to the more prominent proof texts." Ibid., 2:442.

18. Ibid., 2:467.

19. *Having therefore these promises, dearly beloved, let us cleanse ourselves from all filthiness of the flesh and spirit, perfecting holiness in the fear of God* (KJV).

20. Wiley, *Christian Theology*, 2:446.

21. See Ibid., 2:494-96.

22. Ibid., 2:447.

23. Ibid., 2:448-49.

24. Ibid., 2:480.

25. Ibid., 2:479.

26. Ibid., 2:483.

27. Ibid., 2:482.

28. Ibid., 2:480.

29. Ibid., 2:484.

30. Ibid., 2:488-89.

31. Ibid., 2:491.

32. "[E]ntire sanctification is that act of God . . . by which believers are . . . brought into a state of entire devotement to God, and the holy obedience of love made perfect."

33. Wiley, *Christian Theology,* 2:491.

34. Ibid., 2:492.

35. "Holiness in man is the same as holiness in God as to quality, but with this difference, the former is derived, while the latter is absolute." Ibid., 2:492.

36. Ibid., 2:492.

37. Ibid., 2:502.

38. Ibid., 2:505.

39. Ibid., 2:496-97.

40. Ibid., 2:494.

41. Ibid., 2:512.

42. Ibid., 2:512.

43. Ibid., 2:504.

44. Ibid., 2:497.

45. Ibid., 2:497.

46. Ibid., 2:506.

47. Ibid., 2:508.

48. Ibid., 2:510.

49. Ibid., 2:500.

50. John Wesley, "A Plain Account of Christian Perfection." *Works of John Wesley* (Kansas City: Beacon Hill Press of Kansas City, 1986), 11:374.

51. Ruth, C. W. *Entire Sanctification* (Kansas City: Beacon Hill Press, 1944), 47.

52. Ibid., 48.

53. Steele, *Gospel of the Comforter,* 147.

54. Hills, *Fundamental Christian Theology,* 449.

55. Hills, *Holiness and Power,* 189.

Chapter 5

1. Proceedings of the 12th General Assembly: 1948, 154.

2. Ibid., 154.

3. See W. T. Purkiser, *Called unto Holiness* vol. 2 (Kansas City: Nazarene Publishing House, 1983), 256.

4. *Time,* March 8, 1948, cover.

5. Ibid., 70.

6. Ibid., 70.

7. Reinhold Niebuhr, *The Nature and Destiny of Man* 2 vols. (Louisville: Westminster John Knox Press, 1996).

8. Ibid., 137.

9. Reinhold Niebuhr, *The Irony of American History. Cited in Modern Christian Thought* by James Livingston (New York: Macmillan Publishing Company, Inc. , 1971), 473.

10. Proceedings of the Twelfth General Assembly: 1948, 162.

11. Ibid., 163.

12. Proceedings of the 11th General Assembly: 1944, 135.

13. Proceedings of the 10th General Assembly: 1940, 214.

14. Ibid., 207.

15. Proceedings of the 12th General Assembly: 1948, 162.

16. Proceedings of the 10th General Assembly: 1940, 222.

17. Proceedings of the 11th General Assembly: 1944, 50.

18. Ibid., 51.

19. See Purkiser, *Called unto Holiness*, 204-13.

20. Proceedings of the 12th General Assembly: 1948, 177.

21. Henry E. Brockett, *Scriptural Freedom from Sin* (Salem, Ohio: Schmul Publishers, 1984), 7.

22. Ibid., 8.

23. Ibid., 9.

24. Ibid., 17.

25. Ibid., 47.

26. Ibid., 49.

27. Ibid., 50.

28. Ibid., 51.

29. Taylor, Richard S., *A Right Conception of Sin* (Kansas City: Beacon Hill Press, 1945), 9-10.

30. Ibid., 19.

31. Ibid., 33.

32. Ibid., 51.

33. Ibid., 10.

34. Ibid., 63.

35. Ibid.

36. Ibid.

37. Ibid., 66.

38. Ibid., 68.

39. Ibid., 104-5.

40. Ibid., 103.

41. Ibid.

42. Ibid., 104.

43. Ibid.

44. Ibid., 105.

45. Ibid., 104.

46. D. Shelby Corlett, *The Meaning of Holiness* (Kansas City: Beacon Hill Press, 1944), 63.

47. Ibid., 73.

48. Ibid., 74-75.

49. Ibid., 86.

50. Ibid., 90.

51. Ibid., 247.

52. Ibid., 248.

53. Ibid., 249.

54. W. T. Purkiser, *Conflicting Concepts of Holiness* (Kansas City: Beacon Hill Press, 1964), 59.

55. Corlett, *The Meaning of Holiness*, 95-96.

56. Ibid., 100.

57. S. S. White, *Cardinal Elements in Sanctification* (Kansas City: Beacon Hill Press, 1963), 23-24.

58. White, *Cardinal Elements in Sanctification*, 40.

59. Ibid., 47.

60. White, *Eradication: Defined, Explained, Authenticated* (Kansas City: Beacon Hill Press, 1954), 6.
61. Ibid., 38.
62. Ibid., 47.
63. Ibid., 66.
64. White, *Cardinal Elements in Sanctification,* 54.
65. Ibid.
66. White, *Eradication,* 83.
67. Ibid., 85.
68. Ibid., 87.
69. White, *Cardinal Elements in Sanctification,* 55.
70. White, *Eradication,* 90.
71. Ibid., 90-91.
72. White, *Cardinal Elements in Sanctification,* 56.
73. Ibid., 71.
74. Ibid., 78.
75. *And God, which knoweth the hearts, bare them witness, giving them the Holy Ghost, even as he did unto us; and put no difference between us and them, purifying their hearts by faith* (KJV).
76. White, *Cardinal Elements in Sanctification,* 85.
77. *Manual, Church of the Nazarene,* 1948, 27.
78. *Manual, Church of the Nazarene,* 1952, 27 *(emphasis mine).*

Chapter 6
1. Timothy L. Smith, *Revivalism and Social Reform* (Nashville: Abingdon Press) 1957.
2. Ibid., 351.
3. Ibid. *(emphasis mine).*
4. Proceedings of the 17th General Assembly: 1968, 230-33.
5. Proceedings of the 18th General Assembly: 1972, 198, 206-7.
6. Proceedings of the 19th General Assembly: 1976, 234-36.
7. Ibid., 239.
8. Proceedings of the 18th General Assembly: 1972, 199.
9. Proceedings of the 17th General Assembly: 1968, 234.
10. William S. Deal, *Problems of the Spirit-Filled Life* (Kansas City: Beacon Hill Press, 1961), 37.
11. Ibid., 49.
12. Ibid., 50.
13. Ibid., 68.
14. Ibid., 73.
15. Ibid., 75.
16. Ibid., 101.
17. Ibid., 110.
18. Ibid., 111.
19. Richard Taylor, *Life in the Spirit* (Kansas City: Beacon Hill Press of Kansas City, 1966).
20. Ibid., 149.
21. Ibid., 151.

22. Ibid., 165.

23. W. T. Purkiser, ed., *Exploring Our Christian Faith* (Kansas City: Beacon Hill Press, 1960), 371.

24. Ibid., 374.

25. Lowrey, *Possibilities of Grace,* 467.

26. Everett Lewis Cattell, *The Spirit of Holiness* (Grand Rapids: Eerdmans Publishing Company, 1963).

27. Ibid., 7-8.

28. Leo George Cox, *John Wesley's Concept of Perfection* (Kansas City: Beacon Hill Press, 1964).

29. George Allen Turner, *The Vision Which Transforms* (Kansas City: Beacon Hill Press, 1964).

30. Cox, *John Wesley's Concept of Perfection,* 206.

31. Ibid., 207.

32. John Wesley, *The Heart of Wesley's Faith* (Kansas City: Beacon Hill Press, 1961), 23.

33. Ibid., 47.

34. Ibid., 65.

35. Ibid., 32.

36. Ibid., 44.

37. Ibid., 47-48.

38. Ibid., 46.

39. Ibid., 64.

40. Ibid., 66-69.

41. Ibid., 40.

42. Ibid., 38.

43. Ibid., 57-58.

44. Ibid., 82.

45. Cattell, *The Spirit of Holiness,* 8.

46. *Manual, Church of the Nazarene,* 1976, 29.

47. Ibid.

48. Ibid.

Chapter 7

1. *Manual, Church of the Nazarene,* 1985, 25.

2. Ibid.

3. Ibid.

4. Ibid.

5. Proceedings of the 21st General Assembly, 1985, 88.

6. Ibid., 89.

7. The word "eradicated" was ultimately replaced. In the 1997 General Assembly and without much discussion, the word "eradicated" was removed and the phrase "the heart is fully cleansed" was substituted in its place. However the prepositional phrase "by the baptism of the Holy Spirit" was retained.

8. Mildred Bangs Wynkoop had been an evangelist in the Church of the Nazarene prior to her becoming a professor. She received her Th.D. degree from Northern Baptist Theological Seminary. She taught at Western Evangelical Seminary from 1956

to 1961, Japan Nazarene Theological Seminary from 1961 to 1966, Trevecca Nazarene College from 1966 to 1976, and was theologian in residence at Nazarene Theological Seminary from 1976 to 1980.

9. *Seminary Tower,* Summer, 1973, 9.

10. Paul Orjala, "On Doing Theology vs. Rehashing Theology," 1-2 Nazarene Archives.

11. 1973 Nazarene Publishing House Catalog, 42.

12. Mildred Wynkoop, *A Theology of Love* (Kansas City: Beacon Hill Press of Kansas City, 1973), 39.

13. Ibid., 39-40.

14. Ibid., 47.

15. Ibid., 49.

16. Ibid., 49-50.

17. Ibid., 73.

18. Ibid., 154.

19. Ibid., 156.

20. Ibid., 158.

21. Ibid., 177.

22. Ibid., 152.

23. Ibid., 154.

24. Ibid., 155.

25. Ibid., 177.

26. Ibid., 177.

27. Ibid., 171.

28. Ibid., 171, 177.

29. Ibid., 181.

30. 1 John 1:7.

31. Wynkoop, *A Theology of Love,* 251.

32. Søren Kierkegaard, *Purity of Heart Is to Will One Thing* (New York: Harper and Row, 1956).

33. Wynkoop, *A Theology of Love,* 265-67.

34. Ibid., 334.

35. Ibid., 333.

36. Ibid., 331.

37. Wynkoop did attribute this absolute freedom and responsibility to the prevenient grace of God.

38. Wynkoop, *A Theology of Love,* 311.

39. Ibid., 312-13.

40. Ibid., 310.

41. Ibid., 206-7.

42. *Manual, Church of the Nazarene,* 1985, 25.

43. Wynkoop, *A Theology of Love,* 199.

44. Daniel Steele, *Steele's Answers* (Chicago: Christian Witness Company, 1912).

45. Wynkoop, *A Theology of Love,* 189.

46. Ibid., 321.

47. Ibid., 337.

48. Ibid., 357.

49. Cox, *John Wesley's Concept of Perfection,* 130.

50. Turner, *The Vision Which Transforms,* 149.

51. Rob Staples, "The Current Wesleyan Debate on the Baptism with the Holy Spirit," unpublished paper presented to the Breakfast Club, (Mar. 1979), 23.

52. Ibid., 24.

53. Ibid., 25.

54. Ibid.

55. William Greathouse, "Letter to M. A. (Bud) Lunn," Feb. 9, 1980, Nazarene Archives.

56. Ibid.

57. William Greathouse, "Letter to Dr. Ray Dunning," June 22, 1982, Nazarene Archives.

58. *Manual, Church of the Nazarene,* 28.

59. That all of them had at one time or another been associated with Trevecca Nazarene College in Nashville, Tennessee did not go unnoticed and warranted the pejorative appellation, "The Trevecca Connection," which is now the name of the college newsletter.

60. Alex Deasley, "Entire Sanctification and the Baptism with the Holy Spirit: Perspectives on the Biblical View of the Relationship," *Wesleyan Theological Journal* 14, No. 1 (spring 1979): 28.

61. Staples, "Breakfast Paper Addendum," 39.

62. Ibid., 42.

63. William Greathouse, "Letter to Dr. Cunningham," March 2, 1984, Nazarene Archives.

64. Wiley, *Christian Theology,* 2:321.

65. Cunningham, "Letter to Staples."

66. W. T. Purkiser, "Letter to M. A. (Bud) Lunn," August 28, 1986, Nazarene Archives.

67. M. A. (Bud) Lunn, "Letter to Ray Dunning," December 28, 1979, Nazarene Archives.

68. Richard S. Taylor, "Letter to John A. Knight," (no date) Nazarene Archives.

69. Ibid.

70. W. T. Purkiser, "Letter to John Knight," April 18, 1986, Nazarene Archives.

71. Dunning, *Grace, Faith, and Holiness,* 7.

72. Ibid., 7 *(emphasis mine).*

73. Ibid., 11.

74. Ibid., 14.

75. Ibid., 298.

76. Ibid., 17.

77. Ibid., 37.

78. Ibid., 471.

79. Ibid., 275.

80. Ibid., 286.

81. Ibid., 285.

82. Ibid., 290.

83. Ibid., 297.

84. Ibid., 484.

85. Ibid., 488.

86. Ibid., 350.

87. Ibid.
88. Ibid., 351.
89. Ibid.
90. Ibid., 451.
91. Ibid., 489.
92. Ibid., 451.
93. Ibid., 351.
94. Ibid., 352.
95. Ibid., 420.
96. Ibid., 423.
97. Ibid.
98. Ibid.
99. Ibid., 424.
100. Ibid., 465.
101. Ibid., 452.
102. Ibid., 485.
103. Ibid.
104. Ibid., 488.
105. Ibid.
106. Ibid., 486.
107. Ibid., 488.
108. Ibid., 494.
109. Ibid., 496.
110. W. T. Purkiser, *The Biblical Foundations,* vol. 1 of *Exploring Christian Holiness* (Kansas City: Beacon Hill Press of Kansas City, 1983), 7.
111. For some reason, the preface that stated that these volumes were a "comprehensive and definitive summation of the doctrine of holiness" was not included in this third volume.
112. Richard S. Taylor, *The Theological Formulation,* vol. 3 of *Exploring Christian Holiness* (Kansas City: Beacon Hill Press of Kansas City, 1985), 9.
113. Ibid., 99-100.
114. Ibid., 143.
115. Ibid., 154.
116. Ibid., 144.
117. Taylor, *Exploring Christian Holiness,* 146.
118. Ibid., 150.

Chapter 8

1. Richard Taylor, "Why the Holiness Movement Died." *God's Revivalist* (March 1999), 3.
2. Ibid.
3. Ibid., 11.
4. Ibid., 14.
5. Ibid., 14.
6. Ibid., 15.
7. J. Kenneth Grider, *A Wesleyan-Holiness Theology* (Kansas City: Beacon Hill Press of Kansas City, 1994), 367.

8. Donald S. Metz, *Studies in Biblical Holiness* (Kansas City: Beacon Hill Press of Kansas City, 1971), 15.

9. Donald S. Metz, *Some Crucial Issues in the Church of the Nazarene* (Olathe, Kans.: Wesleyan Heritage Press, 1994), 1.

10. Ibid., 15.

11. Ibid.

12. *Core Values: Church of the Nazarene: Christian, Holiness, Missional* (Kansas City: Nazarene Publishing House, 2001), 7-8.

13. Minutes of the 25th General Assembly of the Church of the Nazarene, June 24-29, 2001, 236.

14. Ibid., 237-38.

15. Jim Bond, "Key Note Address to the 'Faith, Living and Learning Conference,'" June 16, 2001.

16. Ibid.

17. Jim Bond, "What About the 'Secondness' of Entire Sanctification?" papers presented at the Global Theology Conference, April 4-7, 2002.

18. Roger Hahn, "Re-Appropriating the Biblical Language of Purity and Cleansing for Holiness," papers presented at the Global Theology Conference, April 4-7, 2002.

19. Subsequent Theology Conferences have already been planned. The next will be in Kansas City in December 2004, with the theme "Holy God, Holy People" guiding the conversation.

20. *Core Values,* 16.

21. Ibid.

22. Lelia N. Morris, *Sing to the Lord* (Kansas City: Lillenas Publishing Company, 1993), 503.

Epilogue

1. General Richard B. Myers, "Remarks at the Liberty Memorial Rededication," May 25, 2002.

BIBLIOGRAPHY

Agnew, Milton S. "Baptized with the Spirit." *Wesleyan Theological Journal* 14 (fall 1979): 7-14.

Arnett, William M. "The Role of the Holy Spirit in Entire Sanctification in the Writings of John Wesley." *Wesleyan Theological Journal* 14 (fall 1979): 15-30.

Bangs, Carl. *Phineas F. Bresee.* Kansas City: Beacon Hill Press of Kansas City, 1995.

Bassett, Paul Merritt. "The Fundamentalist Leavening of the Holiness Movement, 1914-1940 The Church of the Nazarene: A Case Study." *Wesleyan Theological Journal* 13 (spring 1978): 65-89.

———. "The Interplay of "Christology and Ecclesiology in the Theology of the Holiness Movement." *Wesleyan Theological Journal* 16 (fall 1981): 79-94.

———. "The Holiness Movement and the Protestant Principle." *Wesleyan Theological Journal* 18 (spring 1983): 7-29.

———. "Wesleyan Words in the Nineteenth-Century World: 'Sin,' A Case Study." *Evangelical Journal* 8 (spring 1990) 15-40.

———. "Culture and Concupiscence: The Changing Definition of Sanctity in the Wesleyan Holiness Movement, 1867-1920." *Wesleyan Theological Journal* 28 (fall 1993): 59-127.

———. "A Study in the Theology of the Early Holiness Movement." *Methodist History,* 61-84.

Bassett, Paul M. and William M. Greathouse. *Exploring Christian Holiness.* Vol. 2, *The Historical Development.* Kansas City: Beacon Hill Press of Kansas City, 1985.

Bellamy, Edward. *Looking Backward.* New York: Penguin Books, 1986.

Binney, Amos and Daniel Steele. *Binney's Theological Compend Improved.* Nashville: Abingdon-Cokesbury Press, 1902.

Blevins, Dean G. "The Means of Grace: Toward A Wesleyan Praxis of Spiritual Formation." *Wesleyan Theological Journal* 32 (spring 1997): 69-83.

Brockett, Henry E. *The Riches of Holiness.* Kansas City: Beacon Hill Press, 1951.

———. *Scriptural Freedom from Sin.* Salem, Ohio: Schmul Publishers, 1984.

Bundy, David. "The Historiography of the Wesleyan/Holiness Tradition." *Wesleyan Theological Journal* 30 (spring 1995): 55-77.

Carter, Charles W. "Judeo-Christian Ethics: God's Eternal Ethical Ideal for Humanity." *A Contemporary Wesleyan Theology: Biblical, Systematic, and Practical,* ed. Charles W. Carter. Grand Rapids: Francis Asbury Press, 1983.

Cattell, Everett Lewis. *The Spirit of Holiness.* Grand Rapids: Eerdmans Publishing Company, 1963.

Cell, George C. *The Rediscovery of John Wesley.* New York: Henry Holt and Company, 1935.

Chapman, J. B. *A History of the Church of the Nazarene.* Kansas City: Nazarene Publishing House, 1926.

———. *The Terminology of Holiness.* Kansas City: Beacon Hill Press, 1947.

Chiles, Robert E. *Theological Transition in American Methodism: 1790-1935.* Abingdon Press: Nashville, 1965.

Clark, Elmer T. *The Small Sects in America.* Nashville: Abingdon Press, 1965.

Coppedge, Allan. "Entire Sanctification in Early American Methodism: 1812-1835." *Wesleyan Theological Journal* 13 (Spring 1978): 34-50.

Corbin, J. Wesley. "Christian Perfection and the Evangelical Association Through 1875." *Methodist History,* 28-44.

Corlett, D. Shelby. *The Meaning of Holiness.* Kansas City: Beacon Hill Press, 1944.

Cox, Leo George. *John Wesley's Concept of Perfection.* Kansas City: Beacon Hill Press, 1964.

Cubie, David L. "Perfection in Wesley and Fletcher: Inaugural or Teleological?" *Wesleyan Theological Journal* 11 (spring 1976): 22-37.

Culp, John E. "Supernatural and Sanctification: Comparison of Roman Catholic and Wesleyan Views." *Wesleyan Theological Journal* 31 (fall 1996): 147-66.

Dayton, Donald W. *The American Holiness Movement: A Bibliographic Introduction.* Wilmore, Ky.: B. L. Fisher Library, 1971.

————. "Asa Mahan and the Development of American Holiness Theology." *Wesleyan Theological Journal* 9 (spring 1974): 60-69.

————. *Discovering an Evangelical Heritage.* New York: Harper and Row, 1976.

————. "The Doctrine of the Baptism of the Holy Spirit: Its Emergence and Significance." *Wesleyan Theological Journal* 13 (spring 1978): 114-26.

————. *The Higher Christian Life: A Bibliographic Overview.* New York: Garland Publishing, 1985.

————. *Theological Roots of Pentecostalism.* Metuchen, N.J.: The Scarecrow Press, 1987.

Deal, William S. *Problems of the Spirit-Filled Life.* Kansas City: Beacon Hill Press, 1961.

Deasley, Alex R. G. "Entire Sanctification and the Baptism with the Holy Spirit: Perspectives on the Biblical View of the Relationship." *Wesleyan Theological Journal* 14 (spring 1979): 27-44.

Dieter, Melvin E. "From Vineland and Manheim to Brighton and Berlin: The Holiness Revival in Nineteenth-Century Europe." *Wesleyan Theological Journal* 9 (spring 1974): 15-27.

————. "Musings." *Wesleyan Theological Journal* 14 (spring 1979): 7-13.

————. *The Holiness Revival of the Nineteenth Century.* Metuchen, N.J.: The Scarecrow Press, 1980.

————. "The Development of Nineteenth Century Holiness Theology." *Wesleyan Theological Journal* 20 (spring 1985) 61-77.

————. "The Wesleyan/Holiness and Pentecostal Movements: Commonalities, Confrontation, and Dialogue." *Pneuma* 12, No. 1 (spring 1990): 4-13.

————. "Primitivism in the American Holiness Tradition." *Wesleyan Theological Journal* 30 (spring 1995): 78-91.

————, ed. *Five Views on Sanctification.* Grand Rapids: Zondervan Publishing House, 1987.

Dunning, H. Ray. "Nazarene Ethics as Seen in a Theological, Historical, and Sociological Context." Ph.D. Diss., Vanderbilt University, 1969.

———. *Grace, Faith, and Holiness.* Kansas City: Beacon Hill Press of Kansas City, 1988.

———. *Sanctification: A Layman's Guide.* Kansas City: Beacon Hill Press of Kansas City, 1991.

———. *The Second Coming: A Wesleyan Approach to the Doctrine of Last Things.* Kansas City: Beacon Hill Press of Kansas City, 1995.

———, ed. *A Community of Faith.* Kansas City: Beacon Hill Press of Kansas City, 1997.

Flew, R. N. *The Idea of Perfection in Christian Theology.* London: Oxford University Press, 1934.

"Fundamentalism," *The Westminster Dictionary of Church History,* 1971 ed.

Gaddis, Merrill E. "Christian Perfectionism in America." Ph.D. Diss., University of Chicago, 1929.

Girvin, E. A. *P. F. Bresee, A Prince in Israel.* Kansas City: Nazarene Publishing House, 1916.

Greathouse, William M. *From the Apostles to Wesley.* Kansas City: Beacon Hill Press of Kansas City, 1979.

———. *The Fullness of the Spirit.* Kansas City: Beacon Hill Press, 1958.

———, and H. Ray Dunning. *An Introduction to Wesleyan Theology.* Kansas City: Beacon Hill Press of Kansas City, 1982.

Gresham, L. Paul. *Waves Against Gibraltar: A Memoir of Dr. A. M. Hills, 1848-1935.* Bethany, Okla.: Southern Nazarene University Press, 1992.

Grider, J. Kenneth. "Spirit-Baptism the Means of Sanctification: A Response to the Lyon View." *Wesleyan Theological Journal* 14 (fall 1979): 31-50.

———. *Entire Sanctification: The Distinctive Doctrine of Wesleyanism.* Kansas City: Beacon Hill Press of Kansas City, 1980.

———. *A Wesleyan-Holiness Theology.* Kansas City: Beacon Hill Press of Kansas City, 1994.

Guyett, Leroy David. "A Study of the Holiness Preaching of the Past Thirty Years as Represented by the Outlines and Sermons in the Preacher's Magazine (Vols. I-XXX)." B.D. Thesis, Nazarene Theological Seminary, 1957.

Hambrick-Stowe, Charles E. *Charles G. Finney and the Spirit of American Evangelicalism.* Grand Rapids: William B. Eerdmans Publishing Company, 1996.

Hamilton, James E. "Nineteenth Century Philosophy and Holiness Theology: A Study in the Thought of Asa Mahan." *Wesleyan Theological Journal* 13 (spring 1978): 51-64.

———. "The Church as a Universal Reform Society: The Social Vision of Asa Mahan." *Wesleyan Theological Journal* 25 (spring 1990): 42-55.

Harper, Albert F. *Holiness Teaching Today.* Kansas City: Beacon Hill Press of Kansas City, 1987.

Harper, Charles H. "Entire Sanctification as Instantaneous and Gradual from Wesley to the Present." B.D. Thesis, Nazarene Theological Seminary, 1960.

Hills, A. M. *Holiness and Power.* Cincinnati, Ohio: Revivalist Office, 1897.

———. *Fundamental Christian Theology.* Pasadena, Calif.: C. J. Kinne, 1932.

———. *Homiletics and Pastoral Theology.* Salem, Ohio: Schmul Publishing Company, Inc., 1985.

———. *Life of Charles G. Finney.* Salem, Ohio: Schmul Publishing Company, Inc., 1991.

Howard, Ivan. "Wesley Versus Phoebe Palmer: An Extended Controversy." *Wesleyan Theological Journal* 6 (spring 1971): 31-40.

Hynson, Leon Orville. "Remington Rifles or Bows and Arrows? The Post-Bellum Wesleyan Quest for the Transformation of Society." *Wesleyan Theological Journal* 25 (spring 1990): 57-82.

Ingersol, Stan. "Christian Baptism and the Early Nazarenes: The Sources that Shaped A Pluralistic Baptismal Tradition." *Wesleyan Theological Journal* 27 (spring and fall 1992) 161-80.

Jones, Charles E. *A Guide to the Study of the Holiness Movement.* Metuchen, N.J.: The Scarecrow Press, Inc., 1974.

———. *Perfectionist Persuasion: The Holiness Movement in American Methodism, 1867-1936.* Metuchen, N.J.: The Scarecrow Press, 1974.

———. "Anti-Ordinance: A Proto-Pentecostal Phenomenon?" *Wesleyan Theological Journal* 25 (fall 1990): 7-23.

———. "Reclaiming the Text in Methodist-Holiness and Pentecostal Spirituality." *Wesleyan Theological Journal* 30 (fall 1995): 164-81.

———. "The Inverted Shadow of Phoebe Palmer." *Wesleyan Theological Journal* 31 (fall 1996): 120-31.

Kierkegaard, Søren. *Purity of Heart Is to Will One Thing.* New York: Harper and Row, 1956.

Knight, John A. "John Fletcher's Influence on the Development of Wesleyan Theology in America." *Wesleyan Theological Journal* 13 (spring 1978): 13-33.

———. *The Holiness Pilgrimage.* Kansas City: Beacon Hill Press of Kansas City, 1986.

Kostlevy, William. *Holiness Manuscripts.* Metuchen, N.J.: The Scarecrow Press, Inc., 1994.

Langford, Thomas A. *Practical Divinity.* Nashville: Abingdon Press, 1983.

The Liberty Memorial, Perpetuating the American Ideal. Kansas City: The Liberty Memorial, 1941.

Lindsey, Leroy Jr. "Radical Remedy: The Eradication of Sin and Related Terminology in Wesleyan-Holiness Thought, 1875-1925." Ph.D. Diss., Drew University, 1996.

Lindstrom, Harold. *Wesley and Sanctification: Study in the Doctrine of Salvation.* London: Epworth Press, 1950.

Livingston, James. *Modern Christian Thought.* New York: Macmillan Publishing Company, Inc., 1971.

Lowrey, Asbury. *Possibilities of Grace.* Chicago: The Christian Witness Company, 1884.

Lyon, Robert W. "Baptism and Spirit Baptism in the New Testament." *Wesleyan Theological Journal* 14 (spring 1979): 14-26.

Marsden, George M. *Fundamentalism and American Culture.* Oxford: Oxford University Press, 1980.

———. *Understanding Evangelicalism and Fundamentalism.* Grand Rapids: William B. Eerdmans Publishing Company, 1991.

Marston, Leslie R. "The Crisis-Process Issue in Wesleyan Thought." *Wesleyan Theological Journal* 4 (spring 1969): 3-15.

Marty, Martin. *The Righteous Empire: The Protestant Experience in America.* New York: The Dial Press, 1970.

———. *Modern American Religion.* Vol. 3, *Under God, Indivisible: 1941-1960.* Chicago: University of Chicago Press, 1996.

———. *Modern American Religion.* Vol. 1, *The Irony of It All: 1893-1919.* Chicago: University of Chicago Press, 1997.

———. *Modern American Religion.* Vol. 2, *The Noise of the Conflict: 1919-1941.* Chicago: University of Chicago Press, 1997.

Mattke, Robert A. "The Baptism of the Holy Spirit as Related to the Work of Entire Sanctification." *Wesleyan Theological Journal* 5 (spring 1970): 22-32.

McLoughlin, William G. *Modern Revivalism: Charles Grandison Finney to Billy Graham.* New York: Ronald Press, 1959.

Melton, J. Gordon. "An Annotated Bibliography of Publications About the Life and Work of John Wesley." *Methodist History* 29-46.

Metz, Donald S. *Studies in Biblical Holiness.* Kansas City: Beacon Hill Press of Kansas City, 1971.

———. *Some Crucial Issues in the Church of the Nazarene.* Olathe, Kans.: Wesleyan Heritage Press, 1994.

Miley, John. *Systematic Theology* 2 Vols. Peabody, Mass.: Hendrickson Publishers, 1989.

Miller, William Charles. *Holiness Works: A Bibliography.* Kansas City: Nazarene Publishing House, 1986.

Niebuhr, Reinhold. *The Nature and Destiny of Man.* 2 Vols. Louisville: Westminster John Knox Press, 1996.

Noll, Mark A. *Between Faith and Criticism: Evangelicals, Scholarship, and the Bible in America.* San Francisco: Harper and Row, 1986.

Olmstead, Clifton E. *History of Religion in the United States.* Englewood Cliffs, N.J.: Prentice-Hall Inc., 1960.

Palmer, Phoebe. *Faith and Its Effects.* New York: Published for the author at 200 Mulberry St., 1854.

———. *The Way of Holiness.* Salem, Ohio: Schmul Publishing Company, Inc., 1988.

Peters, John Leland. *Christian Perfection and American Methodism.* New York: Abingdon Press, 1956.

Purkiser, W. T. *Beliefs That Matter Most.* Kansas City: Beacon Hill Press, 1959.

———. *Exploring Our Christian Faith.* Kansas City: Beacon Hill Press, 1960.

———. *Conflicting Concepts of Holiness.* Kansas City: Beacon Hill Press, 1964.

———. *Called unto Holiness.* Vol. 2. Kansas City: Nazarene Publishing House, 1983.

———. *Exploring Christian Holiness.* Vol. 1, *The Biblical Foundations.* Kansas City: Beacon Hill Press of Kansas City, 1983.

Purkiser, W. T., Richard S. Taylor, and Willard H. Taylor, eds. *God, Man, and Salvation.* Kansas City: Beacon Hill Press of Kansas City, 1977.

Raser, Harold E. *Phoebe Palmer: Her Life and Thought.* Lewiston/Queenston: The Edwin Mellen Press, 1987.

Rather, Clyde W. "A Compilation of Arguments for Holiness as Found in the Herald of Holiness." B.D. Thesis, Nazarene Theological Seminary, 1948.

Rauschenbusch, Walter. *Christianizing the Social Order.* New York: Macmillan Company, 1913.

Reasoner, Victor Paul. "The American Holiness Movement's Paradigm Shift Concerning Pentecost." *Wesleyan Theological Journal* 31 (fall 1996): 132-46.

Redford, M. E. *The Rise of the Church of the Nazarene.* Kansas City: Nazarene Publishing House, 1951.

Rose, Delbert R. *Vital Holiness: A Theology of Christian Experience.* Minneapolis: Bethany Fellowship, Inc., 1975.

Ruth, C. W. *Entire Sanctification.* Kansas City: Beacon Hill Press, 1944.

Sandeen, Ernest R. *The Roots of Fundamentalism: British and American Millenarianism 1800-1930.* Chicago: University of Chicago Press, 1970.

Sangster, W. E. *The Path to Perfection.* London: Hodder and Stoughton, 1943.

Shaw, S. B. *Echoes of the General Holiness Assembly.* New York: Garland Publishing, Inc., 1984.

Sheldon, Charles M. *In His Steps: What Would Jesus Do?* Chicago: Thompson and Thomas.

Smith, Timothy L. *Revivalism and Social Reform: American Protestantism on the Eve of the Civil War.* Nashville: Abingdon Press, 1957.

————. *Called unto Holiness.* Kansas City: Nazarene Publishing House, 1962.

————. "The Doctrine of the Sanctifying Spirit: Charles G. Finney's Synthesis of Wesleyan and Covenant Theology." *Wesleyan Theological Journal* 13 (spring 1978): 92-113.

————. "How John Fletcher Became the Theologian of Wesleyan Perfectionism: 1770-1776." *Wesleyan Theological Journal* 15 (spring 1980): 68-87.

————. "John Wesley and the Second Blessing." *Wesleyan Theological Journal* 21 (fall 1986): 137-58.

Staples, Rob L. *Outward Sign and Inward Grace.* Kansas City: Beacon Hill Press of Kansas City, 1991.

Steele, Daniel. *Steele's Answers.* Chicago: Christian Witness Co., 1912.

————. *Gospel of the Comforter.* Salem, Ohio: Schmul Publishing Company, Inc., 1960.

Synan, Vinson. *The Holiness-Pentecostal Movement in the United States.* Grand Rapids: William B. Eerdmans Publishing Company, 1971.

————, ed. *Aspects of Pentecostal-Charismatic Origins.* Plainfield, N.J.: Logos International, 1975.

Taylor, Richard S. *A Right Conception of Sin.* Kansas City: Beacon Hill Press, 1945.

————. *Life in the Spirit: Christian Holiness in Doctrine, Experience and Life.* Kansas City: Beacon Hill Press of Kansas City, 1966.

————. "Some Recent Trends in Wesleyan-Arminian Thought." *Wesleyan Theological Journal* 6 (spring 1971): 5-12.

————. *Exploring Christian Holiness.* Vol. 3, *The Theological Formulation.* Kansas City: Beacon Hill Press of Kansas City, 1985.

————. *Leading Wesleyan Thinkers.* Kansas City: Beacon Hill Press of Kansas City, 1985.

————. "Why the Holiness Movement Died." *God's Revivalist* (1999): 1-15.

Thompson, W. Ralph. "An Appraisal of the Keswick and Wesleyan Contemporary Positions." *Wesleyan Theological Journal* 1 (spring 1966): 11-20.

Thorsen, Donald A. D. *The Wesleyan Quadrilateral*. Grand Rapids: Zondervan Publishing House, 1990.

Truesdale, Al. "Reification of the Experience of Entire Sanctification in the American Holiness Movement." *Wesleyan Theological Journal* 31 (fall 1996): 95-119.

Turner, George Allen. *The Vision Which Transforms*. Kansas City: Beacon Hill Press, 1964.

Upham, Thomas C. *The Interior Life*. Kansas City: Beacon Hill Press, 1947.

Walker, James B. *Philosophy of the Plan of Salvation*. New York: The Methodist Book Concern.

Wesley, John. *The Heart of Wesley's Faith*. Kansas City: Beacon Hill Press, 1961.

———. *Works of John Wesley*. 14 Vols. Kansas City: Beacon Hill Press of Kansas City, 1986.

White, Charles E. "What the Holy Spirit Can and Cannot Do: The Ambiguities of Phoebe Palmer's Theology of Experience." *Wesleyan Theological Journal* 23 (spring 1988): 108-21.

White, S. S. *Essential Christian Beliefs*. Kansas City: Beacon Hill Press, 1942.

———. *Eradication: Defined, Explained, Authenticated*. Kansas City: Beacon Hill Press, 1954.

———. *Five Cardinal Elements in the Doctrine of Entire Sanctification*. Kansas City: Beacon Hill Press, 1963.

Wiley, H. Orton. "The Tongues Movement in History." *The Preacher's Magazine* (March 1926): 1-4.

———. *Christian Theology*. 3 Vols. Kansas City: Beacon Hill Press, 1952.

Wood, J. A. *Purity and Maturity*. Boston: The Christian Witness Company, 1899.

———. *Perfect Love*. Kansas City: Beacon Hill Press, 1944.

Wood, Laurence W. "Exegetical-Theological Reflections on the Baptism with the Holy Spirit." *Wesleyan Theological Journal* 14 (fall 1979): 51-63.

———. *Pentecostal Grace*. Wilmore, Ky.: Francis Asbury Publishing Company, 1980.

Wynkoop, Mildred Bangs. *Foundations of Wesleyan-Arminian Theology*. Kansas City: Beacon Hill Press of Kansas City, 1967.

———. *A Theology of Love*. Kansas City: Beacon Hill Press of Kansas City, 1972.

York, William Russell. "The Doctrine of Holiness and Its Effects on the Image of God in Man as Treated by Wesley, Pope, Steele, and Wiley." B.D. Thesis, Nazarene Theological Seminary, 1951.